Standardisation
Processes in IT

Professional Computing

Die Reihe „Professional Computing" des Verlags Vieweg richtet sich an professionelle Anwender bzw. Entwickler von IT-Produkten. Sie will praxisgerechte Lösungen für konkrete Aufgabenstellungen anbieten, die sich durch Effizienz und Kundenorientierung auszeichnen.
Unter anderem sind erschienen:

Die Feinplanung von DV-Systemen
von Georg Liebetrau

Microcontroller-Praxis
von Norbert Heesel und Werner Reichstein

Die Kunst der objektorientierten Programmierung mit C++
von Martin Aupperle

DB2 Common Server
von Heinz Axel Pürner und Beate Pürner

Objektorientierte Programmierung mit VisualSmalltalk
von Sven Tietjen und Edgar Voss

Softwarequalität durch Meßtools
von Reiner Dumke, Erik Foltin u.a.

QM-Verfahrensanweisungen für Softwarehersteller
von Dieter Burgartz und Stefan Schmitz

Die CD-ROM zum Software-Qualitätsmanagement
von Dieter Burgartz und Stefan Schmitz

Businessorientierte Programmierung mit Java
von Claudia Piemont

Methodik der Softwareentwicklung
von Hermann Kaindl, Benedikt Lutz und Peter Tippold

JSP
von Klaus Kilberth

Erfolgreiche Datenbankanwendungen mit SQL
von Jürgen Marsch und Jörg Fritze

Softwaretechnik mit Ada 95
von Manfred Nagl

Unternehmensorientierte Software-Entwicklung mit Delphi
von Daniel Basler

Standardisation Processes in IT
von Kai Jakobs

Vieweg

Kai Jakobs

Standardisation Processes in IT

Impact, Problems and Benefits
of User Participation

vieweg

Die Deutsche Bibliothek – CIP-Cataloguing-in-Publication-Data
A catalogue record for this publication is available from
Die Deutschen Bibliothek
http://www.ddb.de

1st Edition 2000

All rights reserved
© Friedr. Vieweg & Sohn Verlagsgesellschaft mbH, Braunschweig/Wiesbaden, 2000

Vieweg is a subsidiary company of Bertelsmann Professional Information.

No part of this publication may be reproduced, stored in a retrieval system or
transmitted, mechanical, photocopying or otherwise without prior permission
of the copyright holder.

Printing and binding: Lengericher Handelsdruckerei, Lengerich
Printed on acid-free paper
Printed in Germany

ISBN 3-528-05689-4

Table of Contents

List of Tables viii
List of Figures xi
List of Acronyms xi

1 INTRODUCTION AND MOTIVATION 1

2 LITERATURE REVIEW 7

2.1 Standards and Standardisation - A General Overview 8
  2.1.1 What's a Standard Anyway? 9
    2.1.1.1 Definitions and Classifications 9
    2.1.1.2 The Standardisation Universe 18
    2.1.1.3 A Model of the Standards Life Cycle 19
  2.1.2 Policies and Economics in Standardisation -
    Some Brief Deliberations 20
  2.1.3 How to Design the Standardisation Process 32
  2.1.4 Pros and Cons of User Participation 37

2.2 Defining the Term 'User' 40

References and Further Readings 46

3 AN INTRODUCTION TO STANDARDS SETTING BODIES **5 3**

3.1 The International Organization for Standardization (ISO) **5 4**

3.2 The International Telecommunication Union (ITU) .. **6 1**

3.3 The Internet Engineering Task Force (IETF) **6 5**

3.4 Considering User Requirements - The Formal Procedures **6 8**

3.5 Base Standards vs Profiles **7 0**

References and Further Readings **7 3**

4 IMPLEMENTATION OF E-MAIL **7 5**

4.1 Functional Requirements on E-Mail and Directory Services **7 6**

4.2 E-Mail Adoption **7 8**
4.2.1 Top-Down Strategies 81
4.2.2 Hybrid Strategies 83
4.2.2.1 Phases-Based 83
4.2.2.2 Agent-Based 92

4.3 Summary and Analysis **9 3**

References and Further Readings **9 8**

5 USERS AND STANDARDISATION **1 0 1**

5.1 A Simplistic Model of the Standards Setting Process **1 0 2**

5.2 A More Realistic View **104**
  5.2.1 Relations Between Stakeholders 104
  5.2.2 Work Group Members 108
    5.2.2.1 Characterising the Respondents 108
    5.2.2.2 Perceptions 112

5.3 On User Participation on Standardisation **126**
  5.3.1 The Committee Members' Views 128
    5.3.1.1 Integrating User Requirements!? 128
    5.3.1.2 (More) Users on the Committees? 135
  5.3.2 The Users' Views 142

5.4 Summary and Analysis **148**

References and Further Readings **154**

6 OVERALL ANALYSIS AND CONCLUSIONS **169**

6.1 Issues Arising from the Case Studies **171**

6.2 Standardisation, Innovation and Implementation .. **180**

6.3 Users and Standardisation **184**

6.4 A Proposal for a New Standardisation Process ... **189**

6.5 Outlook **203**

References and Further Readings **206**

**ANNEX 1: List of Functional Requirements on
              E-mail and Directories** **209**

ANNEX 2: Questionnaires **219**

**ANNEX 3: The X.400 and X.500 Series of
              Recommendations - A Brief Introduction** ... **227**

Index **237**

List of Tables

Table 2.1.1: The Four Classes of Standards 12

Table 2.1.2: Telecommunications Standards Bodies 15

Table 3.1.1: Project Stages and Associated Documents 58

Table 5.2.1: Respondents' Association With Standards Bodies 108

Table 5.2.2: Affiliations of the Totality of Prospective
Respondents 110

Table 5.2.3: Affiliations of the Actual Respondents 110

Table 5.2.4: How Respondents See Themselves 112

Table 6.4.1: Characteristics of the Phases-Bases Introduction
Process 192

Table A.1.1: Requirements on E-mail and Directory Services
Compiled from Literature 210

Table A.1.2: Requirements on E-mail and Directory Services
Compiled from Interviews 217

List of Figures

Figure 2.1.1: The IT Standardisation Universe in 1970 1
Figure 2.1.2: The IT Standardisation Universe in the 1990s 19
Figure 2.1.3: The Stages of the Standards Life Cycle (sketch) 19
Figure 2.1.4: Summary of the Comprehensive Standards
               Life Cycle 20
Figure 2.2.1: User Hirarchies and the OSI Reference Model 41
Figure 2.2.2: A Three-Level Hierarchy for Standards and Users ... 43
Figure 2.2.3: Categories and Classes of Users 44
Figure 3.1.1: ISO Structure 55
Figure 3.1.2: JTC 1 Organisational Chart 60
Figure 3.2.1: The Structure of the ITU 62
Figure 3.2.2: ITU-T Organisation 63
Figure 3.3.1: Entities Involved in the Internet's
               Standardisation Process 66
Figure 3.5.1: Base Standards vs. Profiles 71
Figure 3.5.2: The MAP Architecture 72
Figure 4.1.1: Functionality as a Contributor to Service Usage 76
Figure 4.2.1: Classes of Introduction Strategies 81
Figure 4.2.2: A Typical Environment at the End of the
               First Phase 85
Figure 4.2.3: A Typical Environment at the End the
               Second Phase 88
Figure 4.2.4: Typical Evolution of Electronic Mail
               Service Platforms 88
Figure 4.2.5: The Envisaged Final Stage of the Process 89

Figure 5.1.1:   The Naive Idea of an Ideal Standards
              Setting Process 102

Figure 5.2.1:   Relations Between Stakeholders 107

Figure 5.2.2:   Different Types of Pro-active and Reactive
              Standards 113

Figure 6.1.1:   'Business Relevant' vs 'Infrastructural' Technology .. 175

Figure 6.1.2:   Application Life Cycles 177

Figure 6.2.1:   Processes Contributing to an Innovation 183

Figure 6.4.1:   Development and Subsequent Deployment
              of a Standard 193

Figure 6.4.2:   The Improved Cycle of Specification Development .. 194

Figure A.1.1:   The Basic MHS Model 228

Figure A.1.2:   Structure of an MHS Message 229

Figure A.1.3:   Use of Distribution Lists 229

Figure A.1.4:   The Message Store 230

Figure A.1.5:   IP-Message Structure 230

Figure A.1.6:   Relations Between Management Domains 231

Figure A.1.7:   Interworking Between MHS and the Directory Service 231

Figure A.1.8:   X.400 Security Scenario 232

Figure A.1.9:   The General Directory Model 233

Figure A.1.10: Model of an Entry (User Information Part) 233

Figure A.1.11: A Sample Distinguished Name (DN) 234

Figure A.1.12: The Directory Schema 234

List of Acronyms

ACTS	Advanced Communications Technologies and Services
AD	Area Director
ADMD	Administration Management Domains
ANSI	American National Standards Institute
AS	Applicability Statement
ATM	Asynchronous Transfer Mode
ATM	Asynchronous Transfer Mode
AU	Access Unit
AUR	Agreed User Requirement
BSI	British Standards Institute
CCIF	International Telephone Consultative Committee
CCIR	International Radio Consultative Committee
CCIT	International Telegraph Consultative Committee
CCITT	International Telegraph and Telephone Consultative Committee
CCR	Commitment, Concurrency and Recovery
CD	Committee Draft
CEU	Commission of the European Union
CFS	Common Functional Specification
CIM	Computer Integrated Manufacturing
CSMS	Cyclic Stage Model of Standardisation
DAP	Directory Access Protocol
DIB	Directory Information Base
DIN	Deutsches Institut für Normung
DIS	Draft International Standard
DIT	Directory Information Tree
DL	Distribution Lists
DL	Distribution List
DN	Distinguished Name

DQDB	Distributed Queue, Dual Bus
DS	Directory Service
DSA	Directory System Agent
DSP	Directory System Protocol
DUA	Directory User Agents
DUA	Directory User Agent
ECMA	European Computer Manufacturers Association
EDI	Electronic Data Interchange
EDIFACT	Electronic Data Interchange for Administration, Commerce and Transport
EEMA	European Electronic Messaging Association
EFTPOS	Electronic Funds transfer at Point-of-Sale
EMA	Electronic Messaging Association
ETSI	European Telecommunications Standards Institute
EWOS	European Workshop on Open Systems
FDIS	Final Draft International Standard
FTAM	File Transfer, Access and Management
GII	Global Information Infrastructure
HCI	Human-Computer Interaction
HTTP	Hypertext Transfer Protocol
IAB	Internet Architecture Board
IBC	Integrated Broadband Communications
ICT	Information and Communication Technology
IEC	International Electrotechnical Commission
IEEE	Institute of Electrical and Electronics Engineers
IERG	Internet Engineering Steering Group
IESG	Internet Engineering Steering Group
IETF	Internet Engineering Task Force
IFIP	International Federation for Information Processing
IP	Internet Protocol
IPM	Interpersonal Messaging
IS	International Standard
IS	Information System
ISA	International Federation of the National Standardizing Associations
ISO	International Organization for Standardization
ISOC	Internet Society
ISP	International Standardized Profile
IT	Information Technology
ITU	International Telecommunication Union
ITU-T	International Telecommunication Union - Telecommunication Standardization
ITUG	International Telecommunications User Group

IWU	Interworking Unit
JTC 1	Joint Technical Committee 1
LAN	Local Area Network
MAP	Manufacturing Automation Protocol
MD	Management Domains
MS	Message Store
MTA	Message Transfer Agent
MTS	Message Transfer System
NII	National Information Infrastructure
NP	New work item proposal
O/R	Originator/Recipient
OECD	Organization for Economic Co-operation and Development
OMG	Object Management Group
OPS	Open Profiling Standard
OSI-RM	OSI Reference Model
PAS	Publicly Available Specification
PDAU	Physical Delivery Access Unit
PKCS	Public Key Cryptosystems
PrMD	Private Management Domains
PTT	Post, Telegraph and Telephone administration
RACE	Research and Development in Advanced Communications Technologies in Europe
RDN	Relative Distinguished Name
RFC	Request for Comments
ROA	Recognised Operating Agency
SC	Sub-committee
SDO	Standards Developing Organisation
SIO	Scientific or Industrial Organisation
SME	Small to Medium Enterprise
SMTP	Simple Mail Transfer Protocol
SNMP	Simple Network Management Protocol
SPAG	Standards Promotion and Application Group
SST	Social shaping o technology
T1	Accredited Standards Committee for Telecommunications - One
TAG	Technical Advisory Group
TC	Technical Committee
TCP	Transmission Control Protocol
TERENA	Trans-European Research and Education Networking Association
TOP	Technical and Office Protocol
TSB	Telecommunication Standardization Bureau
UA	User Agent
VE	Virtual Enterprise

WEMA	World Electronic Messaging Association
WG	Working Group
WP	Working Party
WTSC	World Telecommunication Standardization Conference
WWW	World Wide Web

Chapter 1

Introduction and Motivation

"Standards are not only a technical question. They determine the technology that will implement the Information Society, and consequently the way in which industry, users, consumers and administrations will benefit from it."

Some General Motivation

We are told that Information Technology (IT) will change the world at least as much as did the printing press and the steam engine.

Indeed, our world is becoming networked, and IT is increasingly penetrating our everyday lives. Most prominently, the envisaged Global Information Infrastructure (GII) is going to have a profound impact as the major enabler of the frequently predicted move from an industrial society to the information society. In the meantime the different government initiatives towards national or regional information infrastructures are gaining momentum. This holds particularly for the US, the Pacific Rim and Europe, where the 'Bangemann Report' identifies ten application areas to launch the future information society, including teleworking, distance learning and health care. Likewise, major developments take place in the domestic sector. Here as well stand-alone computers are bound to vanish sooner or later, as ISDN interconnectivity and access to the Internet are becoming increasingly commonplace. As a consequence of these trends network externalities will become more and more visible, and will in turn further speed up the networking process in the non-commercial sector. It may take some time, but ultimately almost every organisation, company, school and household will be interconnected. Or so they say; this frequently evoked development will only happen if globally agreed standards are available.

The single components that will eventually establish the information infrastructure are of extreme heterogeneity, which extends to the physical medium, the communication services and protocols, the application services, and the end systems. These components need to be interconnected to enable the required seamless interoperability between heterogeneous systems and across different networks. As of today, this can only be achieved to a comparably rudimentary degree. Accordingly, a number of new standards have already originated from GII-related activities, and many more are likely to emerge in the near future. In addition, a plethora of existing standards and specifications have been identified as being of importance[1]; there is the need to incorporate the huge installed base of legacy technology, as well as to provide mechanisms to cater for future systems, the nature of which is not yet predictable. Here, standards will play a crucial role as enabler of the integration of diverse networks and services. If they do not emerge the whole concept is bound to fail.

Accepting the importance of standards for future developments, not only with respect to the GII, but for information technology in general, implies that the process leading to such standards should be of particular interest as well.

Background

In the mid nineties, standards setting organisations were complaining about the perceived low level of participation by user companies. Some went to great lengths to increase the number of users in an attempt to improve their standards' visibility and their chances of survival in the market place.

This perception of an increased number of users on standards committees as the panacea of all problems standardisation bodies were facing was one of the cornerstones originally underlying the work described in this book. Yet, the questions to be asked were "Is this really so? Does 'more users' necessarily equate to 'better standards'?"

What Has Been Done

Two lines of research were followed. One looked at the processes that actually generated the standards, to try and find out whether problems could be linked to certain elements of these processes. It should be noted, however, that this exercise did not aim at finding and analysing some kind of 'standards war', as e.g. the recent struggles

---

1   Several hundred standards and specifications, from very different sources, have so far been identified by the EU's 'Open Information Interchange Initiative' as being relevant to GII activities. Areas covered include e.g. colour information interchange, video interchange, data transfer, EDI, electronic conferencing, and geographic information systems [CEU 97].

for HDTV standardisation. Rather, the focus was on the 'lowest' level of the whole process, i.e. on the technical work groups, where the basic technical decisions (as opposed to political or strategic ones) are being made. The interesting issues in this context included the WG members' views on increased user participation (what the official sources of the standards setting organisations were so desperately trying to achieve) in general, if, how and when it should be attempted to achieve, and its potential benefits and drawbacks. On the other hand, user representatives could comment on their perceptions of potential benefits, if any, they would associate with participation in standardisation, and on alternative ways they would pursue to get the functionality they need. The basic idea here was to identify possible ways in which either users could advantageously participate in standards setting, or could put their requirements across in some other way.

What exactly users can contribute to standards setting was the second issue looked at. Common wisdom has it would be their task to identify and communicate real-world requirements, upon which standards work could then be based. The validity of this assumption has neither been challenged nor proved.

In this context, the respective 'histories' of corporate IT (corporate e-mail systems, to be precise), i.e. its diffusion, adaptation and implementation was of potential interest. There might be a link between the corporate messaging 'history' and a company's reluctance - or possibly inability - to play an active role in standards setting. If it had indeed been inability on the users' side thus far, this would have a major impact on the evaluation of the value of user participation in standards setting, and would possibly raise questions regarding the design of the current process in general.

The findings and conclusions reported in the subsequent chapters are primarily based on

- a survey of experienced members of technical committees of ISO, ITU, ANSI, and the IETF,

- a number of case studies on large, internationally operating e-mail user companies.

The remainder of this book is organised as follows: chapter two and three will provide the necessary background information. An introduction to the issues surrounding standards and standardisation will be given in chapter two. In addition, the crucial term 'user' will be thoroughly discussed. The formal processes adopted by the standards setting bodies represented in the study are briefly described in chapter three.

The remaining chapters present an analysis of the compiled data, and offer some conclusions[2]. In particular, chapter four briefly discusses corporate user requirements on messaging services. Yet, the focus will be on the different 'strategies' for the introduction of an electronic mail service in an organisation that could be identified; these are reviewed and discussed as well. Subsequently, chapter five addresses some issues surrounding the standardisation process. The initial naive idea of this process is developed into a more realistic picture, largely based on comments made by committee members. User participation in this process is another focus here; the associated pros and cons, as perceived by different stakeholders, are presented and discussed. Finally, chapter six attempts to form a coherent picture out of the various bits addressed so far. In particular, a new model of the standardisation process is introduced, and its benefits - and potential problems - are discussed. This model takes into account the different aspects discussed previously.

---

[2]   It should be noted that the summaries and analyses, presented in sections 5.3 and 6.3, refer primarily to the respective chapter. The overall analysis is presented in chapter seven.

Chapter 2

Some Necessary Background

This chapter will first address various standards-related issues which are important for the subsequent analyses. This includes including definitions, a classification, and a description of today's standardisation universe, as well as a discussion of the current standards life cycle. A brief closer look at what it actually takes to specify a standard that has the potential to survive in the market place will follow. Finally, some light will be shed on the various possible definitions of the crucial term 'user'

2.1   Standards and Standardisation in IT - A General Overview

The process of standardisation cannot be regarded as a simple, one-dimensional activity required to lay down technical rules and guidelines, taking place in a removed world of its own. Rather, it must be considered in conjunction with the environment within which it takes place. Very different facets need to be taken into account when trying to actually understand this process.

Even if we disregard social, moral and religious rules for the moment, standards - still in a very general sense - have been with us for quite some time: about 5,000 years ago the first alphabets emerged, enabling completely new forms of communication and information storage. Some 2,500 years later, the first national, coin-based currency, invented by the Lydians, established the basis for easier inter-regional and even international trading. The industrial revolution in the 18th century and, more so, the advent of the railroad in the 19th century resulted in a need for technical standards, which was once more reinforced when mass production generated a demand for interchangeable parts. In parallel, the invention of the electric telegraph in 1837 triggered the development of standards in the field of electrical communication technology. In 1865, the International Telegraph Union - to become the International Telecommunication Union (ITU) in 1932 - was founded by twenty states. The other major international standards setting body, the International Organization for Standardization (ISO), was established in 1947.

However, only during the last ten or fifteen years has the economic importance of standards been recognised, and standardisation has been accepted as a strategic tool of major importance. At the same time, the number of 'standards setting bodies' has soared, as has the number of published 'standards' (for a definition of standards, and the explanation of the quotation marks, see below). Almost countless voluntary organisations and, particularly, industry fora keep springing up. Researchers from various disciplines (including, but not limited to, psychology, economy, sociology, and computer science) have begun to analyse different aspects of standards setting. Summaries of some of their insights and results will be presented in this section. However, some limitations also apply. In particular, I am not going to discuss political aspects and intellectual property rights (IPRs)[3].

2.1.1 What's a Standard Anyway?

The term 'standard' defies easy access. It covers too broad a variety of totally different fields, from bolts, paper sizes and character sets to societal norms and moral values. Similarly different are the sources from which standards emerge, including legislative bodies, philosophers, and dedicated standards setting bodies.

If pushed, everyone will have at least a vague idea what a standard is, and what it is supposed to achieve. However, as usual, it is the details that are most tricky. Therefore, a common definition for 'standard' would be very helpful. The search for this definition unearths a wealth of different explanations, from the very general to those limited in one respect or another, to others confined to a single field.

2.1.1.1 Definitions and Classifications

The following definitions are listed to provide an idea of what a standard is, according to a variety of different sources (with a view to IT standards). They range from the very general to the (technology) specific:

1 *"The acceptable behaviour and mores of a society and culture."* [Cargill, 1989].
   In some way this is the broadest definition, yet at the same time largely limited to moral and ethical issues, thus leaving out the more materialistic technological context (unless you consider technology as a special expression of 'behaviour').

2 *"The deliberate acceptance by a group of people having common interests or background of a quantifiable metric that influences their behaviour and activities by permitting a common interchange."* [Cargill, 1989].

---

3 Those who are interested in these topics will find several references in the 'Further Readings' section at the end of this chapter.

Still a rather general definition, regarding a standard as little more than some common ground.

3 *"An authoritative principle or rule that usually implies a model or pattern for guidance, by comparison with which the quantity, excellence, correctness etc. of other things may be determined."* [Webster, 1992].
Perhaps the most complete definition, that is not limited to any specific field, but can be applied to moral and ethical issues as well as to technology. At the same time, however, this universality is a weakness, as it offers little concrete guidance.

4 *"A prescribed set of rules, conditions or requirements concerning definition of terms; classification of components; specification of materials, performance, or operations; delineation of procedures; or measurement of quantity and quality in describing materials, products, systems, or practices."* (quoted in [OECD, 1991]).
According to the source this definition is specifically aimed to the field of IT; however, it can easily be applied to other fields of engineering as well. A potential obstacle to it is the suggested direct association of a standard with a product.

5 *"A set of technical specifications that can be adhered to by a producer, either tacitly, or in accord with some formal agreement, or in conformity with explicit regulatory authority."* (quoted in [Mansell, 1995]).
This definition exhibits a close relation to products in general. Being very pragmatic it fails, however, to recognise that a standard may have many more facets to it than just the 'technical specification' a producer can adhere to. Even more so than the definition above this one rather more defines a standards profile or a functional standard than a base standard.

6 *"The authorized exemplar of a unit of measure or weight; e.g. a measuring rod of unit length; a vessel of unit capacity, preserved in the custody of public officers as a permanent evidence of the legally prescribed magnitude of the unit"* [Encyclopedia, 1987].
This definition is given in the Oxford English Dictionary. It quite accurately describes how the old bases for SI units (e.g.

meter or litre) were established and kept. Unfortunately, it can hardly be applied to anything else.

Given the respective specific limitations and shortcomings of the above definitions it appears that yet another one is needed for the purpose of this work which is, after all, limited to information technology. Thus, in the following the term 'standard' will have the following meaning (unless stated otherwise):

"A publicly available definitive specification of procedures, rules and requirements, issued by a legitimated and recognised authority through voluntary consensus building observing due process, that establishes the baseline of a common understanding of what a given system or service should offer."

This definition restricts the scope of what is colloquially referred to as a standard in three ways:

- It includes only base standards (the 'baseline'); as opposed to functional standards or profiles, which rather more address implementation and interoperability issues.

- It limits the sources from which a standard may emerge to 'recognised authorities'. In particular, this excludes specifications issued by self-styled industry fora like e.g. the ATM Forum (which may - and do - contribute to standards work within e.g. ITU).

- It also excludes legislation, as standards are said to be established 'through voluntary consensus building's.

Thus, the sources from which standards may emerge are limited to recognised national, regional or international standards setting bodies, such as e.g. BSI in the UK or DIN in Germany, ETSI in Europe, and ITU or ISO at the global level, respectively. These organisations are typically referred to as Standards Developing Organisations SDOs).

Standards are the result of a standardisation process, which itself can be described as:

"..... the voluntary and methodical harmonisation of material and non-material objects undertaken jointly by the interests concerned for the benefit of the community as a whole. It shall not lead to individual interests gaining a special economic advantage and requires consensus agreement between all parties concerned." (quoted in [Repussard, 1995]).

There exists an almost impenetrable maze of what is generally called 'standards', ranging from company specific rules, over regional and national regulations, up to globally accepted standards[4]. Moreover, one may distinguish between different types of standards: there are voluntary, regulatory, de jure, de facto, proactive, reactive, public, industry, and proprietary standards; this list is by no means exhaustive. Accordingly, a variety of different classification schemes has been proposed, their different respective scopes, and the originating processes. For example, a four-level classification has been proposed, whereby each class is related to the previous, but introduces an additional level of variation (see Table 2.1.1).

Classes of Standards	Examples	Purpose	Effect
Units	Meter (length)	Sameness	Replication
Similarity	Character sets	Repeatability	Compatible with like
Compatibility	Group 3 facsimile, X.25 interface	Interworking	Transmitter compatible with receiver
Etiquette	CSMA/CD	Expendability	Negotiate the variation

Table 2.1.1:
The Four Classes of Standards (according to [Krechmar, 1996a])

---

4   Please note that, for the sake of a broader discussion, the term 'standard' is used rather more loosely throughout the remainder of this section.

This classification nicely matches the increasing complexity of standards, typical particularly for the IT sector. A number of other categorisations have been proposed in the literature. The more popular ones include:

- **voluntary vs statutory**
  This classification indicates the different natures of the underlying processes as well as the legislative status of its result. A voluntary process is characterised through the lack of both intrinsic benefits associated with participation and penalties for non-participation. Voluntary processes tend to be comparably slow, but this slowness is (more or less?) compensated by the wide range of input that goes into the final specification, and its resulting broad acceptance. Adherence to such standards is voluntary as well; they are a means to 'persuade' the market to move into a certain direction deemed beneficial. This process is embraced by all SDOs. Another crucial characteristic of voluntary standards is the observation of 'due process'. In short, that is, *".. any 'person' with a direct and material interest in the activity's outcome has a right to participate in the activity."* [Baron, 1995]
  A statutory process, on the other hand, can only be initiated by some legislative authority; its outcome will typically materialise faster, but because of its very nature may command less support from the affected communities, who may not have had an adequate say during the process. However, everyone under the legislation of the issuing authority will have to obey those standards.

- **de jure vs de facto**
  This very popular classification should primarily refer to the different ways the respective standards emerge; this includes the characteristics of the respective originating organisations. Frequently, however, this categorisation is used in a way contradicting the above classification, in that the attribute 'de jure' is associated with standards that emerge from an SDO through a voluntary process, and which are indeed only voluntary in nature. Standards that emerge purely through market forces (maybe through the dominant position of one or a

group of players) are referred to as being 'de facto'. With the increasing complexity of the world of standards, and the cross fertilisation between SDOs and consortia, this distinction will eventually become obsolete.

- **public vs industry vs proprietary**
  This distinction is similar to the above one. Typically, standards published by SDOs are referred to as public. de facto standards, which in most cases originate from a single powerful company or a consortium, are referred to as industry standards. Likewise, proprietary standards have been defined by a company, but in contrast to industry standards the specifications have not been made public and are owned by the specifying company.

- **proactive vs reactive**
  These categories (also referred to as 'anticipatory' and 'traditional', respectively) are used to distinguish between the ways the standards emerge, i.e. based on an already existing product (reactive) or in anticipation of future demands and requirements (proactive). In the IT-domain standards setting used to be reactive, this appears to have changed somewhat recently. ATM and ISDN are among the more popular examples of proactive standards. Obviously, any attempt to create proactive standards bears a major risk of failure.

- **base vs functional (this distinction is valid for certain IT standards only)**
  Both ITU-T and ISO, as well as the single national SDOs, primarily produce base standards. These are characterised by the fact that they only address functional matters, as opposed to implementation-specific issues. Particularly in the wake of OSI standards, with their numerous options and even different protocols for the single layers, interoperability problems arose since implementations using different options were no longer able to interoperate, although being standards compliant. Functional standards were introduced to cope with this problem. They identified standard profiles; a profile defines a hierarchy of protocols, and the options to be used within each protocol layer.

Standards setting organisations may be characterised according to the respective type and by whom they are controlled (see Table 2.1.2).

(Standards) Organisation	Type	Controlled by (officially)	Produces
ITU	global governmental standards authority	governments	voluntary base standards
ISO/IEC	global private sector standards authority	national standards authorities	voluntary base standards
ETSI	European membership standards authority	members	voluntary base standards
IETF	global (?) independent consortium	individuals	implementation oriented base standards
ANSI	US private sector standards authority	members	voluntary base standards
(ATM Forum)	global industry consortium	members	technical specifications

Table 2.1.2:
Telecommunications Standards Bodies

The different types of 'standards', as well as the underlying processes, can be characterised through combinations of the above attributes. The fact that the ITU produces 'recommendations' already hints at the non-binding nature of the specifications[5] - although it is an international body under a public intergovernmental organisation (the UN); the same holds for ISO standards (ISO being a private rather

---

5   At least in theory; ITU recommendations, for instance, have almost always been integral part of the procurement procedures of the national PTTs, and Western governments.

than a treaty organisation). The documents produced by these organisations, therefore, can be described as being voluntary, public base standards. In particular, they should not be referred to as 'de jure' since they do not have any legally binding status per se. ITU's and ISO's standards can be either proactive or reactive. On the other hand, it is typically claimed that consortia produce 'de facto' or 'industry' standards (which are no standards at all according to the above new definition, but technical specifications). In any case, these too are voluntary, they may be proactive or reactive, as well as base or functional. Frequently, as in the case of the ATM Forum, these specifications are subsequently submitted to ISO or ITU-T for consideration. ISO has introduced a mechanism allowing reasonably mature specifications to proceed more quickly through the single stages of their process.

The IETF is very much a borderline case. Their process can easily be identified as being voluntary and public; their documents specify base standards. Specifications emerging through this process are regarded by many as 'de jure' standards (i.e. on a par with e.g. the output of ISO and ITU), whereas others consider them as mere 'de facto' standards (akin to specifications originating from consortia). With some reservations I would subscribe to the former[6].

To clarify the confusion apparently surrounding the various types of standards, and the different ways the terms are used in the literature, some additional comments and explanations regarding the above classifications may be helpful. It has already been noted that the terms 'de jure' and 'voluntary' are frequently used interchangeably in the literature. The underlying notion is that both refer to

---

6   Reservations firstly concern the term 'legitimated' in my definition of what constitutes a standard; the IETF is really very much a self-appointed authority. Moreover, the IETF's 'rough consensus' is not quite the same as 'consensus', and very much open to individual interpretation. Finally, none of the relevant IETF documents mentions due process as a guiding principle of their procedure. However, the openness of the procedure, which means that everyone may actively participate in the standards definition process, and the appeal mechanisms established should provide a basis upon which due process can be observed. In general, therefore, I would argue that it appears to be justified to consider the Internet standards as exactly that - standards.

organisations widely considered as 'legitimate' sources of standards - as opposed to, for example, rather more self-styled consortia. Yet, as 'de jure' seems to imply that these standards have been issued by an entity with some kind of statutory power, it should be made very clear that this is not the case; these are truly voluntary standards. Likewise, 'de facto' is frequently used synonymously with both 'industry' and 'proprietary'. Apart from the fact that these refer to very different classes of documents - the former is an 'open' specification, which is publicly available, whereas the latter is, well, proprietary, and possibly safeguarded by patents - these are not really standards at all in the first place. Moreover, 'de facto' could be mistaken for something unique, which is definitely not the case; there may be different competing de facto 'standards'.

Originally, technical standards were exclusively produced by 'official' voluntary standards bodies. Yet, their procedures have been perceived by many as being too time-consuming and too much based on compromise. Moreover, not all important aspects of IT have been addressed by these bodies; for instance, there are no such things as standardised word processors or operating systems. These aspects together with economic considerations led powerful players to try and establish their own proprietary 'standards' (IBM in the sixties and seventies, as well as Microsoft in the nineties are cases in point). Potentially significant economic benefits stood to be gained from successful de facto 'standards'. They could be developed in-house, and be tailored towards the needs of their producer (and possibly towards those of some major customers).

More recently, consortia have been established at an almost alarming rate. Those aiming at the production of technical specifications hope for greater speed of completion, and that real products can easily be produced subsequently. Moreover, consortium members are likely to back the specifications they helped design; with e.g. vendors developing products incorporating these specifications, and users actually buying them. Among the members of such consortia, vendors, suppliers of complementary products or services, and some users may typically be found. Even competitors join forces here in order to establish a market. Unlike proprietary standards, however, consortia specifications (industry standards) are normally openly available, to ensure the broadest support and widest dissemination possible. In fact, for such standards wide acceptance is vital, not least because they do not enjoy the blessing of being an 'official' document, and thus carry less weight for many. They also need to be timely and reasonably well tailored towards their potential customers' needs to be able to either create their own market, or to be condoned by the market.

2.1.1.2   The Standardisation Universe

The maze of standards setting bodies is almost as confusing as the conglomerate of standards itself. Figure 2.1.1 shows the - rather straightforward - standardisation universe in the 1970s.

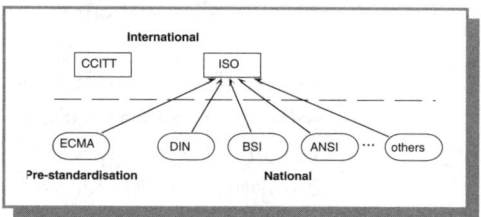

Figure   2.1.1:
The IT Standardisation Universe in 1970

Back in the seventies, the standards setting bodies were few, national bodies contributed to the work of ISO at the international level, which itself was separated from the activities of the then CCITT[7]. The only other international organisation of some importance was the European Computer Manufacturers Association (ECMA).

Since then, the number of players in the global standardisation arena has multiplied, notably through industry consortia, regional organisations such as ETSI, organisations establishing functional standards and profiles, and, of course, the IETF. Likewise, user organisations have been established. Figure 2.1.2 depicts the expanded and far more complex universe of the 1990s (without any claim for completeness).

---

[7]   International Telegraph and Telephone Consultative Committee, the predecessor of ITU-T.

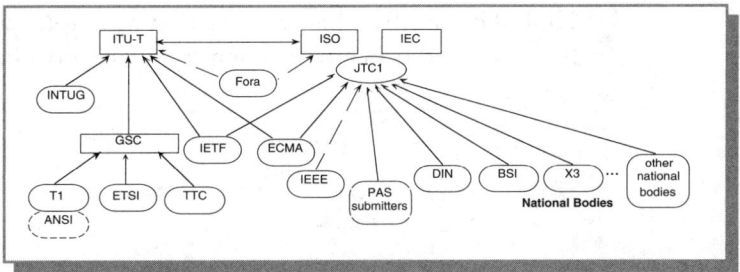

Figure 2.1.2:
The IT Standardisation Universe in the 1990s

Whilst this broader community involved in the process of standardisation gives rise to the hope for more useful standards that can survive in the open market at the same time it potentially lowers the value of a specification as competing documents may be developed in parallel elsewhere

2.1.1.3 A Model of the Standards Life Cycle

A rough sketch of the standards life cycle, which covers standardisation efforts, and follow-up activities like profiling and testing, is depicted in Figure 2.1.3. Similar cycle stages have been identified by other organisations as well.

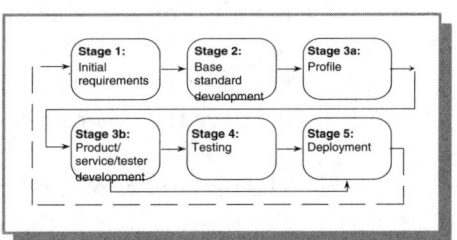

Figure 2.1.3:
The Stages of the Standards Life Cycle (sketch)
(according to [Reilly, 1994])

This figure shows that actually developing and writing a base standard accounts for only part of the overall development cycle. To further refine this model, to show who is doing what at which stage, and especially to include interdependencies, ANSI's Accredited Standards Committee X3 developed a model summarised in Figure

2.1.4. Apparently, this was the first attempt by an SDO to understand the full standards environment they are working in.

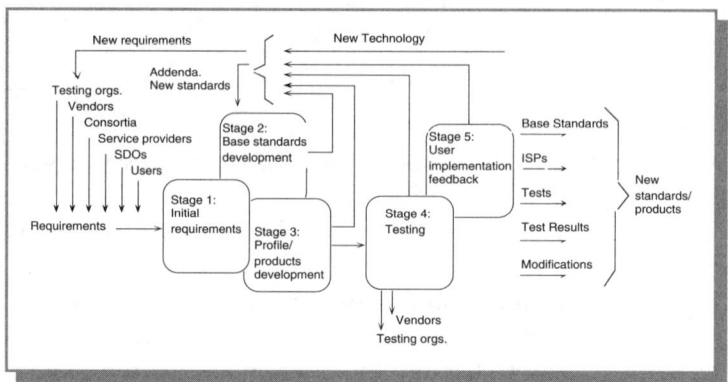

Figure 2.1.4:
Summary of the Comprehensive Standards Life Cycle
(according to [ANSI X3, 1993])

Today, three years is the minimum period for standard production within ISO, which is roughly equivalent to stage two in the above model. Through the 'Fast Track Procedure', this period can be reduced to one year (this does not take into account development efforts that went into a specification prior to submission). X3 states that nine months are *'the *optimum* timeline for approval of a specification that has behind it the full agreement of the technical community'*. Roughly another four years must be added to any of these time spans to cover the other stages as well.

The remainder of this book will primarily focus on the second stage of the life cycle, i.e. the development of base standards, with some additional emphasis also on the requirements compilation stage.

2.1.2 Policies and Economics in Standardisation - Some Brief Deliberations

Standardisation may have far-reaching impact on companies and even on full grown economies. Placing money on a technology that eventually fails to become a standard, and to be adopted by the market, may well lead to the breakdown of a company. Pros and cons of joining the standardisation bandwagon vs trying to push a proprietary solution also need to be considered. Standards based products or services may imply price wars and lower revenues, but may also open new markets and widen the customer base. Offering a proprietary solution may yield (or keep, rather) a loyal customer base, but may also result in a technological lock-in and, eventually, marginalisation for a vendor or service provider.

Consequently, the problem of how to select the 'right' standard, or how to standardise on the 'right' system, needs to be addressed. 'Right', of course, means different things to different people, which is why also the non-technical dimensions of standardisation tend to be very tricky. Something that is 'right' for one country or one company may be disastrous for another. The international and possibly global scale of standards in the field of Information and Communication Technology[8] (ICT) means that players with very different backgrounds from very different economies need to agree on something they deem to be at least more or less 'right'. For obvious reasons, some of which will be outlined below, these problems have been attracting considerable attention, especially against the background of the emerging Global Information Infrastructure (GII).

The 'maze' of standards organisations provides a fertile ground for very different types of standards and technical specifications. In the following, stakeholders' motivations for being active in the standards setting process will be discussed, as well as some of the issues that need to be taken into account by those who seek to influence this process. Prior to that, however, let us first briefly examine why standardisation should be organised in the first place. After all, why not leave it all to the market?

What would happen if the market had to decide upon which technology to standardise? Several results are possible; one, of course, being that an optimal technology (or at least the best alternative available) actually wins. There is no need to discuss this case further. There are other possible outcomes, though. Consider, for example, a situation where different, but roughly equivalent technologies are available, none of which commands sufficient support to establish

---

8　This term is used synonymously with Information Technology (IT).

itself as the 'standard'. It may now well happen that this uncertainty paralyses the market, and that potential buyers postpone their purchases in order not to invest in a losing technology. As a consequence, innovation in that technical domain might come to a standstill. Clearly, nobody would benefit from a situation like this.

The notion of 'uncertainty' is important here. Standards are but a part of a larger socio-economic system, which does exert a certain amount of influence on their development. That is, a standard is subject to path dependencies imposed on it by its broader environment. Unforeseen, and indeed unforeseeable developments may hamper all efforts and may even impose the need to start a standards activity all over again from scratch. Moreover, in most cases a standard is not a stand-alone document. Rather, it is positioned in a network of other standards (some of them possibly only emerging), which influence the boundary conditions within which it can emerge by laying down, for example, stringent compatibility requirements. Last but not least, early decisions made during the standardisation of a technology itself may have significant impact of later decisions. Selecting the telephone network as the carrier for facsimile transmissions, for example, implicitly pre-defined numbering schemes to be used and possible transmission speeds as well as the need to eventually switch from analogue to digital transmission technology. These developments were unforeseeable for those who devised the initial standards. More general, path dependencies were established at an early stage of the process, which to a considerable degree shaped subsequent developments.

It should be obvious that no sufficiently accurate forecasts can realistically be made regarding future developments[9]. Whilst this uncertainty directly affects all predictions, it has a particular strong impact on standardisation. Here, big oaks from minor acorns grow. That is, comparably small events may carry great weight; in the absence of a sound basis for judgement and decisions the adoption of a particular technology by just one firm may encourage others to follow

---

9 Another example is the more recent need for new technologies to be environmentally sound, due to the environmental awareness that came virtually out of the blue. As one result, nuclear power has become less desirable in many parts of the world [Cowan, 1992].

suit. If this happens, chances are that an inferior technology will be adopted, which may suit the initial adopter (who may have evaluated the alternatives and selected the technology to best suit his needs), but does not necessarily meet other entities' demands. They, in turn, will then make their choices solely based on the initial adopter's policy decisions. Little, if any experimentation with alternative technologies or systems will occur, which will rapidly be discarded. A similar effect may be observed when decisions to adopt are based only on initial expressions of a technology (e.g. implementations of IT systems). In such cases, a poor first implementation can easily reduce to zero this technology's chances of being adopted, since possibly superficial, implementation-specific shortcomings hide the technology's inherent advantages. Likewise, observable early benefits of a technology will outweigh all other aspects; in particular, higher benefits to be gained from a different technology at some later stage will be ignored. Indeed, these benefits again cannot be identified at all due to the lack of opportunities for experimentation. It follows that the market can - and frequently will - adopt the 'wrong' technology when left on its own. 'Wrong', like 'right', of course is vague term.

It is most likely that the above course of events could sooner or later be observed if standardisation were left to market forces alone[10]. To prevent this from happening, some form of coordinated standardisation efforts are required. (Prospective) standards surely try to reduce uncertainty by aligning players' views and expectations from the outset. Indeed, the pure existence of a standards setting process might suffice to prevent the development outlined above, as it would then be possible to raise expectations that a standard will soon be emerging from this process

---

10 In fact, it does appear. The DOS operating system may be considered as an example: one strong player, IBM, chose this system, which did not really represent state-of-the-art even at that time, and almost all others followed suit. Obviously, IBM gained significant profits from this development (as did, even more so, Microsoft). In fact, users benefitted as well, albeit not from superior technology, but solely from the emerging network externalities.

The desire to make sure that the 'right' standard emerges normally lies at the heart of firms' involvement in the standards setting process, be it in the 'official' process or in consortium-led activities. Yet, what exactly characterises the 'right', or at least a 'good' standard is far from being clear. Cowan associates a good standard with the attributes 'speed' and 'meet technical requirements'. Whilst these characteristics are valuable for winning stakeholders' support, this is a surprisingly narrow focus. Clearly, any technical specification should meet technical demands, the issue of speed, however, is popular, yet questionable (and will be discussed in more detail in chapter six). Moreover, meeting organisational and, particularly, societal requirements clearly need to play a role in standards setting as well.

Standardisation is becoming all the more important with the increasing economic and corporate globalisation. At the same time, standardisation politics change. Strangely, national interests are becoming more important. A domestic standard successfully introduced into the global arena will not least boost the prospects of the domestic economy. Accordingly, governments have a vested interest in pushing such standards to support domestic firms. These firms, in turn, will look to standards setting for several reasons which are typically, though not necessarily, related to their own economic well-being. Standardisation may thus to some degree be seen as an interface between technical and non-technical (e.g. economic, organisational or social) considerations. That is, standards are not only rooted in technical deliberations, but also result from a process of social interactions between its various stakeholders. These dynamic interactions are projected onto the standardisation bodies' committees, where another dimension is added: that of the individual.

The common engineering background of most committee members has been said to leads to a cooperative situation where all participants work towards the 'best' technical solution. Along a similar, yet more realistic line it may be observed that once the basic choices have been made standardisation work becomes more cooperative at a later stage of the process, now very much resembling joint R&D efforts. Information is shared, and tasks are undertaken cooperatively.

Resources dedicated by the different stakeholders, i.e. commitment demonstrated through their willingness to conduct quality research, prepare high-quality proposals, and take over responsibilities in the committee are important. Likewise, the technical, diplomatic and political capabilities of their representatives, and last but not least the roles they assume must not be underestimated, as they play a decisive role in the process. These commitments and capabilities create asymmetries within the committees which may be exploited by a player (by successfully pushing his ideas).

Gains may result from participation in standards setting others than those purely associated with a successful proposal. Many committee members only participate for reasons related to intelligence gathering. For example, information regarding strategic moves of competitors or recent technical achievements may be gained, yielding a better evaluation of a company's position relative to its competitors. A recent survey showed that about fourteen per cent of committee members belong to that category [Spring, 1995]. Moreover, a company's reputation may rise based on to its commitment to standardisation, which (potential) customers may associate with a dedication to high quality.

If no compromise can be achieved when competing proposals exist, one possible outcome will be the formation of a new 'standards' setting consortium established by one of the rival entities. This might also be an explanation for the alarming expansion of the number of 'standards' consortia. A 'Balkanisation' of the standardisation process, with competing bodies developing competing specifications would be a potential result[11], further introducing incompatibilities.

Being active in standards setting is a costly business. It has been estimated that the costs of the development of an average IT standard amount to about $ 10,000,000 [Spring, 1996] - and that is only one standard. Another estimation says that development cost for a

---

11 Although it is not always necessary to establish a new consortium to push a specification. As we could observe during the standardisation of Local Area Networks (LANs), it is well possible to standardise competing technologies within the same standards setting body. In the case of LANs Token Ring, Token Bus and Ethernet were all standardised by both IEEE and ISO.

'major international telecommunications standard' may amount to some 1,000 person-years of experience, twenty person-years of actual effort, plus $3 million [OTA, 1992]. JTC1 alone has been producing between forty and fifty standards per year over the last decade.

Economics

Only fairly recently have economists addressed the problems associated with compatibility standards. In their terms major differences exist between standards in ICT (or, more generally speaking, in fields where networking effects occur, as also e.g. railroads), and those valid in the 'rest of the world' (i.e. primarily where no such effects may be observed). For the latter, the assumption of 'decreasing returns' holds. That is, benefits derived from producing something decrease with the number of people producing something similar; the revenues of the sole producer of washing machines will decrease once other companies also start offering washing machines. In contrast, increased returns on adoption may be assumed for ICT; the value of an electronic mail service, for instance, will increase potentially manyfold with the number of users with whom communication links can be established. The arrival of competitors offering a compatible service will therefore not necessarily result in lower revenues, it may have the opposite effect and contribute to increasing profits due to the bigger market and the resulting increased value of the first system. Thus, given the increasing returns that stem from the global networks of today, ICT clearly has a major strategic implication, as has the underlying standardisation upon the outcome of which products will be based. Thus, the choice of a standard will have significant impact on the emergence of new technologies, the performance of single companies, and it may affect competitive advantages of whole economies. Standardisation may therefore be considered by some as a useful vehicle to bring a company or a country in a more favourable position in the market by trying to push proprietary or national standards at the international or global level. Yet, with the dramatic increase of players and would-be players in the field of standardisation it remains to seen whether the respective values of the single, and sometimes competing, specifications live up to the expectations.

A company trying to push a proprietary solution towards the status of an international standard is probably the dominant association one has when thinking about the economic dimension of standards and standardisation. Significant increases in market shares - and thus potential gains - may be at stake when a product stands to be ennobled by becoming a standard. At the same time this is the ground upon which turf wars within the committees flourish if competitors try to either push their own ideas, propose a 'neutral' solution, or just attempt to impede the whole process in order to prevent any standard in the field in question. Four distinct situations are possible:

- **Common interests**
  There are no competing proposals, and a decision can quickly be reached by consensus. All parties involved attempt to serve the common good.

- **Opposed interests**
  Each opponent prefers his own proposal to be adopted, but would prefer no standard at all to the adoption of a competitor's proposal. This situation arises when the gains associated with the winning proposal are comparably big compared to the gains of the industry as a whole.

- **Overlapping interests**
  Again, each opponent prefers his own proposal to be adopted, but would rather have a competitor's proposal adopted than no standard at all. This may happen if, conversely to the situation outlined above, the whole industry stands to benefit from the adoption of a standard (regardless from where it originated) rather than the original proposer.

- **Destructive interest**
  At least one player prefers not to have any openly available standard at all, and accordingly tries to slow down the process. Typically, this player is a major vendor largely dominating the market with a proprietary product who would lose market shares if a standard were in place.

Obviously, these alternatives all come down to the question of competition vs cooperation. The path towards competition may eventually lead to a company's dominating market position with a product or service based on their own proprietary specification. Yet, at the same time the virtual absence of other players may render this particular market insignificant[12]. On the other hand, cooperation establishes a broader market for products or services based on open specifications, created through, and capable of accommodating, a number of different players. A product that succeeds in creating an environment in which other vendors consider it beneficial to produce compatible products will prove considerably more successful than its competitors. Such compatible products can only emerge if the underlying original specifications have been made public, or if a very liberal licensing policy has been pursued. That is, potential benefits are to be gained from open specifications, even if the product itself is inferior to its (less open) rivals in terms of functionality provided. Here, the range of products compatible to the original specification strengthen its status as a de facto 'standard', which in turn triggers the development of even more compliant products. As a result, a bigger market has been established, leading to increasing revenues.

Another popular (and to some degree valid) perception has it that standards, once established, tend to suppress the development of superior technology. This is true, however, only if 'superior' at the same times means 'incompatible', which is not necessarily, though often, the case. Customers waiting for the advent of Asynchronous Transfer Mode (ATM) systems, for instance, severely hampered and, in fact, virtually thwarted the take-off of another, earlier high-speed communication system, DQDB. In the same way, an established standard may not only hinder progress, but also reduce the variety of alternative technologies. After all, that is what compatibility standards are all about. The resulting limited variety of technological options carries the risk of the market being left with a less-than-optimal solution, which in turn may eventually yield the need for an expensive move towards a better, but incompatible system. At the same time, however, because of its dominant position in the

---

12 Basically, this happened to Apple Computers Inc., who implemented a very restrictive licensing policy and eventually lost the battle against Microsoft and were left stranded with a rapidly diminishing market.

market the winning standard-based system may trigger follow-up developments. For example, a wealth of different applications were soon available once the PC and DOS had established themselves as (de facto) standards. This example also illustrates another potential economic effect of standardisation: increased price competition. As functionality or other product characteristics have been eliminated as means of competition, prices become even more important. This development will most likely result in price cuts which will, in turn, push the diffusion of the system. It does not really matter here if the standard in question has evolved through sheer market power as a de facto standard, originated from an industry consortium, or proceeded through 'official' standardisation processes.

Against this background it is no big surprise that, at least initially, the major players in the ICT field were very reluctant when it came to open standardisation. With large customer bases for their proprietary systems they had little incentive to open up this lucrative market to competitors; IBM in the sixties and seventies being a case in point. Such dominant companies, who control the market, or at least major segments of it, have to lose the most from openly available standards. More recently, however, even major players seem to realise that their products hardly stand a chance of dominating an ever growing and increasingly competitive market. Strategic alliances are formed with producers of complementary products, users, and competitors. Even arch-enemies (e.g. Netscape and Microsoft) have agreed to cooperate in certain areas to enable the development of de facto 'standards'.

The Users

Thus far, the discussion has been somewhat focussed on the vendor's views on standardisation. Obviously, things look slightly different from the users' perspective. For them, standards serve three major purposes:

- **Avoid technological dead-ends**
  Users want to avoid purchasing products that eventually leave them stranded with an incompatible, and inferior, technology. A number of issues need to be considered in this context. For instance, it has to be decided if and when a new technology should be purchased, and which one should be selected. Too early

adoptions not only bear the risk of adopting a technology that eventually fails in being successful in the market, but also ignore the considerable time and money that have gone into the old technology. It has to be decided if and when to switch from a well-established technology to a new one. Investments in the old technology need to be balanced with the prospective benefits potentially to be gained from this move. On the other hand, late adopters may lose competitive advantage while being stuck with outdated technology.

- **Reduce dependency on vendors**
  Being locked in into a vendor-specific environment is increasingly becoming a major risk for a user, despite the advantages that can be associated with integrated proprietary solutions. In particular, problems occur if a vendor misses an emerging development, and its users are forced to switch to completely new (and different) systems; a very costly exercise. Accordingly, standard compliant products from a choice of vendors appeal to the users, who can pursue a pick-and-mix purchasing strategy, and also stand to benefit from price cuts as a result of increased competition.

- **Promote universality**
  Ultimately, users would like to see seamless interoperability between all hardware and software, both internally (between different departments and sites) and externally (with customers and business partners). With the ongoing globalisation of markets this can only be achieved through international standards. Clearly, this holds especially for communications products. Ideally, it should not matter at all which vendor or service provider has been selected; interoperability should always be guaranteed. This implies that user needs and requirements are met by the standards (and the implementations). In addition to seamless communication - and the business value that lies herein alone - there is another major economic benefit to be gained: the costs of incompatibility may be tremendous. For instance, in 1980 half of General Motors' automation budget went into the design of specific interfaces between incompatible machines, a situation that would not have

occurred if adequate standards had been available in the first place.

An issue closely related to the above is the timing of standards. A typical complaint about today's 'official' standards setting processes has it that standards emerge too late, that they are overtaken by the technological development, especially in the realm of IT, and that accordingly new ways of producing standards need to be found. Whilst it is certainly true that a standard needs to meet its window of opportunity, it is equally true that a specification done hastily bears the risk of producing an inferior specification. This may easily happen since the long-term values of a proposed standard are difficult to evaluate, potentially giving advantage to proposals with well understood short-term benefits. Thus, a lengthy process may well make sense in the long term.

Funding - or rather the lack of it - is another aspect which is of particular importance to the user community. In fact, it is one of the most prominent explanations for users' abstention from standardisation. Active involvement in standardisation not only demands regular participation in meetings; additional time for preparation is also required. A standard worker will not be available to his/her employer for a considerable length of time if the engagement is taken seriously, thus incurring potentially major expenses. Various suggestions have been made if and how funding should be provided to attract more users. Views differ widely in this respect; it has been argued that no special funding needs to be made available to users because they already are adequately represented on the committees. On the other hand it has been claimed that additional funding should be made available by interested parties (e.g. governments) to enable and promote participation of smaller users.

This discussion on the economic importance of standards induces the question how to guarantee, to the greatest possible extent, that standardisation activities yield a result that is widely adopted and can survive on the market. This, in turn, leads to the question how the standards setting process should be designed.

2.1.3   How to Design the Standardisation Process

Developing a standard is not an end in itself. The yardstick for a standard's success or failure is its acceptance in the market. That is, users must feel that they will benefit from employing products and services based on, or incorporating, this standard. It follows that its origin (proprietary, consortium, standards body) may be of less importance in many cases. In fact, it has been noted that wide distribution of a standard is more significant for many than its technical quality. This leads to the question what exactly establishes a 'successful' standard. Crucial attributes of an ideal standard may include:

- high technical quality,
- effective solution to the initial problem,
- timeliness,
- wide adoption.

The last point may well be the most important one. The other criteria should not be ignored, though, as they also contribute significantly to actual adoption. However, it might be argued that 'high technical quality' and 'wide adoption' are almost mutually exclusive, as the latter will almost always be based on compromises, which, in turn, stand in the way of the former. Alternatively, inclusion of options has become a popular way of accommodating the desires of different players.

It is easily conceivable that no single factor exists to guarantee a successful outcome of a standards setting activity. Rather, we can observe a complex interplay of different contributors. A standardisation process must

- be driven by a commitment to business value,
- engage interested parties,
- be based on real requirements,
- have vendor implementation commitment,
- establish confidence in conformance,
- reflect due process,
- attract a critical mass of purchasing power,
- recognise IPRs.

From the business process point of view, standardisation is an extremely simple procedure: a perceived need is identified somehow within (or possibly outside) a standards setting body; if a specified number of members subscribe to this view and offer support and commitment a work group or committee is established to identify and specify a technical solution to the problem in question. All standards setting bodies have well-defined rules in place to guide committees from deliverable to deliverable until eventually the proposal is ready for voting, which is again governed by a set of precisely defined procedures. However, very little is available in terms of guidelines for the management of the actual work in the committees, and no policies exist within ISO or IETF to prevent a committee from being dominated by an interested party or group. In an era of multinational companies ISO's 'one country, one vote' balloting approach, for example, seems ill suited; it should not be too difficult for a sufficiently interested multinational to dominate balloting through company representatives on the single national committees, or through 'proxies', who exist in the form of standards consultants[13].

Moreover, nothing is being done to establish whether or not the perceived need actually justifies the effort. Given, for example, that the costs associated with OSI have been estimated at over $4 billion standards setting bodies would seem to be well advised to produce a business case prior to the technical work (see Figure 2.1.5). A major task, therefore, is to sell the planned activity to those who would actually have to carry most of the financial burden, and who may be expected to be most interested in the final product, including particularly vendors and users. It is them who need to be convinced of the benefits to be gained from the proposed standard setting activity, and that it is in their best interest to participate and commit resources to it. Issues to be addressed here include requirements compilation and verification, ability to meet these requirements, identification of resources required, expected stability of the standard, likelihood of meeting a window of opportunity, establishment of appropriate liaisons, etc.

---

[13] Within ITU, only Members, i.e. states, typically represented by their national PTTs or equivalent organisations, have the right to vote. Only individuals, not institutional representatives, participate in the IETF.

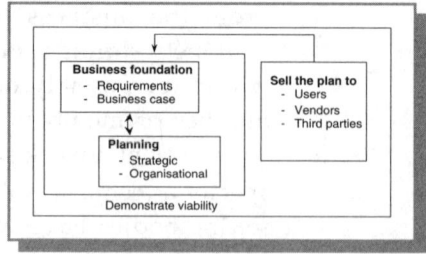

Figure 2.1.5:
Establishing a Standards Activity (adapted from [Morell, 1996])

To come up with a meaningful set of requirements, however, implies that users actually know to what use the proposed new standard will be put within their respective organisation. This, in turn, implies that corporate strategists also need to be involved at least for requirements compilation, in addition to the engineers who typically populate standards committees. Likewise, users from different types of companies, and from different backgrounds have to contribute. Only if users can be assured that their needs and requirements will establish the basis of the proposed standard can their commitment to eventually purchase products based on this standard be secured. Likewise, commitment from vendors to actually implement the standard needs to be obtained.

Following these 'preliminary' activities, the standards development can commence. In addition to the technical work of actually specifying the standard this process also comprises market development activities. That is, users need to contribute their - potentially changing - exploitation plans, the windows of opportunity have to be considered, and market awareness needs to be established. Related activities include early demonstrators, which will also serve to increase confidence of both vendors and users in the standard. This whole development process has to be managed effectively, strict scheduling has to be enforced through milestones, checkpoints and deliverables. Moreover, personnel whose job descriptions explicitly include standards development (as opposed to the rather more 'voluntary' workers today) need to be made available. Even if all this has been considered two more issues need to be resolved: how to assure that all stakeholders have an equal say during the process, and where to locate this process (i.e. whether to have a consortium or an official body do the work).

Due Process and Consensus

Due process and consensus are widely considered as the fundamental cornerstones of any 'official' standardisation process. They may be observed to a slightly lesser degree in consortia, and are completely absent in the case of a proprietary standard.

Due process is originally a legal term; the underlying concept was designed to limit arbitrary use of power by some (government) entity. Consensus is achieved when substantial agreement has been reached by all participants. This signifies more than a simple majority, but not necessarily unanimity. When applied to the standards setting process, due process means "*... that any person (organisation, company, government agency, individual, etc.) with a direct and material interest has the right to participate by a) expressing a position and its basis, b) having that position considered, and c) appealing if adversely affected.*" [ANSI, 1995]. This implies, among other things, advance notice of meetings and timely distribution of all related documents, the equal right to speak for all interested parties, strict rules on balloting procedures, availability and accessibility of an appeal body for those who feel have they suffered from improper actions, and parliamentary courtesy between committee members. Due process guarantees that everyone who might potentially be affected by a standard has the right to participate in the process on equal terms. It is a basic requirement for the development of consensus which in turn requires that all views and objections be considered, and that an effort be made towards their resolution.

Due process and consensus are indeed indispensable if a sufficiently high level of trust into a standards setting procedure is to be established. However, achieving consensus, both among the individual members of a technical group and among the high-level entities that take the ultimate decision on a proposed standard (e.g. the national bodies in ISO) takes time, which may in turn lead to a lost window of opportunity. In fact, consensus is at the same time the strength and the weakness of the official bodies.

Several measures have been embraced by these bodies to reduce the time span for balloting, and possibly for consensus building as well:

- Better utilisation of various electronic communication media.
- Implementation of management strategies to guide the projects.
- Re-design balloting procedures.
- Mechanisms to integrate proprietary specifications into the process.

Indeed, consortia which exhibit a more relaxed attitude towards strict due process and consensus, and which have far less stringent and time consuming balloting procedures appear to have an advantage here; they can move faster. Moreover, dedicated personnel (and employers) are readily available, thanks to the well defined common (business) goal, and the underlying understanding that this goal cannot be reached by any one member alone. Compared to this situation the measures proposed by the 'official' bodies outlined above appear to do little else than fiddling about with the symptoms rather than offering a cure.

It remains to be seen, however, whether the process of consensus building actually needs to be reconsidered. After all, while preventing rapid development of standards, consensus offers a quality potentially much more valuable than speed: longevity. Any standard that has gone through the painstaking procedure of consensus building, during which (ideally) all concerns have been considered, eliminated or, if deemed necessary, integrated may stand a far better chance of surviving for a reasonably long period of time than does a consortium specification. As often as not the output of a consortium tends to reflect the views of a single company, possibly its major sponsor, who may have invested heavily in the consortium and is looking for some return on investment.

Judging by the list of requirements on the standardisation process listed above, and taking into account the arguments presented, it would seem that a combination of a consortium-style process (because of its speed), followed by the official sanctioning of its - potentially modified - outcome (to preserve the public good character of a standard) could combine the best of both worlds.

2.1.4   Pros and Cons of User[14] Participation

The issues surrounding the problem of user participation in standards setting have for quite some time been high on the agenda of both researchers and the standards setting bodies themselves. There is a wide agreement that user participation is a sine qua non for a standardisation activity to be successful, particularly in the field of information technology. In fact, increased user participation is often considered as the panacea for all problems[15]. However, today very few users are represented in the major international standards organisations. Looking at the list of ITU-T members, for example, reveals the virtually complete absence of users. Those members with the right to vote represent their respective national PTTs or equivalent organisations. Among the private sector members there is an almost one hundred per cent dominance of vendors and manufacturers. Within ETSI, the list of full and associated user members comprises twenty-two names, only about half of which, however, really are users. Moreover, user members, even those who actually deserve this description, do not always contribute.

Moreover, users do not see standards as a means in itself; rather, they need systems that work smoothly in networked environments, that can easily be interconnected and are interoperable across both network and organisational boundaries. Their choices will therefore be pragmatic, and standards are only one way to achieve these goals, albeit an obvious and convenient one. This needs to be accepted by standards bodies if they want to produce standards which stand a chance of survival in the market place. As a consequence, these bodies must realise that only business users can provide this crucial input. Taking these thoughts one step further, users need to ensure that not only their compatibility needs be addressed, but also their overall

---

14 The term 'user' denotes corporate users, as opposed to individual end-users.

15 There is a strange exception, though. [ISO, 1990] states that negotiations in the case of emerging technologies (i.e. for anticipatory standards) *"... do not need to be conducted under the traditional multi-interest consensus procedures..."*. This holds because *"... an emerging technology has no users yet"*. In effect this means that users may be excluded from the specification of anticipatory standards.

'computing' needs, i.e. those requirements that originate from their organisational and strategic environments.

If users participate at all in standards setting, they will do so with motivations very different from those of vendors and service providers, who seek to protect their own business interests by either trying to push proprietary solutions or by joining the 'open systems' bandwagon, whatever is deemed most profitable. Above all, though, they want to keep - better yet, increase - their customer base. Users, in turn, will primarily try and push their specific requirements during the process. While typically wishing to have standards-based systems, users at the same time also want to have solutions which are adaptable as much as possible to their specific needs. Thus, clashes are pre-programmed not only between single vendors, but also between vendors and users. Not least in an attempt to circumvent these clashes, and to accommodate their customers, vendors tend to incorporate enhancements into their products to meet their customers' actual demand. Similarly, every now and then users tend to design their own standards, which then eventually compete with their official counterparts. This happened for example in the case of EDI, where the official standard (EDIFACT) was preceded by, and has to compete with, several sector standards. Ultimately, such activities are likely to undermine the general idea of compatibility standards.

The above thoughts unveil a number of questions directly related to the issue of user participation in standardisation - why, what, how, where, and when to participate.

First, why participate at all? After all, such commitment implies major expenses on the part of the user, with a very uncertain return on investment. Yet, users need to recognise that they are the ultimate sponsors of standardisation (the costs of which are included in product prices). Indeed, as customers they have a tremendous hold over the industry. This holds especially in telecommunications, where the benefits to be gained from network externalities will either rapidly attract more and more users, or where their absence will throw a standard into obscurity Moreover, users will suffer most from inadequate standards that will leave them struggling with incompatibilities. Likewise, they will benefit from well-designed standards addressing real needs; for one, they stand to gain major benefits from backward-compatible standards, which offer a degree of protection against obsolescence.

What could users contribute? Two prominent areas may be identified, the most obvious one being their needs and requirements. User requirements are rarely, if ever, specified in a way that renders further discussions, refinements and elaborations in the committees dispensable.

The second area is somewhat similar. Users will go through a learning process when employing services. At some stage, therefore, they will be able to contribute their experiences gained from real-life day-to-day work to the process. These experiences may eventually bring users in a position to make contributions well beyond pure requirements compilations. At this point, however, opinions vary between the view that users are well able to contribute to the technical work, and that the technical nuts and bolts should be left to the vendors. This discussion will be taken up again later in the light of further findings.

The next issue to be considered is 'how to participate'. Whereas the 'why' has been addressed at length in the literature, this question remains somewhat less touched. Rather vague suggestions have been made regarding mechanisms to enable users to express their needs, and to contribute resources to standards setting. However, few concrete recommendations as to how exactly this could be done have been brought forward. In general, though, there seems to be consensus that large users, especially those with an urgent need for standardised systems or services should participate directly in the technical work. However, especially for smaller companies there are obvious barriers to this form of participation, rooted in the lack of sufficient financial resources and knowledgeable personnel. They could, for instance, participate through trade associations Likewise, a similar, popular suggestion to overcome these barriers is the formation of 'user coalitions', i.e. users have to organise themselves to play an adequate role in the process.

The standards setting process comprises a variety of different types of organisations. Thus, 'Where to participate?' is another question to be addressed. In most cases 'the standardisation process' is looked at as something akin to an atomic entity, which cannot be subdivided any further. In particular, rarely is a distinction being made between organisations producing base standards and those in charge of functional standards. However, it is far from clear where participation is most beneficial for users. Participation in profile development would be the option of choice if interoperability of implementations were to be assured. On the other hand, there is little point in specifying a profile for a base standard that does not meet the requirements.

Finally, when should users participate? This problem is closely related to the question of what users can contribute to standardisation. The two genuine user domains, requirements and operating experience, seem to suggest that the crucial periods of user contributions are prior to, or at a very early stage of, a standards activity (requirements), and either following field trials - which may or may not be part of the process - or after the project has finished and products are available on the market (experience). Whilst these suggestions appear to be straightforward, they too will need additional discussion, which will be postponed until the final chapter.

2.2   Defining the Term 'User'

The concept of the 'user' is becoming progressively more complex. For example, an ISO Working Group charged with identifying user requirements reportedly failed, and was disbanded in the early 1990s, not least because they could not come up with a meaningful, and agreed, definition of what actually constitutes a 'user'. In 1996, the same happened to ITU-T's Study Group 1, the task of which was to provide 'service definitions'. The former activities of SG 1 have now been merged with those of other SGs.

Typically, the term 'user' is employed in very different contexts, and with very different meanings. Several attempts have been made to get a grasp of the 'user'. For example, the OSI Reference Model may be used as an analogy for a hierarchy of users (Figure 2.2.1). Within this model, an entity of layer (N) uses services provided by layer (N-1), and offers services to layer (N+1) (Figure 2.2.1a). The overall communication functionality is provided by a hierarchy of seven layers (Figure 2.2.1b). Applying this model to users is intuitive; for instance, an end-user has a requirement, passes it to the system administrator who, in turn, translates it into a system requirement which is passed to a system integrator, who will forward it to the network operator if necessary (see Figure 2.2.1c).

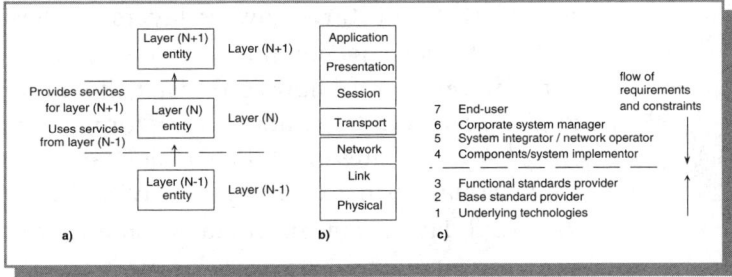

Figure 2.2.1:
User Hierarchies and the OSI Reference Model
a) Interaction Between Layers in the OSI/RM (slightly modified)
b) The Seven Layers of the OSI/RM
c) The Layered Model of User Classes (according to [Naemura, 1995])

Yet, even this apparently straightforward model has its weaknesses. Whilst it shows the likely flow of requirements within the upper four layers it fails to do so for the lower three layers, where this flow is rather more in the reverse direction, if a real flow can be identified at all. The underlying technology imposes constraints upon a base standard (provider), which in turn leaves only options to be implemented by the functional standard (provider). Moreover, it does not show a real hierarchy of users. I would argue that, at least as far as telecommunication systems are concerned, in terms of requirements a system manager is little else than just another type of end-user. A corporate network manager's needs will focus on other aspects of the system than those of the end users, i.e. he will be interested in functionality supporting administrative and operational tasks, but nevertheless will concentrate on functionality rather than strategic issues. Thus, I would further argue that the class of users who make the strategic decisions is completely missing in the above model. These users, who are likely to draw upon advice from system managers, are focussing on their respective organisation's business needs rather than technical matters. They establish the class of the 'corporate users'; their requirements are largely dictated by their environment (market power, relations to customers, suppliers and business partners, etc).

Still, using the OSI-RM as a tool for modelling different classes of users is quite helpful. Indeed, we can take the similarities between the hierarchy of user classes and the layers of the OSI-RM even one step further: the three lowest layers of the OSI-RM are generally referred to as being 'communication oriented', that is, they deal solely with the problem of how to transfer the information form the sender to the receiver. In contrast, the topmost three layers are called 'application oriented', as their major task is to present and organise the information in a meaningful way to the user. The functionality of the fourth layer, 'Transport', falls somewhere in between.

We can now identify an analogous three-level hierarchy for standards and users as well (see Figure 2.2.2). The lower three layers are 'standards oriented', they provide a framework within which standards compliant systems and services can be built. The two upper layers are 'user oriented', a specific technology is not that important at this level; it is more important that it fits into the existing or envisaged environment (primarily for corporate users) and that it provides adequate functionality (primarily for end-users). In between there are the service providers and vendors, who have to deal with both aspects to produce something useful for their customers, and thus have to consider their requirements as well.

If we take the abstraction yet another step further we will come to a well-known classification of users that distinguishes between

- users of implementations or services and
- users of standards.

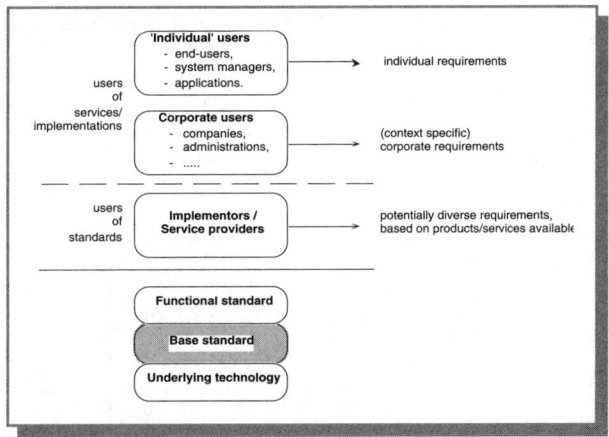

Figure 2.2.2:
A Three-Level Hierarchy for Standards and Users

A user of an e-mail *service*, for instance, may be a corporate user (e.g. a company or a government agency), or an actual end-user; it may also be a system administrator or even an application. These groups will each have very different requirements, visibility of which will vary from 'potentially considerable' in case of a really large corporate user to 'virtually non-existent' for human end-users.

Yet, vendors and providers are also users, albeit users of *standards specifications* (as opposed to services). Accordingly, from a standard's point of view, the former category may be referred to as 'indirect' users of standards, as they are typically only employing services based on or around implementations of standards, rather than the standards themselves. In contrast to that, the latter category may be termed 'direct' users of standards, as the products and services they are offering incorporate, and/or are directly based on the standards specifications. Figure 2.2.3 once more depicts these different relations, but from another angle. Looking at a 'user' from yet another angle, we find that several differentiation schemes have been suggested in the literature on innovations and on the social shaping of technology. Typically, these schemes have been based on computing skills. Identified categories include users who develop their own systems, who control development of their systems, data processing professionals, and programmers. However, not least with the emergence of end-user computing these boundaries have vanished to some extent.

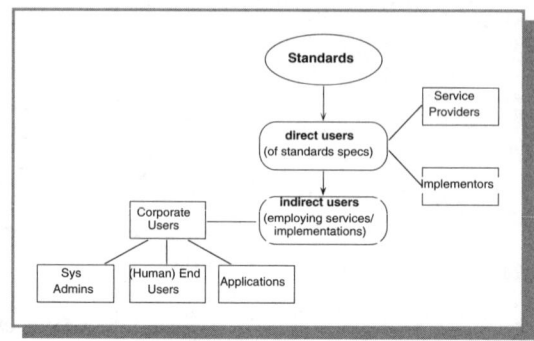

Figure 2.2.3:
Categories and Classes of Users

Yet another classification has been based on the variables of organisational power and IT expertise, and distinguishing between in-house IT specialist, non-programming user, functional support personnel, computer-skilled business programmers, and (unskilled) organisational groups. Moreover, a corporate IT department, for instance, may well assume a dual role, acting as a user as regards an external vendor, and being the supplier itself for local end-users or other departments. In any case, and whichever classification is applied, it should be obvious that again 'user' in no way denotes a homogeneous group with similar requirements, expertise and perceptions.

During the implementation of ICT systems, knowledge regarding technological, organisational and economical problems is distributed among vendors and users; only cooperation and collaboration will yield positive results. In particular, it is the users' task to develop and communicate knowledge of their respective working environment, including organisational aspects as for instance the respective organisational framework, local administrative structures, specific information channels, and characteristics of the work organisation, but also technical information as e.g. existing legacy systems that need to be integrated. It follows from this diversity that representatives of all types of users have to be involved in, and have to contribute their specific knowledge and requirements to, the implementation of a new IT system.

References

[ANSI 1995]   American National Standards Institute
                       Procedures for the Development and
                       Coordination of American National Standards
                       http://www.ansi.org/procttl.html

[ANSI X3 1993]   ANSI X3
                       Standards Life Cycle
                       ASC X3/93-0884-L, 1993

[Baron 1995]   Baron, S.N.
                       The Standards Development Process and the
                       NII: A View from the Trenches
                       In: Kahin, B.; Abbate, J. (eds): S"tandards
                       Policy for Information Infrastructure". MIT
                       Press, 1995.

[Cargil 1989]   Cargil, C.F.
                       Information Technology Standardization -
                       Theory, Process and Organizations
                       Digital Press, 1989

[Cowan 1992]   Cowan, R.
                       High Technology and the Economics of
                       Standardization
                       In: Dierkes, M.; Hoffmann, U. (eds): New
                       Technologies at the Outset - Social Forces in
                       the Shaping of Technological Innovations.
                       Campus/Westview, 1992.

[Encyclopedia 1987]   The New Encyclopædia Britannica, 15th
                       Edition, 1987.

[ISO 1990]   International Organization for
                       Standardization
                       A Vision for the Future. Standards Needs foe
                       Emerging Technologies
                       ISO/IEC, ISBN 92-67-10154-4, 1990.

[Krechmar 1996a]   Krechmer, K.
                       Technical Standards: Foundations of the
                       Future
                       ACM Standard View, vol 4, no 1, 1996.

[Krechmar 1996b]   Krechmer, K.
                      Standards Make the GIH Possible
                      IEEE Communications Magazine, vol. 34, no. 8,
                      1996.

[Mansell 1995]   Mansell, R.
                      Standards, Industrial Policy and Innovation
                      in: In: Hawkins, R.W. et al. (eds): "Standards,
                      Innovation and Competitiveness". Edward
                      Elgar Publishers, 1995.

[Morell 1996]   Morell, J.A.; Stewart, S.L.
                      Standards Development for Information
                      Technology: Best Practices for the United
                      States
                      ACM StandardView, vol. 4, no. 1, 1996

[Naemura 1995]   Naemura, K.
                      User involvement in the lifecycle of
                      information technology and telecommunication
                      standards
                      In: Hawkins, R.W. et al. (eds): "Standards,
                      Innovation and Competitiveness". Edward
                      Elgar Publishers, 1995.

[OECD 1991]   Organization for Economic Co-operation and
                      Development
                      Information Technology Standards: The
                      Economic Dimension
                      Information Computer Communications Policy,
                      no. 25, 1991

[OTA 1992]   Office of Technology Assesnt
                      Global Standards - Buidling Blocks for the
                      Future
                      OTA-TCT-512, 1992

[Reilly 1994]   Reilly, A.K.
                      A US Perspective on Standards Development
                      IEEE Communications Magazine, 1/94

[Repussard 1995]   Repussard, J.
                          Problems and Issues for Public Sector
                          Involvement in Voluntary Standardisation
                           In: Hawkins, R.W. et al. (eds): "Standards,
                          Innovation and Competitiveness". Edward
                          Elgar Publishers, 1995.

[Spring 1995]   Spring, M.B. et al.
                          Improving the Standardization Process:
                          Working with Bulldogs an Turtles
                          In: Kahin, B.; Abbate, J. (eds): S"tandards
                          Policy for Information Infrastructure". MIT
                          Press, 1995.

[Spring 1996]   Spring, M.B. et al
                          System Design for an Integrated Document
                          System and Its Impact on Standards
                          Development Efficiency
                          Managing Virtual Enterprises; Proc. IEMC 96,
                          1996.

[Webster 1992]   Webster's New Universal Unabridged
                          Dictionary
                          Barnes & Noble Books, New York, 1992.

Further Readings

Alexander, D.: "Infrastructure evolution and the global electronic marketplace: a European IT user's perspective". In: Hawkins, R.W. et al. (eds): "Standards, Innovation and Competitiveness". Edward Elgar Publishers, 1995.

American National Standards Institute - Accredited Committee X3: "Standards Life Cycle". ASC X3/93-0884-L, 1993.

Ask, F.: "Interoperability and Intellectual Property". In: Kahin, B.; Abbate, J. (eds): Standards Policy for Information Infrastructure. MIT Press, 1995.

Baron, S.N.: "The Standards Development Process and the NII: A View from the Trenches". In: Kahin, B.; Abbate, J. (eds): Standards Policy for Information Infrastructure, MIT Press, 1995.

Besen, F.M.: "The standards process in telecommunication and information technology". In: Hawkins, R.W. et al. (eds): "Standards, Innovation and Competitiveness". Edward Elgar Publishers, 1995.

Bogod, J.L.: "Information Technology Standardization". In: Berg, J.L.; Schumny, H. (eds): An Analysis of the Information Technology Standardization Process. North-Holland, 1990.

Cargill, C.F.: "A Five-Segment Model for Standardization". In Kahin, B.; Abbate, J. (eds): Standards Policy for Information Infrastructure. MIT Press, 1995.

Cotterman, W.W.; Kumar, K.: "User Cube: A taxonomy of End Users". Communications of the ACM, vol. 32, no. 11, 1989.

Cowan, R.: "High Technology and the Economics of Standardization". In: Dierkes, M.; Hoffmann, U. (eds): New Technologies at the Outset - Social Forces in the Shaping of Technological Innovations. Campus/Westview, 1992.

Dankbaar, B.; v. Tulder, R.: "The Influence of Users in Standardization: The Case of MAP". In: Dierkes, M.; Hoffmann, U. (eds): "New Technologies at the Outset - Social Forces in the Shaping of Technological Innovations". Campus/Westview, 1992.

David, P.A.: "Standardization Policies for Network Technologies: The Flux Between Freedom and Order Revisited". In: Hawkins, R.W. et al. (eds): "Standards, Innovation and Competitiveness". Edward Elgar Publishers, 1995.

David, P.A.; Monroe, H.K.: "Standards Development Strategies Under Incompete Information - Isn't the 'Battle of the Sexes' Really a Revelation Game?". MERIT Working Paper 2/94-039, 1994.

Ellis, W.: "Intellectual Property Rights and High Technology Standards". In Kahin, B.; Abbate, J. (eds): Standards Policy for Information Infrastructure. MIT Press, 1995.

ETSI Directorate: "Progress on User Participation in the Standardization Process". Presented at 3rd Interregional Telecommunications Standards Conference, Tokyo 1992

Farrell, J.: "Arguments for Weaker Interlectual Property Protection in Network Industries". ACM StandardView, vol. 3, no. 2, 1995.

Ferné, G.: "Information Technology Standardization and Users: International Challenges Move the Process Forward". In: Kahin, B.; Abbate, J. (eds): Standards Policy for Information Infrastructure. MIT Press, 1995.

Fincham, R. et al.: "Expertise and Innovation - Information Technology Strategies in the Financial Services Sector". Oxford University Press, 1994.

Fischer, P.: "The Role of the User in the Standardization Process - Workshop Report". In: Berg, J.L.; Schumny, H.: "An Analysis of the Information Technology Standardization Process". North-Holland, 1990.

Foray, D.: "Coalitions and Committees: How Users Get Involved in Information Technology Standardisation". In: Hawkins, R.W. et al. (eds): "Standards, Innovation and Competitiveness". Edward Elgar Publishers, 1995., 1995.

Genschel, P.: "Standards in der Informationstechnik (Standards in Information Technology)". Campus Publishers, 1995.

Gray, E.M.; Bodson, D.: "Preserving Due Process in Standards Work". ACM StandardView, vol 3, no 4, 1995.

Hanrahan, W.F.: "Standards and the Information Infrastructure". In: Kahin, B.; Abbate, J. (eds): Standards Policy for Information Infrastructure. MIT Press, 1995.

International Organization for Standardization: "IEC/ISO Directives - Part 1 - Procedures for the technical work of ISO/IEC JTC1 on information technology, Supplement 1: The transposition of publicly available specifications into international standards". ISO 1995

International Organization for Standardization: "IEC/ISO Directives - Procedures for the technical work of ISO/IECJTC1 on information technology". ISO 1995

International Organization for Standardization: "Raising Standards for the World - ISO's Long Range Strategies 1996 - 1998". http://www.iso.ch/presse/strategy/strategy.html

International Organization for Standardization: "Transposition of publicly available specifications into international standards - A management guide". ISO 1995

International Organization for Standardization: "ISO/IEC Directives - Part 1 - Procedures for the Technical Work,". ISO 1995.

International Telecommunication Union: "The World Standardization Summit Sets New Directions for the ITU-T". http://www.itu.int/press/releases96/np96-07/e.htm

Isaak, J.: "Information Infrastructure Meta-Architecture and Cross-Industry Standardization". In: Kahin, B.; Abbate, J. (eds): Standards Policy for Information Infrastructure. MIT Press, 1995.

Jakobs, K.: "Standardisation of Global Telecommunication Services - Expertise or Market Shares". Proc. 7th Int. Symposium on Technology and Society, ISTAS '96, IEEE Press, 1996

Jakobs, K.; Procter, R.; Williams, R.: "Usability vs. Standardization". Proceedings CHI '95 Research Symposium, ACM, 1995

Jakobs, K.:: "On the Relevance of Global IT-Standardisation - Should User Companies Participate?". Proc. 5th Annual Bayer Conf., Strategies for Global Involvement, 1996

Kahin, B.; Abbate, J.: "Standards Policy for Information Infrastructure". MIT Press, 1995

Mazza, S.: "The Future for ANSI". ACM StandardView, vol. 3, no. 4, 1995.

Morell, J.A.; Stewart, S.L.: "Standards Development for Information Technology: Best Practices for the United States". ACM StandardView, vol. 4, no. 1, 1996

Office of Technology Assesnt: "Global Standards - Buidling Blocks for the Future". OTA-TCT-512, 1992.

Organization for Economic Co-operation and Development: "OECD Workshop on the Economics of the Information Society. OECD". Paris 1996.

Organization for Economic Co-operation and Development: "Information Technology (IT) Diffusion Policies for Small and Medium-Sized Enterprises (SMEs)". OECD, Paris 1995.

Rankine, L.J.: "Information Technology Standards - Can the Challenges be Met". In: Berg, J.L.; Schumny, H.: "An Analysis of the Information Technology Standardization Process". North-Holland, 1990.

Richardson, G.B.: "Economic Analysis, Public Policy and the Software Industry". DRUID Working Paper 97-4, 1997.

Salter, L.: "User Participation in Standardization - New or Merely Recycled". Managing Virtual Enterprises, Proc. IEMC 1996.

Salter, L.: "User Involvment in IT&T Standardization". Proc. Multimedia Communications, ICCC 1993.

Salter, L.: "D Reforms Make a Difference Gearing Methodology to Assessments of Standardization Practice". In: Hawkins, R.W. et al. (eds): "Standards, Innovation and Competitiveness". Edward Elgar Publishers, 1995.

Schmidt, S.K.; Werle, R.: "The Development of Compatibility Standards in Telecommunications: Conceptual Framework and Theoretical Perspective". In: Dierkes, M.; Hoffmann, U. (eds): "New Technologies at the Outset - Social Forces in the Shaping of Technological Innovations". Campus/Westview, 1992.

Shurmer, M.; Lea, G.: "Telecommunications Standardization and Intellectual Property Rights: A Fundamental Dilemma". ACM Standard View, vol. 3, no. 2, 1995.

Smoot, O.R.: "Tension and Synergism Between Standards and Interlectual Property". ACM StandardView, vol. 3, no. 2, 1995.

Spring, M.B.; Weiss, M.B.H.: "Selected Intellectual Property Issues in Standardization". Proc. 20th Telecommunications Policy Research Conference, Solomons, MD, 1992.

Steinmueller, W.E.: "The political economy of data communication standards". In: Hawkins, R.W. et al. (eds): "Standards, Innovation and Competitiveness". Edward Elgar Publishers, 1995.

The New Encyclopædia Britannica, 15th Edition, 1987.

Updegrove, A.: "Standard Setting and Consortium Structures". ACM StandardView, vol. 3, no. 4, 1995.

Chapter 3

An Introduction to Standards Setting Bodies

This section will first introduce those international standards setting bodies this book looks at, and their respective procedures. This will be followed by a brief discussion of if, and how, user requirements are fed into the individual processes. Finally, the fundamental differences between base standards and profiles are outlined.

3.1   The International Organization for Standardization (ISO)

The International Organization for Standardization[16] (ISO) is a global, non-governmental federation of national standards bodies from about 120 countries. ISO was established in 1947, with the mission *"to promote the development of standardization and related activities in the world with a view to facilitating the international exchange of goods and services, and to developing cooperation in the spheres of intellectual, scientific, technological and economic activity."*[ISO, 1995d]. Prior to that, standardisation was done under the auspices of either the International Electrotechnical Commission (IEC), created in 1906, in the electrotechnical field, or by the International Federation of the National Standardizing Associations (ISA), established in 1926.

Following the break in standards activities caused by World War II, ISO was founded by twenty-five countries. Its work commenced in 1947, with the first standard published in 1951.

Membership in ISO is on a per-country basis, with one organisation - typically the respective national standards body - representing its country. There are full members, correspondent members (which do not actively participate, but are kept fully informed), and subscriber members which normally represent those countries that cannot afford one of the other categories. Depending on a full member country's interests its representative may decide to become a P(anticipating)-member or an O(bserving)-member in a committee, or no member at all. P-members participate actively in the work, with an obligation to vote on all questions formally submitted for voting within the technical committee or subcommittee, and, whenever possible, to participate in meetings. O-members follow the work as an observer, and therefore receive committee documents and have the right to submit comments and to attend meetings (but not to vote).

The operations of ISO are governed by the Council consisting of the principal officers and eighteen elected member bodies. Inter alia, it

---

[16] 'ISO' is not an acronym, but a word derived from the Greek word 'isos', meaning 'equal'.

appoints the twelve members of the Technical Management Board, and the Chairmen of the policy development committees. It also decides on the annual budget of the Central Secretariat. The Officers and delegates nominated by the member bodies constitute the General Assembly. Its tasks include actions relating to the ISO annual report and the ISO multi-year strategic plan with its financial implications. It may also establish policy development committees. The Technical Management Board is in charge of all aspects related to the technical work. Among others, it establishes and dissolves Technical Committees (TCs), allocates their secretariats and appoints their chairpersons, handles the technical coordination between ISO TCs and their respective counterparts within other organisations, and acts as the 'court of appeal' against committee decisions. It also appoints Technical Advisory Groups if expert advice on particular areas is needed. Figure 3.1.1 shows the general structure.

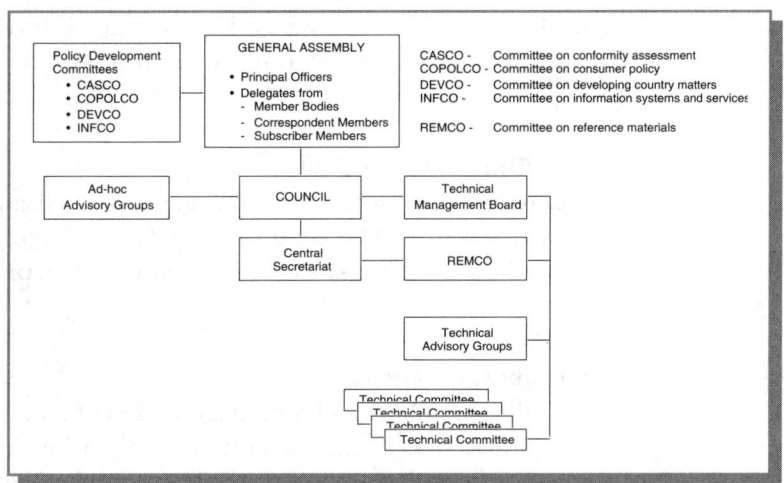

Figure 3.1.1:
ISO Structure (based on [ISO, 1995e])

The actual standardisation work is almost fully decentralised, and performed in 187 TCs (1999) and their respective Sub-committees (SC) and Working Groups (WG), with a total number of about 2,700. Participants come from the respective national member bodies, which are also in charge of providing secretarial services for the committees and groups. In general, participation within any TC or SC is open to every national member body and to all A-liaisons (as e.g. ITU-T Study

Groups). Development and revision of standards are carried out as 'projects' within a committee. Typically, a project is assigned to a Working Group comprised of individually appointed experts. It should be noted that *"The experts act in a personal capacity and not as the official representatives of the P-member or A-liaison organisation by which they have been appointed."*[ISO, 1995a]. ISO itself - being very much a meta-organisation - primarily provides for a central coordination entity, does the final editing of documents prior to publication, and maintains an overall schedule.

In the following the process and procedures governing ISO's standards setting process are described in some more detail, since largely similar rules have been adopted by almost all national and regional private sector standards setting organisations.

The 1995 revision of the ISO/IEC Directives specifies the accepted procedures for developing and approving International Standards. The following is a brief outline of this seven-stage development process:

- **Preliminary Stage (0)**
  During this stage preliminary work items are addressed, covering,for instance, emerging technologies that have not yet reached a sufficiently mature status for progressing to other stages.

- **Proposal Stage (1)**
  Voting members ballot on the creation of a new standards project. The first step in the development of an international standard is to confirm that this particular standard is needed. A new work item proposal (NP) is submitted for vote by the members of the relevant TC/SC to determine the inclusion of the work item in the programme of work. The proposal is accepted if a majority of the P-members of the TC/SC vote in favour and at least five P-members declare their commitment to actively participate in the project. At this stage a project leader responsible for the work item is normally appointed.

- **Preparatory Stage (2)**
  The project leader manages the development of a Working Draft. Usually, a working group of experts is set up by the TC/SC for the preparation of a working draft. Successive working drafts may be considered until the working group is satisfied that it has developed the best technical solution possible. At this stage, the Committee Draft is forwarded to the working group's parent committee for the consensus-building phase.

- **Committee Stage (3)**
  Consensus is achieved on a Committee Draft.
  As soon as a first committee draft is available, it is registered with ISO's Central Secretariat. It is distributed for comments from and, if required, voting by the P-members of the TC/SC. Again it may be necessary to consider successive committee drafts until consensus is reached. Once consensus has been attained, the text is finalised for submission as a Draft International Standard (DIS).

- **Enquiry Stage (4)**
  National bodies vote (and comment) on a DIS.
  The DIS is circulated to all ISO member bodies for voting and comment. It is approved for submission as a Final Draft International Standard (FDIS) if a two-thirds majority of the P-members of the TC/SC are in favour and not more than one-quarter of the total number of votes are negative. Otherwise, the text is returned to the originating TC/SC for further study. In this case a revised document will eventually be circulated for voting and comment as a DIS.

- **Approval Stage (5)**
  Yes/No vote on Final Draft International Standard (FDIS).
  The FDIS is circulated to all ISO member bodies for a final yes/no vote. If technical comments are received during this period, they are no longer considered, but registered for consideration during a future revision of the International Standard (IS). The majority of votes required for approval is the same as above. If these criteria are not met, the standard is referred back to the originating TC/SC for reconsideration in the

light of the technical reasons submitted in support of the negative votes received.

- **Publication Stage (6)**
  ISO publishes the International Standard.
  Once an FDIS has been approved, only minor editorial changes, if and where necessary, are introduced into the final text, which is sent to the Central Secretariat for publication.

Target dates have been established for stages two through six. If these dates are not met by a project it may be cancelled unless suitable justification for the delay can be produced by the secretariat in charge. Target dates are:

- six months until Working Draft status,
- two years until Committee Draft status,
- three years until Final Draft International Standard status.

Table 3.1.1 summarises the different stages and the respective outcomes.

Stage #	Project stage name	Associated document	Abbrev.
0	Preliminary stage	Preliminary work item	PWI
1	Proposal stage	New work item proposal	NP
2	Preparatory stage	Working draft(s)	WD
3	Committee stage	Committee draft(s)	CD
4	Enquiry stage	Draft International Standard	DIS
5	Approval stage	Final DIS	FDIS
6	Publication stage	International Standard	IS

Table 3.1.1:
Project Stages and Associated Documents

In case of technical errors or ambiguities, or outdated information included in the document detected after publication, a Technical Corrigendum will be produced, or the corrections may be incorporated into a new edition of the standard. Alternatively, an Amendment modifies and/or adds information. Amendments too follow the procedures for a new project.

If a document with a certain degree of maturity is available at the start of a standardisation project, for example a standard developed by a national standards organisation, it will be possible to omit certain stages. In the so-called 'Fast track procedure', a document is submitted directly for approval as a DIS to the ISO member bodies (stage 4). If the document has been developed by an international standardising body recognised by the ISO Council (as e.g. ITU-T), it can be submitted for approval as an FDIS (stage 5), without passing through the previous stages.

Following publication a standard will be subject to reviews by the P-members of the TC/SC in five-year intervals. Outcome of this review decides whether the standard is confirmed, revised or withdrawn. A document to be revised will be dealt with like a new project and will have to go through stages two through six.

JTC 1

To adequately deal with all aspects of information technology ISO and IEC jointly established their Joint Technical Committee One (JTC1) in 1986. In 1999, 26 countries actively participated in the work of JTC1 (P-members), another 36 are O-members. The total number of ISO (draft) standards under the direct responsibility of the JTC1 secretariat is around 500. Figure 3.1.2 shows the position of JTC 1 in relation to its parent organisations ISO and IEC.

JTC 1 has developed its own set of procedures and guidelines, taking into account the special circumstances of, and requirements on IT standardisation. The rules specifying the steps towards an international standard differ slightly from those adopted by ISO.

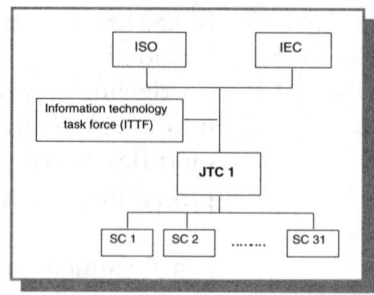

Figure 3.1.2:
JTC 1 Organisational Chart

For one, they comprise only six stages, basically combining Enquiry and Approval stages into one. The most important difference, however, has been the implementation of a Transposition Procedure for Publicly Available Specifications (PAS) [ISO, 1995b]. Based on the fast track procedure, this is an even more extensive policy for proprietary specifications to be transposed into international standards. As with the fast track procedure, this reflects the recognised need for a speed-up of the standards setting process, and even more so, the fact that considerable expertise - and almost readily usable specifications - may be available from companies or consortia. The procedure works as follows:

An organisation wishing to have one of its proprietary specifications transposed into an international standard (termed the 'PAS originator') first applies for recognition as a 'PAS submitter' to the JTC 1 secretariat. This application includes information on the specifications to be submitted and on the PAS submitter. Upon approval, the PAS submitter gains the right to submit specifications for an initial period of two years. The remainder of the procedure follows the fast track procedure as described above. A set of criteria has been developed by which the submitted document will be judged regarding quality, consensus and alignment[17].

---

17 Sun Microsystems applied for being permitted to become a PAS provider in an attempt to standardise JAVA. This move caused much excitement. The story is captured nicely in [Cargill, 1997].

3.2   The International Telecommunication Union (ITU)

The International Telegraph Union, the predecessor of the ITU, was set up as a treaty organisation in 1865 by twenty European countries. At the same time, the first International Telegraph Convention was signed.

Following the invention of the telephone in 1876, the Telegraph Union began to cover international legislation in this area as well. The invention of wireless telegraphy in 1896 triggered the initiation of the first International Radiotelegraph Conference, held in 1906. This was the first Plenipotentiary Conference through which the work of the Union - and later of ITU - has since been directed. The International Telephone Consultative Committee (CCIF) was set up in 1924, followed by the establishment of the International Telegraph Consultative Committee (CCIT) in 1925, and in 1927 the International Radio Consultative Committee (CCIR) was founded. In 1934, the Union's name was changed into 'International Telecommunication Union' (ITU), which became a specialised agency of the United Nations in 1947. The International Telephone and Telegraph Consultative Committee (CCITT) was founded in 1956, through the merger of the CCIT and the CCIF.

In an attempt to adapt to the more complex and, particularly, more competitive environment it was working in the ITU was restructured in 1992. According to article 7 of the ITU Constitution [ITU, 1993], the Union comprises of (see also Figure 3.2.1):

- the Plenipotentiary Conference, which is its supreme organ,
- the Council, which acts on behalf of the Plenipotentiary Conference,
- World Conferences on International Telecommunications,
- the General Secretariat, in charge of administrative and organisational tasks,
- Telecommunication Standardization (ITU-T; formerly CCITT),
- Radiocommunication (ITU-R; formerly CCIR; the standards setting activities have been moved to ITU-T),
- Telecommunication Development (ITU-D).

Fundamental policy and organisational decisions as well as long term strategic resolutions are made at 'Plenipotentiary Conferences' which are convened every four years. Between two such conferences the ITU Council, which is composed of forty-six members, is in charge of monitoring the implementation of decisions taken. It also considers policy and strategic issues, and is generally conducting the day-to-day business. If necessary, telecommunications regulations are revised at a 'World Conference on International Telecommunications'.

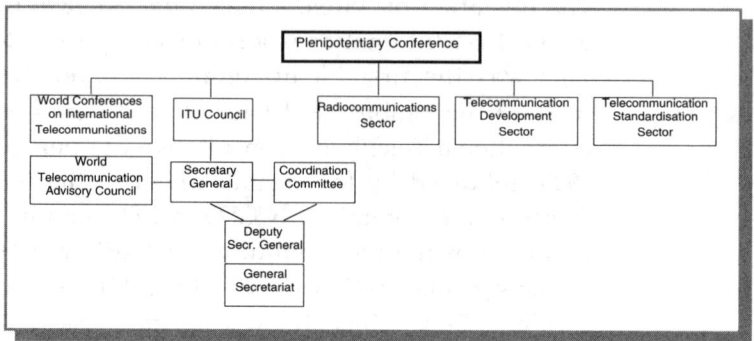

Figure 3.2.1:
The Structure of the ITU

In mid-1999, the ITU comprised of 188 Member States and 371 members (scientific and industrial companies, public and private operators, broadcasters, regional/international organisations) in the three sectors. However, the right to vote is restricted to one representative per Member Country, i.e. almost exclusively to the respective national PTTs (Post, Telegraph and Telephone administration) or, as a result of the liberalisation of the telecommunication market, to one of the respective national Recognised Operating Agencies (ROAs, e.g. AT&T in the US). Other companies, notably those referred to as Scientific or Industrial Organisations (SIOs), need to be approved by their respective governments, and only have a right to participate and to contribute to the technical work, but are not allowed to vote.

As another result of the increasingly competitive standardisation environment the goals identified in the ITU strategy document include adoption of a market-oriented approach to standardisation, among others through delivery of high-quality products (i.e.

recommendations) on time and enhancement of participation and involvement by non-administration entities and organisations.

The Telecommunication Standardization Sector (ITU-T)

All technical and organisational work on standardisation is done within ITU-T, which since 1993 operates through (see also Figure 3.2.2):

- World Telecommunication Standardization Conferences (WTSC) supported by study groups (legislative),
- an Advisory Group on Standardization (strategic advice) and,
- a Standardization Bureau (administrative).

In analogy to the organisational structure of its parent organisation, ITU-T convenes quadrennial 'World Telecommunication Standardization Conferences' as the top-level decision making organisational institution. They approve, modify or reject proposed draft standards ('recommendations') and approve the technical programme of work, which is subdivided into 'Questions'.

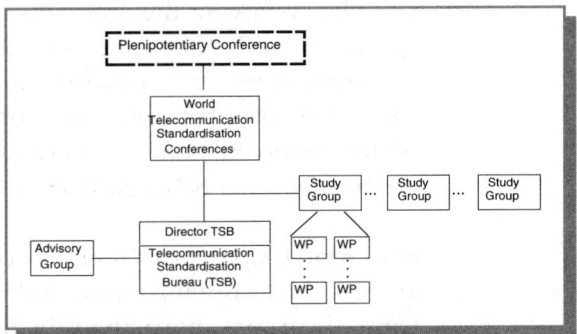

Figure 3.2.2:
ITU-T Organisation

Again as a result of the restructuring exercise Advisory Groups have been established in ITU-T to:

- review priorities and strategies for activities,
- review progress in the implementation of the work programme,
- provide guidelines for the work of study groups,

- recommend measures, inter alia, to foster cooperation and coordination with other standards bodies.

Day-to-day management is performed by the 'Telecommunication Standardization Bureau' (TSB), which organises and coordinates the work of the sector.

Study Groups (SGs) do the technical work. These are groups of experts from administrations, the public sector, and private organisations. Membership in study groups is limited to representatives of ITU Members. During the current study period (1997 - 2000), fourteen Study Groups are active.

SGs are established by the WTSC which also assigns to them the Questions to be studied. That is, rather than addressing a specific topic to be standardised a SG has to deal with pretty broad Questions each of which may cover very diverse topics[18]. The SGs produce draft recommendations within the scope of the questions assigned to them. These are to be approved by a qualified majority of members of the WTSC. Until 1992, this resulted in the well-known four-years study periods. Following the reorganisation of ITU in 1992, and in order to speed up and streamline the process, this strict formalism was abandoned; recommendations may now be decided upon through correspondence between two Conferences in which case 70% of the replies received must indicate approval. Similarly, new Questions can be identified between WTSCs.

Both representatives of Member countries (typically from the PTT or an equivalent organisation) and other organisational members (e.g. from SIOs) may participate in the technical work at SG level and submit contributions. However, representatives of organisational members need to be approved by their respective member country. Every SG is headed by a chairman and a (possibly several) vice-chairman, who are appointed by the WTSC, based on their technical and management skills.

---

[18] Two sample questions, to be addressed by SG 7, are '15/7 Directory systems', and '16/7 Message handling services'.

To adequately deal with this variety of topics an SG typically needs to be further subdivided into Working Parties (WPs, see Figure 3.2.2), and possibly sub-working parties. Like Study Groups, WPs are headed by chairpersons, who are appointed by the chairperson of the respective parent SG. In addition, Rapporteurs may be appointed by the chairperson in charge to perform in-depth studies of specific technical questions. Rapporteurs play a crucial role in the development phase of a draft recommendation in that they are not only in charge of solving technical problems, but may also act as Liaison Rapporteurs, that is, they are the interfaces between SGs or WPs working on related subjects, and the contact points for liaisons with external groups. Rapporteur group meetings are convened to discuss technical details and to ensure that overlap between activities performed in different groups is minimised.

ITU-T has recognised that communication with consortia and fora is essential in order to produce high-quality specifications based on real user needs. Formal communication has been established with a number of such organisations, including the ATM Forum, the Network Management Forum, and the Object Management Group.

3.3 The Internet Engineering Task Force (IETF)

The Internet's standardisation process has changed over the years, from very informal ad-hoc implementations driven by a few enthusiastic people to a reasonably - some would say overly - formal procedure today. There are, however, quite a few things that survived this transformation, most notably the openly available Request for Comments (RFC) series of documents, which provides a forum for discussion on new protocols, mechanisms, and ideas. RFCs are not necessarily related to standardisation, but approved Internet standards remain part of this series as well.

The process has been designed to provide quick solutions to immediate problems. Obviously, this approach tends to produce specifications with a somewhat limited scope. This is in clear contrast to the strategy adopted, for instance, by ISO. However, extension mechanisms exist in most specifications, to enable integration of further developments.

Figure 3.3.1 shows the entities involved in the IETF standards setting process. The Internet Society (ISOC) was established in 1991 as an international organisation to oversee growth and evolution of the Internet and the social, political, and technical issues that arise from its use. It is managed by a Board of Trustees elected by the worldwide membership. Internet standardisation is an activity under the auspices of the ISOC. The need for this professional control unit originated in the Internet's expanding commercial market and international scope.

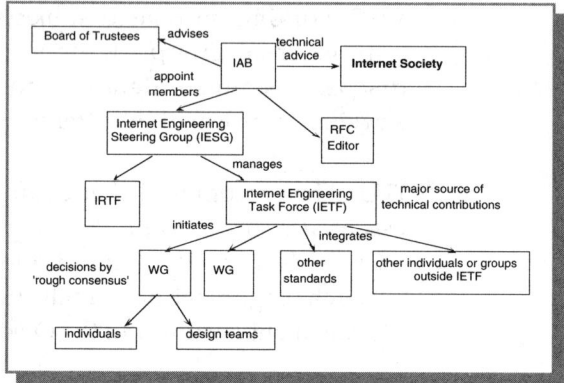

Figure   3.3.1:
Entities Involved in the Internet' Standardisation Process

The Internet Architecture Board (IAB), the former top management entity, was placed under the ISOC with the responsibility for ".. *oversight of the architecture of the worldwide multi-protocol Internet"* [Crocker, 1993]. The IAB is also responsible for approving appointments to the Internet Engineering Steering Group (IESG). It provides architectural oversight and does the final technical review of Internet standards, and provides leadership in the IETF, based on skills and years of experience.

The IESG in turn is responsible for technical management of the Internet Research Task Force (IRTF) and the Internet Engineering Task Force (IETF). Members of the IESG include the IETF chair and the directors of the different IETF technical areas. Its responsibilities include the management of the standards process, and the final approval of specifications as Internet Standards.

The IRTF is in charge of considering long-term developments, work on topics which are considered as too premature or too uncertain for immediate standardisation work. However, the outcome of the IRTF activities may well lead to standardisation efforts.

The actual technical standardisation work is done within the IETF Working Groups (WGs) which are chartered by the IESG. They are the primary mechanism for development of IETF specifications. A working group may be established at the initiative of an Area Director (AD), or it may be initiated by an individual or group of individuals. The goals of the standards process, as pursued within the WGs are:

- technical excellence,
- prior implementation and testing,
- clear, short, and easily understandable documentation,
- openness and fairness,
- timeliness.

The IETF working groups are grouped into areas, each of which is managed by an AD. The ADs are members of the IESG. Membership of WGs is open to all interested individuals; with e-mail distribution lists being used as the major communication medium. In fact, an IETF 'member' is someone whose address appears on one of the IETF's distribution lists. In addition, there are three annual IETF meetings. A rough consensus of all WG members is required before a specification can proceed on the standards track, which is another major difference to the approaches adopted by ISO or ITU. In particular, there is no formal voting procedure. If rough consensus cannot be achieved, the IESG will undertake to solve the problem. If this fails, the IAB will be the final authority for an appeal and may, for instance, establish a new working group to consider the matter.

Typically, a standards action is initiated by a work group having produced a specification they consider as satisfactory. The document is made available for comments as an Internet Draft for a certain time, and is subsequently submitted to the IESG. If a specification is found to be of sufficient importance to the Internet community, the IESG commissions an independent review committee. Having gone through a final review, the specification, then referred to as Proposed Standard, is published as an RFC. It remains at this level for at least six months, thus allowing sufficient time for public consideration and, very likely, revision. After this period, if at least two independent and interoperable implementations exist, the specification is considered as sufficiently stable, and will become a Draft Standard for at least four months. Finally, when significant operational experience has been gained, the specification will be raised to the Internet Standard level. If a specification fails to reach the Internet Standard level after two years, it will be reviewed and possibly withdrawn. All decisions relating to advances along the standards track, including final approval and withdrawal, are under IESG responsibility.

Besides this formal standardisation process there is an additional way to foster and publish new ideas, which may ultimately also lead to standardisation. These so called non-standards track RFCs primarily serve as a discussion platform for a wide range of topics, possibly originating from outside the IETF. The formal process associated with those contribution is less strict, with the IESG making an recommendation on whether to publish or to bring the work within the IETF.

3.4 Considering User Requirements - The Formal Procedures

The question of how user requirements are integrated into a standard specification has several aspects. One, for instance, is whether or not there actually are any requirements at all prior to a particular standard setting activity, and who has defined them. This is related to the question of whether real-world requirements need to be proved prior to the initiation of any activities, and if they are properly considered subsequently. In the increasingly competitive standardisation environment it would definitely make sense for the standards setting bodies to make sure that the outcome of a prospective new activity meets real user demands, as opposed, for example, to being technically challenging, and that these demands are adhered to during the process. The two aspects that need to be considered in this context are the formal provisions (if any) made by the single standards setting bodies to ensure that both new and ongoing activities are based on real-world requirements, and the way committees translate these provisions into standards (if at all). This section discusses the former, the latter will be addressed in chapter 5.

Both ISO/IEC JTC1 and ITU-T have established strict formal procedures on how user requirements are to be incorporated into the documents. The JTC1/SC18 user requirements procedures stipulate that preliminary user requirements have to be included with the document during proposal stage and commented upon by national bodies as part of the balloting process. During the further course of development, the WG in charge shall establish a set of user requirements to be submitted to SC18 for agreement. It should be noted that these requirements are supposed to originate from many sources, including user groups, technical committees and personal contributions. Once a set of requirements has been approved they will be registered as 'Agreed User Requirements' (AURs); subsequent changes must be agreed upon within the WG and reported to SC 18. During preparation of a committee draft an additional document outlining if and how AURs are met by the CD has to be produced and distributed for balloting, along with the proposed CD. No user requirements are considered during the following stages of the process. That is, the formal procedure requires:

- the identification of preliminary user requirements as a mandatory part of a New Work Item Proposal,

- the subsequent agreement of the relevant sub-committee on these requirements, yielding a set of Agreed User Requirements,

- statements identifying how the standards document conforms to these requirements.

Within ITU, responsibilities are assigned to Study Groups (SGs). At present, fourteen SGs are working actively, covering the entire field of telecommunications. Until recently SG1 was in charge of producing 'Service Definitions', which were supposed to reflect user requirements. However, this group was abandoned in late 1996; its responsibilities were transferred primarily to SG 2. As SG 2 is also in charge of a number of other, technical questions, this move seems to hint at a lower priority assigned to user requirements. Yet, ITU has always recognised that requirements could as well come from within 'technical' groups, in which case any requirements identified have to be sent to the SG in charge of service definitions for approval through 'Liaison Statements'. This is a highly formalised process. However, no mechanisms have been in place to verify the actual origin of purported user requirements.

Reportedly, cooperation between e.g. SG7 ('Data Networks and Open System Communications') and SG1 worked reasonably well in the past; they had co-located meetings, and SG 1 didn't really interfere with the technical work. More recently, the co-located meetings had been abandoned, and contact limited to the exchange of liaison statements.

In contrast to the other bodies, the IETF does not have any regulations governing the integration of user requirements into their work. The only mechanism that may be used to provide requirements are the 'Applicability Statements' (AS). The broadest type of AS is a conformance specification, called a 'requirements document', for a particular class of Internet systems.

3.5   Base Standards vs Profiles

The standards documents published by ISO and ITU (and others) normally describe what can be coined 'Base Standards'. In the area of data communications these have typically been designed within the framework of the OSI Reference Model. This model subdivides the tasks to be performed for establishment, management and release of a communication link, and the actual transmission of information, into a stack of seven distinct layers. For each of these layers two or more service definitions and associated protocol specifications are available. Moreover, base standards typically comprise both mandatory and optional functional elements. This variety of functional elements, protocols and services yields an extremely complex hierarchy of possible configurations and resulting functionalities. As a result, there is no guarantee that even implementations fully compliant with a standard (or a stack of standards) can interoperate. Thus, something had to be done to limit the variety of options and to provide guidelines on what should be implemented to actually achieve interoperability. The solution offered by standards setting bodies is the specification of a) which protocols should be implemented and b) which parts of each protocol should be implemented. These specifications are commonly referred to as 'Functional Standards' or 'Profiles'. They establish the platform for implementations.

Figure 3.5.1 shows the basic differences between base standards and profiles. A profile defines only one protocol per layer and specifies which options to be implemented. Thus, an implementation that sticks to a certain profile will more likely be able to communicate with other implementations of this profile.

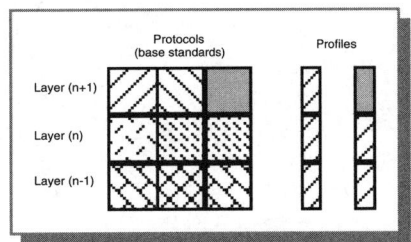

Figure 3.5.1:
Base Standards vs. Profiles

Although profiles typically originate from other bodies they may well be published by ISO as International Standardized Profiles (ISPs), *"An International Standardized Profile is an internationally agreed, harmonised document which identifies a standard or group of standards, together with options and parameters, necessary to accomplish a function or set of functions"*.

Specific, user-driven profile specification activities emerged in the US, where two major user companies, General Motors and Boeing, established MAP (Manufacturing Automation Protocol) and TOP (Technical and Office Protocol), respectively, in the late 1980s. Figure 3.5.2 shows the general MAP architecture; TOP looks pretty similar.

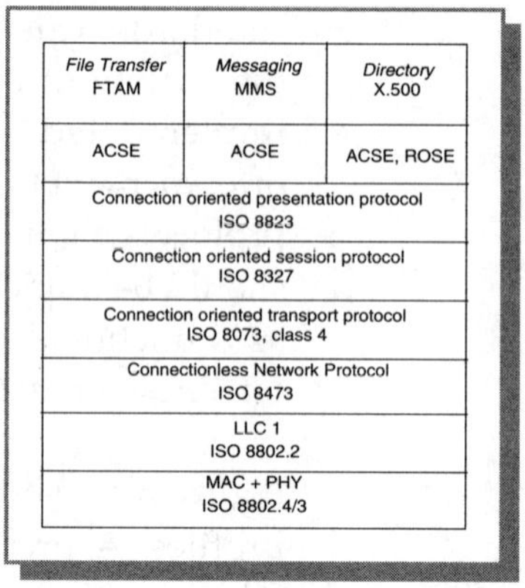

File Transfer FTAM	Messaging MMS	Directory X.500
ACSE	ACSE	ACSE, ROSE
Connection oriented presentation protocol ISO 8823		
Connection oriented session protocol ISO 8327		
Connection oriented transport protocol ISO 8073, class 4		
Connectionless Network Protocol ISO 8473		
LLC 1 ISO 8802.2		
MAC + PHY ISO 8802.4/3		

Figure 3.5.2:
The MAP Architecture

References

[Cargill, 1997]　　Cargill, C.
　　　　　　　　Standardizing Java (special issue)
　　　　　　　　ACM StandardView, vol. 5, no. 4, 1997

[Crocker 1993]　　Crocker, D.
　　　　　　　　Making Standards the IETF Way
　　　　　　　　ACM StandardView, vol. 1, no. 1, 1993.

[ISO 95a]　　　　International Organization for Standardization
　　　　　　　　ISO/IEC Directives - Part 1 - Procedures for the
　　　　　　　　Technical Work, ISO 1995

[ISO 95b]　　　　International Organization for Standardization
　　　　　　　　IEC/ISO Directives - Part 1 - Procedures for the
　　　　　　　　technical work of ISO/IEC JTC1 on information
　　　　　　　　technology, Supplement 1: The transposition of
　　　　　　　　publicly available specifications into
　　　　　　　　international standards, ISO 1995

[ISO 95c]　　　　International Organization for Standardization
　　　　　　　　Transposition of publicly available specifications
　　　　　　　　into international standards - A management
　　　　　　　　guide, ISO 1995

[ISO 95d]　　　　International Organization for Standardization
　　　　　　　　Introduction to ISO
　　　　　　　　http://www.iso.ch/infoe/intro.html

[ISO 95e]　　　　International Organization for Standardization
　　　　　　　　ISO Structure
　　　　　　　　http://www.iso.ch/infoe/isostr.html

[ITU 1993]　　　International Telecommunication Union
　　　　　　　　Final Acts of the Additional Plenipotentiary
　　　　　　　　Conference - Constitution and Convention of the
　　　　　　　　International Telecommunication Union, Geneva
　　　　　　　　1993.

Further Readings

Foray, D.: "Coalitions and Committees: How Users Get Involved in Information Technology Standardisation". In: [Hawk 95b], 1995.

International Organization for Standardization: "A Vision for the Future. Standards Needs foe Emerging Technologies". ISO/IEC, ISBN 92-67-10154-4, 1990.

International Organization for Standardization: "User Requirements Procedures for ISO/IEC JTC1/SC18". ISO/IEC JTC1/SC18/WG4/N3101, 1995.

International Organization for Standardization: "IEC/ISO Directives - Procedures for the technical work of ISO/IEC JTC1 on information technology" ISO 1995.

International Telecommunication Union: "The World Standardization Summit Sets New Directions for the ITU-T". http://www.itu.int/press/releases96/np96-07/e.htm

International Telecommunication Union: "Strategic plan 1995 - 1999". ITU 1994.

Bradner, S.: "The Internet Standards Process -- Revision 3". Internet RFC 2026, 1996

Hovey, R.: "The Organizations Involved in the IETF Standards Process". Internet RFC 2028, 1996

Huitema, C.: "Charter of the Internet Architecture Board". Internet RFC 1601, 1994

Valenzano, A.; Demartini, C.; Ciminiera, L.: "MAP and TOP Communications: Standards and Applications". Addison-Wesley, 1992.

Chapter 4

Adoption of E-Mail

This chapter will look at the problems and issues surrounding the introduction, and subsequent use, of messaging systems in large, internationally operating organisations. Requirements on messaging services - identified through in-depth literature studies and interviews - will be discussed. This can be related to the corporate history of e-mail usage, and therefore, the different adoption strategies that have been identified through case studies will be described and discussed. Finally, a summary and an analysis will be presented.

4.1   Functional Requirements on E-Mail and Directory Services

Functionality is one of the crucial contributors to a service's usability and, particularly, to its usage. Accordingly, in order to provide a usable service it is important to assure that its functionality actually meets users' requirements. This, in turn, implies that these requirements need to be known from the outset, i.e. prior to the actual implementation of the service, prior to the decision how to implement it and, in fact, prior to the decision whether or not to implement it at all. The question to be asked at this stage is "Will this particular implementation of this particular service suit my current and likely future needs?".

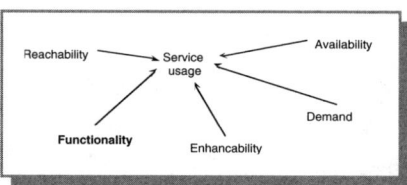

Figure 4.1.1:
Functionality as a Contributor to Service Usage (adapted from [RACE, 1994])

It will be helpful to recap the distinct definitions of two terms (as they are used in this context) which should not be confused:

- 'Service' refers to the functionality as specified in some (standard) document. For instance, the X.400 series of recommendations define the ISO/ITU e-mail service (and related aspects), the Internet e-mail service is specified by a number of RFCs.

- An 'Implementation' of a service is one particular expression of (a subset of) this service, offered by a service provider or by vendor.

Please note that neither Internet e-mail nor proprietary e-mail services will be considered. Although these days both are arguably far more popular than X.400, this is the more function-rich system by far; in terms of functionality the X.400 specifications may well be considered a superset of the other systems. Things look slightly different as far as directory services are concerned. Whilst X.500 has been just around the corner for some time now, it has still not quite managed a breakthrough. Yet, today both commercially available directory systems and work done by the IETF concentrate on slightly modified X.500 systems.

The compiled requirements on electronic mail and directory services originate from a variety of sources. However, it has to be stressed that this compilation only provides a snapshot, catching the situation in the mid-nineties. New, additional requirements are likely to surface continuously, others may disappear. Thus, the compilation and the subsequent analysis should only be seen as a case study exemplifying to what extent - if at all - the two sample standards manage - or fail - to live up to their users' needs and requirements, and why.

The full list of identified requirements, together with some brief comments and explanations, will be given in Annex A. This list has been compiled from a broad range of publications and from case studies. Both represent the demands of very heterogeneous users from different domains, including government agencies, R&D institutions, and corporate users. In addition, a number of non sector-specific requirements have been included.

Only those requirements identified by several users will subsequently be considered. It should also be noted that these requirements result from considerable experience with corporate e-mail systems; each of the companies studied has been using e-mail for at least ten years. A significant number of additional requirements identified should therefore be expected.

To cut a long story short: the analysis of the compiled requirements shows that their vast majority are actually met by the standards specifications. As far as the scope of a standard goes, X.400 plus X.500 provide for almost all functionality required by users. Most functions currently not included are outside the scope of base standards, and can be attributed to either inadequate service implementations, lack of agreements between service providers, or need to be resolved locally. Only four requirements (out of forty-five that were identified, i.e. less than 10%) that actually address functionality to be included in the standards must be considered as not being met. Out of these, however, none is likely to be met by the specifications in the near future. Still, the predicted gap expected between user requirements and services provided by the standards could not be confirmed. This, of course, implies that reasons other than purely technical functionality need to be found to explain users' perceived lack of enthusiasm about e-mail systems.

4.2   E-Mail Adoption in Organisations

Despite the popular view that standard IT-services do not adequately meet their users' requirements even long-standing corporate users of electronic messaging services are apparently not (yet) in a position to identify technical requirements that go much beyond the functionality provided by today's e-mail and directory services. One possible explanation, which will be explored in more detail in this section, is based on the assumption that systems have not been employed to their full potential.

Indeed, it appears that until very recently e-mail has been little else than a convenient means for interpersonal communication for most large corporate users. This finding may explain the absence of detailed technical requirements on the services. Yet, it should be interesting to look at the reasons behind this phenomenon. After all, one would expect that after years of service utilisation at least large, globally operating organisations would have moved beyond this simple use, and employ both e-mail and directories in a more sophisticated way (as the basis for strategic applications, e.g. in the domains of electronic commerce or workflow).

This is indeed a startling question: how can it be that even technically advanced organisations, operating on an international scale and thus being in urgent need of sophisticated communication services, after long years of usage still have not realised, let alone exploited, the full potential of electronic mail and directory services? This is all the more surprising if we consider that especially over the last ten or so years four crucial business trends have resulted in a dramatically increased need for seamless global communication and information exchange:

- **Internationalisation**
  Moving into new markets requires adaptation to the respective dominant local system.

- **Integration**
  Companies are merging or acquired, with a very high likelihood of resulting heterogeneous IT and communication environments.

- **Cooperation**
  The degree of cooperation even between possible competitors is increasing, again yielding the need for reliably working inter-company communication services.

- **'Virtualisation'**
  Virtual enterprises, i.e. temporary joint ventures of different departments or companies to achieve a certain, rather short-term goal are becoming increasingly popular.

For the business community each of these trends alone implies an urgent need for global communication services, enabling seamless communication both internally between different groups or departments and externally with business partners and customers.

Indeed, one of the major recent developments in the IT sector reflected these trends: the move from proprietary e-mail systems - almost exclusively employed until about the early eighties - towards 'open' systems - i.e. TCP/IP or OSI-based communication networks in general and e-mail services in particular. Yet, these observations make the situation even more baffling: if organisations have realised the importance of open, standards based communication, why are its potentials still not fully exploited? Based on evidence obtained from the case studies it can be shown that this situation was almost inevitable.

There is a central dilemma associated with the organisational implementation of Information Technology today, concerning the relationship between the central and the local. On the one hand, the vision of the strategic application of IT advanced, for example, by proponents of Business Process Re-engineering, implies a centrally planned, top-down design and implementation of systems coupled to a radical transformation of organisational practice. On the other hand, research into IT implementations has revealed the importance of bottom-up strategies aligned to local individual and collective learning processes in which technical potential is explored and fitted to the specific current and emerging requirements of groups of organisational end-users. The latter points to the contingency and heterogeneity of organisational information systems, viewed as complex configurations of diverse technologies and working practices. However, such a heterogeneous approach to IT systems remains problematic in relation to distributed IT systems, which exhibit strong network externalities, i.e. where the value for each user of being on the network increases with every new player joining the network. For example, if different local systems are incompatible, this will limit the benefits available from using the system.

For distributed IT systems such as electronic messaging services, two kinds of barriers to successful implementation are particularly important. The one most commonly recognised is at the technical level of interoperability, where differences between various proprietary solutions or different generations of technology may mean that systems cannot interoperate or that some functions cannot be shared. However, another, potentially more significant barrier in terms of the cost and effort needed to overcome it arises from the commitment of end-users to their own locally-chosen systems -- which may represent a substantial investment made by large numbers of people to learning how to use a system and to apply its functionality to their working activities. This may result, for example, in a reluctance on the part of many end-users to comply with the imposition of organisation-wide, standardised services.

In the following the different strategies for the adoption and development of company-wide e-mail services, as revealed through the case studies, will be categorised and described; their respective pros and cons will be discussed. In this context it will be necessary to link these strategies to the respective previous history of messaging services, that is, to the situation that had emerged within each organisation before a corporate, centrally led system was imposed. It will become clear that in the vast majority of cases such a strategy was implemented only at a rather late stage.

Figure 4.2.1 shows the different development paths identified in the case studies. Only rarely was there evidence of a top-down strategy being followed throughout adoption and development. The case studies show that it were either the smaller organisations, and particularly those that were 'born' into the Information Age which adopted this approach, often initiated by a top executive. In fact, in most cases a hybrid strategy could be observed, with a distributed and largely uncontrolled bottom-up phase eventually being succeeded by a centrally-led top-down phase. No examples of a pure bottom-up strategy were found, a fact that may most likely be attributed to the massive technical incompatibilities this approach is bound to produce, and which can only be overcome through centrally coordinated counter measures[19].

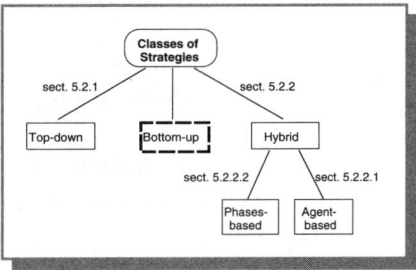

Figure 4.2.1:
Classes of Introduction Strategies

4.2.1   Top-Down Strategies

The advantage of pursuing a top-down strategy right from the beginning of e-mail service implementation is that compatibility issues are more easily resolved and a solution providing homogeneous services throughout the whole organisation will be much more cost-

---

19 Competing standards and technical specifications contribute to this situation, which could (theoretically) be avoided if only one standard were available. On the other hand, given the need for this standard to cater for a wide range of environments and applications, its sheer scope would inherently carry incompatibilities due to the various optional functionalities that would have to be offered. Basically, this happened to X.400.

effective. Also, the backing of senior management removes many obstacles.

> "The decision to use electronic messaging was backed by the board of directors. Accordingly, the introduction brought at least very few organisational problems." (company representative, 1994).

However, one of the major drawbacks of pursuing a top-down strategy from the outset is that it removes the opportunity for individual and organisational learning, which may have serious consequences for the success of the project. This was also the experience of one of our case study organisations, where the introduction of e-mail was initially confounded by users' resistance to change. This resistance was itself directly linked to the fact that at that time the project began, e-mail's benefits were not really understood.

> "In 1984, it was extremely difficult to convince people that e-mail was part of their job. People considered distributing information via e-mail as something vexatious." (company representative, 1994).

Another, related effect was reported from another company, which experienced problems in terms of service utilisation.

> "Generating usage. People tend to use voice mail." (company representative, 1996).

This is not too surprising at all; there is little point in introducing a service for which no need has been identified on the part of the end-users. The same company reports that e-mail has been

> "Moderately successful. Very useful." (same representative, 1996).

Generally, the organisations which followed a top-down strategy from the outset were either the smaller ones, or relatively young organisations founded within the last twenty years.

> "The company was lucky in that one of its founders was quite keen on IT, so funding has not really been a problem. In the

early days, decisions related to information technology in general, and to e-mail in particular, were very much taken by this person." (company representative, 1994).

Even in these cases, it was noted that following a top-down strategy only eased the introduction of the first system; subsequent moves, e.g. from mainframe-based towards LAN-based systems, still caused considerable problems, largely identical to those discussed below.

4.2.2   Hybrid Strategies

Overall, it appears that large, international enterprises do not normally make top-down strategic decisions about electronic messaging services from the very beginning. This result may partly reflect the structure of the case study organisations, the majority of which are subdivided into a number of almost autonomous companies or branches, located around the globe. The result was that end-users typically took the lead in e-mail adoption.

> *"Management plans, users do. Thus, ultimately we are bottom-up driven though us central guys pretend it's the other way around. Only rarely is it top-down."* (company representative, 1995).

Typically, early e-mail related decisions had been made at departmental or site level. As a result the initial messaging environments in the case study organisations were in most cases very heterogeneous. In general, this situation was at some stage aggravated by the existence of different generations of equipment, including mainframes, minis, workstations and an ever increasing number of PCs. The consequence of this pattern of local, end-user led adoption on the one hand and the obstacles created by heterogeneous systems to interoperability on the other was the emergence of two distinct hybrid 'strategies' which combined elements of bottom-up and top-down strategies, but in rather different ways.

4.2.2.1   Phases-Based Strategy

The first hybrid strategy found holds for about two thirds of the organisations studied. In it, bottom-up adoption and top-down development strategies were pursued at different phases within the overall implementation process.

The Initial Phase - Introduction

In classical bottom-up fashion, a group of employees obtained a messaging tool, either to fulfil a specific work requirement, or, more or less coincidentally, bundled in with other software.

> *"The first e-mail system was installed as part of a major IT project, when it was merely considered a tool enabling cooperation between project teams in 17 European countries. Its introduction was part of the project roll-out, and based on a management decision."* (company representative, 1994).

> *"Use of e-mail emerged from the use of VAX-mail, which came for free with the operating system."* (company representative, 1994).

The new service became more and more popular. Slowly, mainly by word of mouth, information about its benefits spread throughout the department.

> *"E-Mail started within 15 years ago as a tool for Human Resource clerks located at different sites to communicate with each other. It grew at the request of our scientists who wanted to communicate with collegues at other institutions. Executive management discovered it about 2 years ago. Development was bottom up." (company representative, 1996).*

The number of users increased steadily, though still within the department or site, rather than at the organisational level. However, at the same time very similar developments took place at many sites, eventually resulting in an extremely heterogeneous environment. Indeed, this (typical) outcome of the bottom-up approach was next to inevitable, since all departments purchased a system that best met their particular local needs and requirements. At this phase mainframe-based systems were used, yet a few unix-based services were installed as well.

Due to the lack of any overall management, the situation outlined above was bound to last (i.e. continue to generate problems without sufficiently solving others), unless some central entity would take over. Users had recognised the need for integration as they experienced the problems of incompatibilities between the patchwork of systems adopted at the different sites. In some cases, there were more than ten different mail systems installed, interconnected through a (not fully meshed) network of point-to-point gateways (see Figure 4.2.2). As a result inter-department messages had to be routed through several gateways. As gateways are rarely (if at all) able to map the full functionality of one system completely onto the capabilities of a different one, this led to sometimes significant losses in overall functionality; in extreme cases of incompatibilities it could even happen that some departments could not be reached at all from some other sites.

The resulting poor quality of inter-departmental communication quality was a major obstacle and often costly and frustrating for users. Thus, the conditions existed to justify the intervention of a central IT entity, which would subsequently pursue a top-down strategy to increase the benefits expected from a company-wide, smoothly operating and, therefore, far more useful e-mail service.

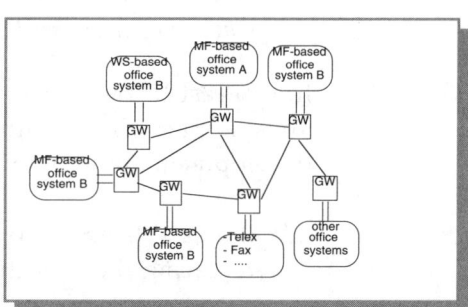

Figure   4.2.2:
A Typical Environment at the End of the First Phase
(MF = Mainframe, WS = Workstation, GW = Gateway)

The Second Phase - Interconnection

At that time the case for following a central, top-down development strategy as a solution to these problems was very strong.

> *"[E-mail emerged] Isolated at different sites and then everyone had this great idea. Hey why can't the whole company use e-mail. Unfortunely, no-one architected the thing from the beginning -- this is changing."* (company representative, 1996).

Unfortunately, its acceptance depended upon senior management being convinced that the major expenditures necessary for purchasing, installing and maintaining a (more or less) homogeneous e-mail service were justified by the benefits.

> *"Funding at times has been a problem. Management did not believe that a mail system this large required yearly funding for training and upgrades. I was able to get a budget for the last two years and the system has improved a thousand fold. Errors dropped from 1240 a month to 20 in one month."* (company representative, 1996).

Eventually, attempts to establish a top-down development strategy started: a central entity - typically the central IT or IS (information systems) department - tried to integrate the different services with management backing.

> *"Originally it was an effort led by techies, now it has much management support."* (company representative, 1996).

In contrast to the initial service introduction, this consolidation was always part of a centrally managed and organised top-down development strategy, which aimed at

- the establishment of a homogeneous, company-wide backbone replacing the collection of point-to-point gateways,

- the reduction of the number of locally used systems to an acceptable level.

The former was a comparably straightforward task; the point-to-point gateways had to be replaced by either an Internet- and/or X.400-based backbone, or by a central multi-protocol converter.

"7 independent Email systems evolved into the 4 integrated networks we have today. One major system - mainframe based CA-Email - was migrated directly to cc:Mail about 3 years ago." (company representative, 1996).

Regarding the latter, the ideal situation of just one company-wide e-mail front-end system (i.e. user agent) could not realistically be achieved. This was primarily due to some groups with very specific functional requirements.

"We have consolidated to 4 Email systems, fully interconnected: cc:Mail, representing over 1/2 our installed base. The other 3 are Lotus Notes, primarily used by the field sales force and marketing, SMTP, used by Engineering, and DEC Pathworks used in many of the factories." (company representative, 1996).

As this was a centrally initiated move, problems similar to those experienced by companies that pursued a top-down strategy from the outset surfaced at this point. That is to say, resistance to change on the users' side turned out to be an important issue.

"All of the above [convince management, get funding, technical issues], but the biggest was inherent resistance to change and fear of new technology." (company representative, 1995).

This quote hints at a problem that must not be underestimated - there is little point in pushing a new system or service, even if it is significantly superior in technological and/or organisational terms. This holds although it slows down the introduction process even further.

Figure 4.2.3 depicts part of a typical e-mail environment once the consolidation phase had been finished. The typical scenario comprised a limited number of different systems, which were interconnected by one or, more commonly, a small number of backbone networks. These, in turn, were interconnected through dedicated Interworking Units.

"We use a centralized integrated messaging architecture which includes an X.400 backbone, a message transfer agent (MTA) which routes messages between E-mail systems, gateways to the various messaging systems, an extended LAN facility (ELF) to exchange messages between similar LAN E-mail systems, and a global directory service that synchronizes changes nightly." (company representative, 1996).

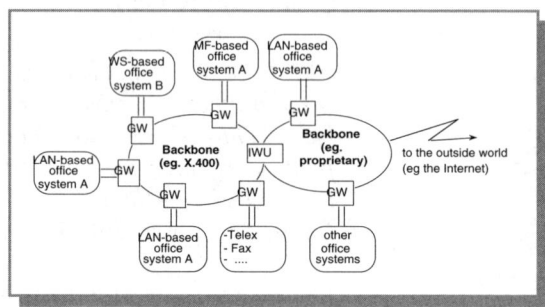

Figure 4.2.3:
A Typical Environment at the End of the Second Phase
MF = Mainframe, WS = Workstation, GW = Gateway, IWU = Interworking Unit

Also at this phase most organisations started looking at more flexible and feature-rich systems, which were typically either PC- or Unix-based. Another development supporting this migration was the then popular general move away from mainframe machines to smaller systems. Whereas there was a general trend towards a higher degree of service distribution, this was achieved via different evolution paths (see Figure 4.2.4). Some companies followed different such paths in parallel.

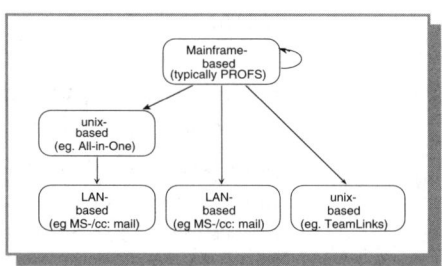

Figure 4.2.4:
Typical Evolution of Electronic Mail Service Platforms

Quite a few companies seemed to be satisfied having reached this stage and had no plans to push integration any further. Others, though, intended to move on.

The Third Phase - Interoperation

This phase, which some of the case study organisations were pursuing in the mid-nineties, was a continuation of the top-down development strategy, and was characterised by the attempt to introduce an almost uniform local e-mail environment (typically utilising MS-Mail or cc:Mail), interconnected through one messaging backbone (typically an X.400-based system or the Internet), which also offered access to the respective other e-mail world (i.e. the Internet or X.400, see Figure 4.2.5). Completion of this step meant that a homogeneous service would be available for most users, and that the number of different gateways will be minimised.

> *"Until we've got to the stage we've got an entire user population on one e-mail system we're going to have a degree of user annoyance."* (company representative, 1994).

Whilst this may be an unrealistic goal for the time being, there is no doubt that this statement is true. As noted earlier, interconnection of different mail systems via gateways always leads to a loss of functionality, which in turn will frustrate affected users. Some of the case study organisations have gone to great lengths to push forward an architecture similar to the one depicted above, employing LAN-based systems interconnected through one homogeneous backbone.

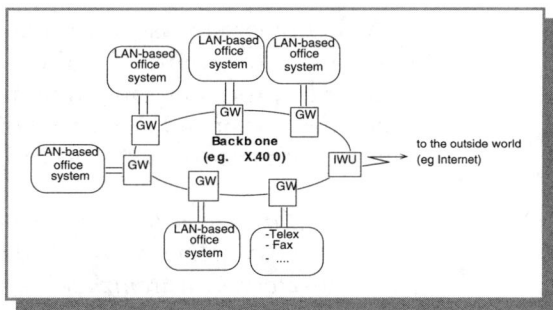

Figure 4.2.5:
The Envisaged Final Stage of the Process

This move, which is still far from being completed in most companies, typically also resulted in some problems, including:

- **Convincing management**
  The establishment of the first e-mail systems was achieved fairly painlessly and without major financial expenditure. However, convincing top management that a move from an apparently well working service towards something new was typically quite difficult.

- **Service uptake**
  Despite their various advantages, LAN-based systems incurred a considerable extra overhead compared to centralised mainframes, including, for example, additional local administration staff, extra management tasks, and directory synchronisation.

- **Convincing users**
  Once staff got accustomed to using to a certain service, organisations found it hard to persuade them to use something else instead. This was even more the case if the new service was still in its infancy, and likely to cause problems for some time.

- **System interconnection**
  There was almost universal agreement that a single, company-wide e-mail service was the best solution for organisational messaging needs. However, this proved to be very difficult to achieve in practice. Consequently, most organisations have opted to establish an interconnecting (and integrating) e-mail backbone instead.

Then popular envisaged future steps (in the mid-nineties) which were supposed to eventually allow a closer integration of e-mail into business processes, and thus a better utilisation of its capabilities, included use of an X.500 based directory service and the move towards an increased use of electronic commerce.

"Future plans for the corporate mail system in 1996 include the installation of an X.500 directory that will assist in the directory synchronization effort. In early 1997, X.400 will be installed to permit seamless communication with the diverse systems of external partners. The X.500 directory will be the foundation for electronic commerce and electronic

signature in late 1997. By early 1998, cc:Mail will be the mechanism for the transmittal of invoices, receipts and payment of bills." (company representative, 1996).

The Next Phase - Integration

Developments like those outlined above could probably be observed in many companies, including especially the very large ones, with the most urgent need for a seamlessly working global IT-infrastructure. In particular, as a first step towards more sophisticated usage mail-enabled applications were envisaged to become increasingly important.

"Yes to your initial list [interpersonal messaging, mail-enabled applications like eg. EDI and groupware] and also add in calendaring and scheduling. Really, Email is generally useful." (company representative, 1995).

Whilst up to then the single phases occurred pretty much sequentially over time, this phase seems to overlap in part with the previous ones, in that mail-enabled applications were used over a still rather heterogeneous underlying e-mail infrastructure.

However, the major characteristic of this phase, which makes it stand out from the others and, indeed, defines it, is the recognition of e-mail as a strategic corporate tool. In 1996, only three of the case study organisations had at least partly progressed to this stage, in that they considered e-mail as being mission critical and as a strategic tool in its own right, and as an enabler of strategic applications.

"We have a corporate-wide Email strategy with tactical and strategic plans and several important projects currently running. Email is beginning to be viewed as an important tool for accomplishing business processes. That is why we have emphasized it so." (same company representative, 1995).

It should be noted that this company, despite being 'only' a user, has long been a major player in the data communications field. Even such a leading edge user company, which had recognised the business potential that lies in the use of e-mail, and which started phase two in 1987, had not completed this phase by 1996. This again points at the tremendous problems that come along with e-mail introduction and implementation. A similar situation could be observed at another early adopter, who stated that

> *"LAN based IPM is the primary usage. Just starting to deploy MEAs* [Mail-enabled Application]." *(same company representative, 1996).*

Indeed, it seems to be a very long way from the first adoption of e-mail in an organisation to a stage were its full potential is entirely exploited.

4.2.2.2   Agent-Based Strategy

In contrast to the first hybrid strategy, where bottom-up and top-down strategies were pursued sequentially and contingently, the second hybrid strategy that could be identified integrated the two in a systematic and pre-planned way: bottom-up adoption was steered and controlled through a parallel, overarching, top-down implementation strategy.

Use of this strategy was for instance observed within a large chemical group. Sales staff and a special communications group where the first to be involved in the project. A simple adoption strategy was followed: people known be interested in trying and testing new technologies were persuaded to use the new e-mail service. Those people - the agents - then had something like a catalyst function within their respective departments, serving to promote the further introduction of the system. Electronic messaging could be demonstrated as being an attractive service. Yet, it was always made very clear that it was not intended to be a replacement of other established communication media, but an additional service, and that electronic messaging would be as easy to use, and at least as effective as other communication services. Stressing these facts was considered crucial, as gaining users' confidence has always been a vital part of the internal marketing strategy.

Eventually, management and other senior personnel learned about the benefits of e-mail, largely by word of mouth. Once these people were enthusiastic about messaging, it became an important tool in their departments within very short time. It turned out that people suddenly found they had various obligations that forced them to use e-mail. In fact, this was simply because colleagues or superiors were using the system. This development was supported by group meetings, where messaging benefits had been presented, with senior staff sharing their related experiences. Such private success stories and experiences, as well as concrete business cases, contributed significantly to the system's further uptake.

This hybrid approach is of particular interest because it represents an attempt to combine the advantages of a pure top-down implementation strategy - i.e. its speed and resulting homogeneity - with the advantages of a bottom-up adoption strategy - i.e. the opportunities for organisational learning - but without the latter's disadvantages - i.e. the problems of incompatibility. However, judging by the outcome of the case study, this approach is not too widely used.

4.3   Summary and Analysis

One of our initial assumptions was the notion that functionality provided by today's specifications of electronic mail systems is inadequate and fails to live up to actual user needs and requirements. To verify this hypothesis, user requirements on two sample services, electronic mail and the directory service, were compiled and subsequently been matched against functionality actually specified in the standards.

It turned out that very few of these requirements went beyond what is already provided by the X.400 and X.500 series of recommendations. This holds particularly for those requirements gathered from various literature sources, the majority of which were specified a-priori, that is, they had been identified prior to actual usage of the service. It is little wonder that such requirements remained particularly sketchy, focussing on rather general issues such as reliability, reachability, provision of distribution lists, or security features.

Thus, despite the original assumption of inadequate standard functionality, it does not come as too much of a surprise that almost all functionality necessary to meet the identified user requirements was included in the standards. In fact, most of those requirements that were not met were outside the scope of any standardisation anyway, in that they related either to functionality to be provided locally (as e.g. virus checking), or to user behaviour (as e.g. up-to-date directory information).

Despite being somewhat sketchy, the identified gaps in the standards' functionality were generally valid. The frequent mention of other, more trivial requirements (notifications, security, etc), however, came as the real surprise. It may be concluded that at least some service providers had not implemented the full standard. Indeed, typically only those elements of service had been implemented that are classified as 'essential' in the standard, excluding most of those features that serve to make a messaging system more user-friendly and useful. In particular, this holds for all security-related service elements, which had been implemented by less than a handful of vendors.

Whilst the above may help to explain why experienced users considered such evidently trivial requirements as not being met by e-mail services, it does not go into the problem why even supposedly sophisticated users apparently did not have any further, more specific requirements.

To solve this puzzle it was helpful to look at the state of e-mail exploitation in organisations, and the underlying typical history and development of corporate e-mail systems. The degree of e-mail usage, the sophistication of mail-enabled applications in use, and corporations' judgements regarding the strategic importance of electronic mail provided valuable insight as to why no more detailed requirements were available.

The vast majority of companies in the case study share a common past in terms of e-mail implementation. They typically experienced a distributed user-led bottom-up approach resulting in a variety of different messaging systems, that at some point had to be integrated through a centrally designed and implemented backbone network. This happened around the mid to late eighties. From then on, e-mail implementation has been under corporate control and management, and further developments have been directed by central IT or IS departments.

E-mail had almost exclusively been used for interpersonal communication in many companies (apart from maybe scheduling and calendaring, which have been around for a while). Only recently have more sophisticated uses of the service got of the ground, and early adopter companies have been looking closely at mail-enabled applications for some time.

In general, the dilemma between centralised top-down and distributed bottom-up strategies for system implementation is perhaps unavoidable in very large, multi-divisional organisations trying to employ new and evolving technologies. For instance, departments and other sub-units are positioning themselves closer to their information resources in an attempt to circumvent central IS. As a result departments hope to minimise coordination costs between supplier (central IS) and user (themselves) of IT. Moreover, with information technology increasingly being perceived as easy to use even for non-specialists, and with hardware prices dropping steadily, inclination rises on the side of departmental managers to have their own staff design and develop tailor-made applications. As a logical consequence end-user computing[20] has emerged more recently in most companies, and has established itself as a top priority for IS managers, with related management issues becoming more and more important as well. One reported consequence of this development is *"... a shift in the primary function of the central (IT) organization from systems design and development to systems integration and from the role of developer to that of advisor."* This is exactly what could be observed in the case study companies, where integration of heterogeneous e-mail systems had been the major task of the central IT departments.

---

[20] "End-user computing may be defined as the adoption and use of information technology by personnel outside the information systems department to develop software applications in support of organizational tasks." .

Characteristics of the recent trend of end-user computing to a considerable degree resemble the situation that arose during the first phase of the e-mail introduction process. It may be concluded with some justification that this first phase in fact represented an early form of end-user computing, although none of the interviewees actually put it that way. Indeed, a department installing the e-mail system that suits its needs is well within the scope of the definition of 'end-user computing'. However, whilst this approach is perfectly valid on the purely local scale, it does not take into account company-wide implications, which may indeed not be foreseeable at all at the time of implementation. In consequence, problems in terms of incompatibility and heterogeneity are likely to occur eventually at the corporate level. If and when this happens, central IT will be called upon for systems integration. Even if this were the accepted major task for a central IT department, early planning, issuing of guidelines, and requiring use of standardised components from the early stages on, which would only marginally interfere with the single departments' freedom of choice, could help avoid a lot of problems later. Against this background, insights gained especially from studies of introduction strategies of interactive services - and the subsequent development - may attain additional relevance.

On the other hand, the findings of the case studies also suggest that the influence of managerial planning on departmental decisions regarding e.g. questions like 'which e-mail system shall we use?' and 'how can we put e-mail to good use?' should not be over-estimated. In many cases, purchase and subsequent use of e-mail systems just happened, almost by accident. In one company, for example, e-mail came for free with the newly purchased operating system, for another it came bundled with a word processor for secretarial staff; subsequent increase of usage was again achieved mainly by word of mouth (i.e. bottom-up) rather than through dedicated departmental strategies (i.e. top-down).

While extra problems at the corporate level are likely to surface through end-user computing, measures to limit experimentation with new technical alternatives to centralised functions would establish a barrier to innovation by reducing the scope for individual and organisational learning. This is, for instance, one of the reasons why large bureaucracies in public administration were much slower than e.g. manufacturing organisations in successfully adopting distributed computing. Management responses to end-user computing have been characterised variously as 'monopolist', 'laissez-faire' and 'managed free economy'. The evidence of our case studies points to the apparent domination of laissez-faire strategies which, as we have seen, leads to major problems once organisations are forced to grasp the nettle of interoperability and system incompatibilities.

Of the alternatives, a better strategy than the monopolist approach of suppressing locally-generated innovation, might be to develop policies that cater for it, and allow it to be fostered within a more overarching strategy. An example might be the agent-based strategy identified in the case studies, where seemingly local innovations were pushed and, in fact, guided through a central entity. This approach was considered highly successful by those in charge. Similar strategies involving 'change agents' are also known from the literature. More specifically, given the importance of compatibility for services like e-mail, it might be useful to encourage local innovations on the condition that the need for migration strategies to eventual organisation standards is addressed. This might, for example, involve giving preference to systems built on open standards, possibly including proprietary industry standards that have been opened out to complementary suppliers, and especially to 'architectural technologies' where some elements of a product remain constant, providing some guarantee of compatibility over several product generations.

References

[RACE 94]   RACE Consensus Management Project
              RACE Common Functional Specifications and Common
              Practice Recommendations, Document 14 - Usability and
              Generic Applications, Issue E
              RACE Industrial Consortium, 1994

Further Reading

Bälter, O.: "Electronic mail from a user perspective: Problems and Remedies". KTH, IPLab, Stockholm, 1995.

Bogod, J.L.: "Information Technology Standardization". In: Berg, J.L.; Schumny, H. (eds). "An Analysis of the Information Technology Standardization Process". North-Holland, 1990.

Brancheau, J.C.; Brown, C.V.: "The Management of End-User Computing: Status and Directions". ACM Computing Surveys, vol. 25, no. 4, December 1993

Clark, T.D.: "Corporate Systems Management: An Overview and Research Perspective". Communications of the ACM, vol. 35, no. 2, Feb. 1992.

Dodson, B.: "Harnessing End-User Computing within the Enterprise". http://www.theic.com/dodson.html

Jakobs, K.; Lenssen, K.: "Successful Applications of Electronic Messaging in International Organizations - Strategies, Results, Experiences, Part I". Report of the European Electronic Messaging Association, 1994

ETSI Directorate: "Progress on User Participation in the Standardization Process". Presented at 3rd Interregional Telecommunications Standards Conference, Tokyo 1992

Ferné, G.: "Information Technology Standardization and Users: International Challenges Move the Process Forward". In: Kahin, B.; Abbate, J. (eds): "Standards Policy for Information Infrastructure". MIT Press, 1995

Fischer, P.: "The Role of the User in the Standardization Process - Workshop Report". In: Berg, J.L.; Schumny, H. (eds). "An Analysis of the Information Technology Standardization Process". North-Holland, 1990.

Gerrity, T. P.; Rockart, J. F.: "End-user computing: Are you a leader or a laggard". Sloan Management Review, Vol. 27 (4), 1986.

Hawkins, R.W.: "Enhancing the User Role in the Development of Technical Standards for Telecommunications". Technology Analysis and Strategy Management, vol. 7, no. 1, 1995.

Jakobs, K.: "Future (Data) Communication Networks - The Challenge to (Public) Service Providers". Computer Communications, vol. 18, no. 11, Butterworth-Heineman, 1995

Jakobs, K.; Procter, R.; Williams, R.; Fichtner, M. : "Corporate E-Mail in Europe - Requirements, Usage and Ways Ahead". Proc. 4th Int. Conf. on Telecommunication Systems, Modelling and Analysis, 1996

Rogers, E.M.: "Diffusion of Innovations, 4th ed". Free Press, New York, 1995

Chapter 5

Users and Standardisation

This chapter first introduces a simplistic initial description of the standards setting process. A discussion of the relation between the different stakeholders of this process will lead to a more realistic description, which will draw upon standards setting professionals' comments. Subsequently, both committee members and users' views on perceived potential benefits and drawbacks that may come with increased user involvement will be reported. Finally, some explanations for the reluctance on the users' side to commit resources to standards setting activities will be given.

5.1 A Simplistic Model of the Standards Setting Process

The various procedures adopted by the different standards setting bodies may well lead to the assumption that the degree of control over, and influence on the standards setting process is about equally distributed between the different stakeholders (including vendors, service providers, the government, and users). This, in turn, yields the model of the standardisation process as depicted in Figure 5.1.1. It shows the 'ideal' situation, with all stakeholders having a (more or less equal) say in the standards setting process. It assumes that interested parties meet, compile and review their - possibly only anticipated - needs and requirements, define the best technical approaches and mechanisms realistically feasible, and eventually come up with a standard that should survive in the market and should pretty much suit all needs.

Indeed, this model reflects the technocratic view apparently quite popular with the standards setting bodies themselves. It can easily be derived from the descriptions of, and rules for the 'official' processes. Unfortunately, it does not quite capture reality; for instance, the non-technical dimensions (i.e. organisational or social) are completely ignored. Moreover, it does not assume any links or interrelations between the different stakeholders apart from the common work in a committee.

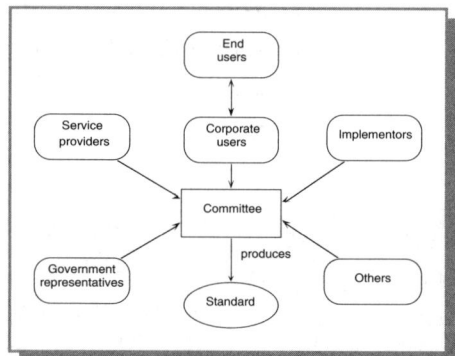

Figure 5.1.1:
The Naive Idea of an Ideal Standards Setting Process

As a consequence, this scenario is far removed from reality. In fact, it appears that so far especially the development of communication services has almost exclusively been technology driven; services offered tend to reflect the providers' and/or implementors' priorities, like, for example, manageability rather than e.g. usability. This can largely be attributed to the fact that relevant standardisation committees have typically been dominated by vendors and service providers. Asked what kind of organisations are represented in the committees, and which are perceived as being the most dominant ones, the responses were pretty much unanimous. In the words of members from four different organisations:

> "All kinds of organizations are represented - and, in fact, strong measures are taken to get wide representation. However, end user participation is generally quite small - it is hard for an end user to make the economic commitments necessary to be a successful player in standardization." (ANSI committee member, 1995).

> "Manufacturers, PTTs, Governments, and research institutions dominate more or less in that order within the committees on which I served." (ITU committee member, 1996).

> "Manufacturers and service providers (including standard's consultants) are the major participants; it is too expensive for small companies and user groups to attend and commit the resources necessary for effective participation (one cannot be effective in standards development and only attend part-time)." (ISO committee member, 1995).

> "I am primarily interested in the applications area. The subsets of the working groups that actually do the design and documentation work, in general come from the manufacturing community. Participants not representing implementors tend to come and go and rarely involve themselves with the design teams." (IETF work group member, 1996).

These brief quotes, which are representative for the committees considered in the case studies, already suggest that the original model is in need of some modifications, and that insufficient resources on the users' side is a popular explanation for this situation. The former is beyond doubt, and will be elaborated on in the following sections. Regarding the latter it remains to be seen whether it actually represents the correct interpretation of the current situation.

5.2   A More Realistic View

Having dismissed the view outlined above as being overly simplistic, the following sections attempt to provide a more realistic description.

5.2.1   Relations Between Stakeholders

The major stakeholders of the overall standards setting process can easily be identified. As already depicted in Figure 5.1.1 above, they include users, vendors, service providers, and the government. At the technical work group level, however, the picture looks slightly different. Here, the government, for instance, is little else than another corporate user.

Obviously, there are also relations between these various stakeholders outside the standards setting process, the most obvious one being customer - supplier. Those relations may well have considerable impact on both sides' activities and conduct in standardisation. For instance, it would seem - in contrast to the assumption outlined above - that users consider talking to their system vendors and/or service providers, and buying tailor-made products, as the most effective and convenient way towards a useful system, rather than getting involved in setting standards.

> *"We do talk to our vendors quite a bit, if you like, they're proxies for us.... They probably sit on the committees..... They can say their customers are asking for this... You hope the vendors and service providers do actually listen to their customers."* (user representative, 1995).

A vendor's market share, and actual market presence, are important factors influencing users' decisions about what to purchase. Asked for the initial criteria for the e-mail system of choice, a typical response was:

> *"Very much a point in time decision. If we had made the cc:Mail decision 2 years earlier we would have gone with Novell MHS. If we had made it 2 years later we would probably have gone with MS-Mail."* (user representative, 1996).

This comment suggests a certain 'follow the leader' approach; the selection of a corporate system depends on the respective market leader. In particular, this aspect appears to be considerably more important than criteria like e.g. adequate functionality or potential for integration into the existing environment.

A user's relations to business partners and customers also appear to play an important role when it comes to purchasing an e-mail system.

> *"We selected Microsoft mail because a major customer had it, and we were able to interconnect our e-mail systems."* (user representative, 1996).

Improving communication links with customers or business partners is a strategic goal. Yet, the simple (tactical) solution described above - i.e. to buy the same LAN-based system a customer has and to interconnect them - will not necessarily yield the best overall solution, not to mention the problems that arise if another equally important customer happens to use a different system.

The users' positions outlined above become somewhat more understandable in the light of the typical pattern of adoption of corporate e-mail. Yet, if these were really major factors influencing purchasing decisions - which the responses from users seem to suggest - this could at least partly explain users' reluctance to go that extra mile and participate in standards setting. At the same time, it demonstrates a severe lack of strategic thinking on the user side.

Most organisations are using LAN-based e-mail systems as their front-ends, and use X.400 or the Internet only to interconnect these local networks. Thus, these wide-area systems are hidden behind the respective local systems and their interfaces, reducing the perceived need for standardised services even further, as provision of adequate functionality appears to rest with the vendor of the LAN-based systems. Accordingly, product user groups (for LAN-based mail systems) are another popular means to exchange information and convey requirements. Membership in such groups, whether product specific (as e.g. for MS-mail) or related to a certain class of services (as e.g. EEMA) serves a similar purpose as do direct talks with vendors, but offers the additional benefit of regular information interchange with other users.

> "We are members of the Microsoft Mail user group. We do seem to get benefits from user groups. We seem to get major benefits from meeting an talking to people that have been in the same situation." (user representative, 1995).

Given the (realistic) perception of costly, cumbersome and time consuming 'official' standardisation processes (i.e. those embraced by e.g. ISO and ITU), which bring no guarantee of success, it may not come as a big surprise that users seek alternative ways to communicate their needs to those entities they feel are in charge. Surely users want the immediate benefits of currently available systems rather than to forego these in favour of possibly better future systems.

> "We are much wiser about the value of standards than we were in the '80s. The promises never became reality. This is one reason we focus much more on market/de facto standards rather than de jure "paper tiger" standards." (user representative, 1996).

From Figure 5.2.1 it could be concluded that implementors and service providers (deliberately or not) act as a 'buffer' between users and standards committees. One potential result might be that many user requirements simply do not make it into the standardisation process because of this 'buffering' phenomenon. Worse, helping customers (the users) to resolve short-term problems in an ad-hoc manner implies that established processes and procedures are being bypassed for the sake of a quick solution. Whilst this approach helps users solve urgent problems quickly (a point which must not be underestimated), it still remains a short-sighted short-term approach. As this 'bypass effect' accumulates there is a real danger that the standardisation process will be undermined, and that at the end of the day users are locked in to enhanced, but mutually incompatible systems. This, in turn, means that they are virtually stuck with their respective vendor, which is exactly the situation open systems were designed to overcome. Another potential result is that such ad-hoc 'solutions' may lead to additional functionality added to local implementations rather than global functional enhancements, thus again causing system incompatibilities.

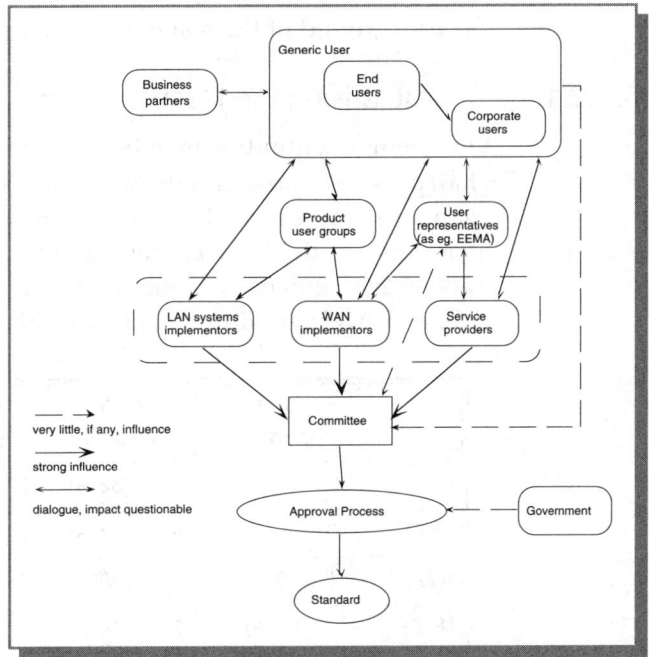

Figure 5.2.1:
Relations Between Stakeholders
(Reflecting the actual situation in the technical work groups)

In summary, it may be stated that established consumer-supplier relations between the different stakeholders in the standardisation process, and the resulting chance to get (proprietary non-standard) solutions fairly quickly, form a major barrier to user participation in standards setting. However, as participation in user groups (as e.g. the MS-mail user group) is also considered very useful, and as user groups become increasingly involved in (pre-) standardisation, this may be used as a vehicle to convey user input to the relevant committees.

5.2.2   Work Group Members

Thus far only the rules and regulations governing the different bodies' standards setting processes have been addressed. Yet, such rules do not necessarily describe how things work in reality. Moreover, they focus on the overall standardisation process rather than the technical work going on in the work groups. Therefore, to get a fuller picture, we need to have a look inside these groups. Here, some more information on the background of the respondents might be beneficial.

5.2.2.1   Characterising the Respondents

Only senior committee members were represented in the survey (e.g., chairpersons, project editors and rapporteurs) form a caste of 'standards professionals'. The vast majority of respondents have been active in the field for a considerable time in various positions (see Table 5.2.1). Indeed, it appears that at least the 'official' bodies ITU, ISO, and ANSI are dominated by particularly long-standing members.

	0-4 years		5-9 years		10-14 years		>14 years		Total
ITU	0		8	(32%)	13	(52%)	4	(16%)	25
ISO	0		8	(57%)	5	(36%)	1	(7%)	14
ANSI	1	(7%)	4	(29%)	3	(21%)	6	(43%)	14
IETF	8	(50%)	7	(44%)	0		1	(6%)	16
Total	9	(13%)	27	(39%)	21	(30%)	12	(18%)	69

Table 5.2.1:
Respondents' Association With Standards Bodies

Table 5.2.1 reveals a striking difference between particularly IETF on the one hand side and ITU and ANSI on the other, with ISO being placed somewhere in between. This difference, however, is not as unexpected as it may appear at first glance. Until as recently as 1988, CCITT (International Telegraph and Telephone Consultative Committee, the predecessor of ITU-T) was basically a closed community, made up largely from PTTs and equivalent national organisations. Vendors, users, research and academia were allowed to participate as experts, but with no voting rights. Moreover, the monopoly positions of the national PTTs had led to well-established relationships with the respective major domestic vendors. Consequently, the environment within which standards setting took place could be described as 'static', to say the least. Against this background, the high percentage of long-standing ITU committee members does not come as a surprise.

Things look slightly different as far as ANSI's JTC1-TAG is concerned. This TAG is less a technical work group, but a committee primarily in charge of strategic decisions related to the US involvement in JTC1. Accordingly, this group is made up from representatives who need to be more experienced and more senior than the members of the technical groups. Both these attributes take time to acquire. Thus, it is little wonder that the members of the TAG have been active in the standardisation area for a considerable length of time.

At the opposite extreme, the IETF is a very young organisation by comparison, established to address Internet-specific technical problems. Accordingly, procedures adopted differ from those of the older 'official' bodies in more than one respect. One of these differences is the non-existence of a formal membership in the IETF, another one is the comparably short life-span of the individual working groups, which typically address only a narrow and well-defined problem. If you add the strong academic roots of the Internet, which resulted in strong academic participation in the WGs, the combination of these facts may well account for the lack of long-standing members (academics tend to change their employer eventually, move on to industry jobs and give up standardisation).

> "Sofar I think the most dominant ones have come from the research institutes and the universities. That is changeing [....] the persons now active are moving to the companies to earn some money on their knowledge ....." (committee member, 1996).

A notable exception is the caste of the 'gurus' who have been involved in the Internet from its earliest stages, many of whom now capitalise on their experience by running their own consultancy firms.

Information about the interviewees' respective affiliations might also help to interpret the responses. Tables 5.2.2 and 5.2.3 show that the vast majority of prospective respondents (i.e. the totality of individuals who received a questionnaire) were working for service providers or vendors. In fact, more than two thirds of this group came from this side, as do almost 60% of the actual respondents. In particular, it turned out that user companies are strikingly under-represented (with the exception of ANSI, where they form the second-strongest group).

	Service providers Vendors		Consult's		Academia and Research		Users		Total
ITU	146	(83%)	8	(4.5%)	9	(5%)	13	(7.5%)	176
ISO	31	(53%)	6	(11%)	10	(17%)	11	(19%)	58
ANSI	33	(54%)	2	(3%)	2	(3%)	24	(40%)	61
IETF	32	(55%)	3	(5%)	16	(28%)	7	(12%)	58
Total	242	(68%)	19	(5%)	37	(11%)	55	(16%)	353

Table 5.2.2:
Affiliations of the Totality of Prospective Respondents

	Service providers Vendors		Consult's		Academia and Research		Users		Total
ITU	19	(76%)	1	(4%)	1	(4%)	4	(16%)	25
ISO	6	(43%)	0	(0%)	6	(43%)	2	(14%)	14
ANSI	6	(43%)	0	(0%)	1	(7%)	7	(50%)	14
IETF	9	(56%)	1	(6%)	3	(19%)	3	(19%)	16
Total	40	(58%)	2	(3%)	11	(16%)	16	(23%)	69

Table 5.2.3:
Affiliations of the Actual Respondents

The distribution of professional affiliations already suggests who dominates the committees. Yet, WG members might choose to adopt a more altruistic approach and see themselves as impartial champions of a technically sound, usable and useful system or service, regardless of their employers' commercial interests. However, it seems that this would be asking too much.

Asked how they would characterise their role in the standardisation process a relative majority of the respondents (41%) basically said 'company representative'.

> *"Predominantly company representative (even at the international level), though I represented the USA at international meetings."* (committee member, 1995).

Yet, some actually wear the hat of a 'user representative':

> *"End user representative seeking non-proprietary solutions."* *(committee member, 1995).*

Most, however, see themselves in varying roles, depending either on the respective group or the actual level (i.e. national/international):

> *"Company representative at the national level, USA National representative at the international level, and AFII Professional Association liaison at the national and international levels."* (committee member, 1995).

> *"Community representative and promoter of technically superior solutions. Later, as chair, I helped guide the IETF community to consensus on solutions."* (committee member, 1996).

Table 5.2.4 summarises the roles respondents assume for their standardisation work ('others' includes for instance responses like *"No idea"*). If several roles were mentioned, only the one perceived as most important has been included. Again, considerable variations between the single organisations cam be observed.

	National rep.	Company Rep.	User advocate	'Techie'	Other
ITU	7 (28%)	13 (52%)	2 (8%)	2 (8%)	1 (4%)
ISO	3 (21.5%)	3 (21.5%)	2 (14%)	3 (21.5%)	3 (21.5%)
ANSI	n/a	10 (72%)	4 (28%)	0	0
IETF	1 (6%)	3 (19%)	2 (13%)	9 (56%)	1 (6%)
Total	11 (16%)	28 (41%)	10 (15%)	14 (21%)	5 (7%)

Table 5.2.4:
How Respondents See Themselves

One thing that leaps to the eye is the vast majority of 'techies' in the IETF (i.e. respondents who see themselves as 'promoters of technically superior solutions'). However, this is not at all surprising: the framework within which IETF works, i.e. the narrow scale of the WGs and particularly the requirement for *"A specification from which at least two independent and interoperable implementations from different code bases have been developed, and for which sufficient successful operational experience has been obtained"* if a specification is to be promoted to the level of 'Draft Standard', pave the way for a very technology-centric view.

5.2.2.2   Perceptions

The standardisation process starts with the formal recognition of an open question by a standards setting body and the subsequent establishment of a work group in charge of addressing this question. Prior to that, however, other interests may well have played a crucial role. For example, a vendor wishing to have a piece of proprietary technology being standardised may have been instrumental in the establishment of the WG.

Proactive vs Reactive Standardisation

Whilst these terms seem to be intuitively clear, they may need some further elaboration and explanation. 'Reactive' refers to the fact that standardisation draws upon something that is already available. Yet, there are different alternatives what exactly establishes the basis for a reactive standardisation project. For example, in the 'purest' case of reactivity, an activity may be based on an already existing product or service, for which the vendor seeks the consecration of standardisation. One such example is the Ethernet, which existed as a product before standardisation started. In another, more open alternative some entity (a company, a research lab) tries to push an idea through the process which may not yet have reached the maturity level required for a product. Finally, the need to resolve incompatibility issues between existing systems may also be a starting point for a standardisation activity. This is a borderline case, very much verging on proactive standardisation, with X.400 being a good example.

Anticipatory (proactive) standards may emerge based on an identified demand for which no products or services exist that meet the requirements. Again, X.400 can be taken as an example, as can be ATM (Asynchronous Transfer Mode) to some extent. X.400, for instance, emerged from the very real need to overcome communication barriers established by various incompatible, proprietary e-mail systems. Alternatively, there are the truly proactive standards, which attempt to anticipate future requirements and try to meet them in advance. The X.500 Directory Service, and the Open Systems Interconnection (OSI) initiative are fine examples of this category. Figure 5.2.2 summarises the different expressions.

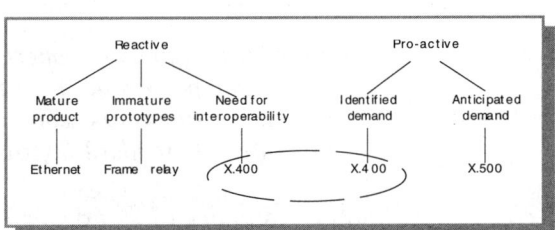

Figure 5.2.2:
Different Types of Proactive and Reactive Standards

It is typically claimed that there has been a shift from reactive standards setting towards a proactive approach, and that the amount of proactive standardisation work has been increasing dramatically in recent years, at least in the area of information technology in general and telecommunications in particular. This claim is hardly surprising and appears to be very convincing in a fast moving area like this. Yet, committee members' responses give a slightly different impression. For instance, the shift from reactive to proactive has been confirmed only by a very small group (about 7%) of committee members. According to one interviewee, this shift was initiated by OSI.

"Believe this is changing somewhat. For the most part, standards were based on an existing offering that others wanted the opportunity to provide once its value to the marketplace had been demonstrated. When users wanted integrated platforms, they began to demand that their favorite service be available across all the various platforms. This was taking an already available technology and making it standard. When Open Systems came along, standards developers began with concepts that were beyond any single vendor solution. That concept started anticipatory standards development --- trying to determine what customers want before you have product to show and trying to solve 100% of the problem up front through consensus." (committee member, 1995).

On the other hand, about one third of the respondents stated that activities still typically emerge based on existing products or services. This perception is almost equally valid across all 'traditional' voluntary standardisation bodies looked at.

"Standards typically emerge as de facto standards created by one company and in one way or another provided to the voluntary standards community to pursue a national or international standard." (committee member, 1995).

Another category of standards is based on identified - or conceived - user needs.

"In my experience it is mostly based on identified demand. For example, the Aviation Industry needed a way of encoding data that minimized the bandwidth requirements, so the Packed Encoding Rules project was born." (committee member, 1995).

Finally, a large group of respondents (some 30%) observed that proactive and reactive standardisation exist in parallel. They did not note any particular change over time, but found that whether the process is reactive or anticipatory largely depends on the type of product or service to be standardised, even within IT. For rather more 'traditional' IT components the reactive approach seems to be fairly common; a new mass storage device, for instance, is likely to be based on established technology. The same holds for e.g. programming languages and character sets. In contrast, technologies like e.g. ATM typically tend to be based on early lab developments (ATM) or anticipated needs (OSI-RM).

> "At times, multiple competing approaches are in the market place that cause incompatibity issues, stds are sought to resolve problems between existing products. (Magnetic tape and radio stds are examples). At other times the lack a standard prevents the industry from moving forward to a higher level of performance, so the industry is waiting for the stardard (X500, EDI/EDIFACT - for electronic commerce are examples)." (committee member, 1995).

As a result of the persisting reactive standardisation, standards committees continue to be a battleground for vendors and providers trying to push their respective ideas and solutions. To summarise this situation in the words of a committee member:

> "A product will often give rise to a standards activity but that doesn't mean that the product specification will be adopted as a standard. Sometimes, depending on who originated the specification, it may actually cause other vendors to dig in their heels and oppose such a spec moving towards a standard. Specifications developed by industry consortia have a much better chance of being accepted as stds. On the other hand, standards work may sometimes be initiated as a result of a perceived need even though there may not be any candidate specs waiting in the wings. Standards developing in the latter case are likely to take time to develop as it is often necessary to get agreement on concepts that may be imature or may not be widely agreed in general." (committee member, 1995).

Regarding the latter, the OSI initiative is a case in point. A (perceived?) user need for vendor independent interworking triggered the development of a framework encompassing all communication-related tasks and establishing an 'open' communication platform. It has taken a considerable time span to establish sufficiently mature specifications in the OSI context. With a few notable exceptions, however, OSI products have not been accepted by the market, for various reasons), in spite of strong backing from various governments). This suggests that timeliness and, particularly, simplicity are more important for a standards specification to be successful in the market than fully meeting perceived user demands. As one committee member observed:

> *"In recent years it has been clear that anticipatory standards (e.g. OSI) produce much better technical solutions but fail in the marketplace. This seems to be a byproduct of the apparent fact that designing something from the top down is not as good a mechanism for commercial success as getting something simple out quickly and then changing it based on customer demand."* (committee member, 1995).

It appears to be safe to say that anticipatory standardisation occurs far less frequently than typically claimed. Even worse, one can easily identify several examples of anticipatory standards that did not quite make it in the marketplace. The most notable of these is again the OSI suite of protocols and services, most of which eke out a miserable existence in the shade of the ubiquitous Internet.

The current success enjoyed by the Internet - and its protocols - also seems to stress this observation. Whilst important other factors are playing major roles in this success story, the contribution of the standardisation process adopted by the IETF, where the scope of a work group is comparably narrow, and thus the overall standards setting activities very flexible, should not be underestimated. Regarding for instance the establishment of a standards setting activity, the IETF process works as follows (according to a WG member):

> *"... Someone (or several people) identify an area that they believe needs an Internet standard. They propose a BOF to*

> *the relevant IETF area director. If the people (self-*
> *selected) who show up at the BOF decide there is enough*
> *interest to pursue the activity, someone is nominated to*
> *write-up a working group proposal. Upon IESG approval,*
> *the WG convenes. ...."* (WG member, 1996).

Of course, this informal approach does not guarantee success. Yet, if the respective initiators are sufficiently knowledgeable, experienced and enthusiastic, some useful initiatives will result. On the other hand, this also makes it easy for vendors to bring in their own specifications, representing their proprietary interests and preferences.

Influential Factors

It is also worthwhile to have a closer look at what members feel about who dominates the respective committees, and which factors are considered as being most influential when it comes to actual decision making.

Perceptions mostly reflect the affiliations of the committees' senior member. That is, committees are indeed seen as being dominated by representatives of vendors and service providers. Yet, two notable exceptions can be identified: first, the perceived influence of government within ITU bears no relation to the actual number of government employees, which was about 5% among the interviewees (and only slightly higher for all senior committee members). This perception may partly be a relic from the past, when the ITU was pretty much a playground for national PTTs and administrations. In any case, at least in terms of numbers government representatives do not play a major role any more. It should be noted, though, that the upper levels of ITU are still dominated exclusively by PTTs and equivalent organisations, which continue to be the only ones with a right to vote in ITU. However, the ongoing process of deregulation is changing the environment they are operating in, as well as their positions within this environment. Accordingly, PTTs will rather more act like service providers in the future, rather than national representatives. Some of the responses confirm this likely trend:

> *"Before, PTTs and/or governments were represented, but now*
> *it is changing. At moment the most dominent bodies are*

> *manufacturers and service providers." (committee member, 1996).*

Second, about one out of three respondents from ISO observed that an individual's personality plays the most important role. As one committee member put it:

> *"Oddly enough, it's been my experience that _individuals_ dominate ISO. Sometimes the individual will have a powerful multinational corporation or government/national interest on their side, but the bully pulpit is controlled by individuals, and only those with a strong sense of purpose survive." (committee member, 1995).*

This may be attributed to the fact that ISO WG members are less inclined to act in a particular role (officially they act in a personal capacity). Within ANSI and ITU a huge majority of members see themselves as representing company and/or national interests. Thus, their tasks are much more pre-defined by company/national strategies and leave less room to move. Much in line with this observation, respondents (again from ANSI, ISO and ITU) stressed that speaking out at meetings for or against a proposal was the most important single factor influencing technical decisions. That is, even good proposals will hardly be considered if nobody is available to explain or defend them at meetings (and vice versa).

> *"For any given technical decision the presence of supporters/opponents weighs heavily, for in practice unless there is someone or some organization that champions a solution and pushes it forward it does not get as much consideration/exposure as alternate solutions. That is, group members typically do not delve into researching solutions that someone happened to send us unless such solution at first glance seems to be overwhelmingly good. More likely the members push the solutions that they already understand."* (committee member, 1995).

The other two factors identified as influencing decisions are a proposal's technical merits and underlying company interests, both of which were attributed with roughly the same - though considerably less - importance.

> *"The technical viability of a decision does carry great weight. As almost all members at the technical committee meeting level are engineers, the technical prowess of the solution, tied with the credibility (knowledge) of the person presenting it are very influential. On occasion, a company which already has a product back in their labs will also prove to be a formidible opponent."* (committee member, 1995).

These priorities are particularly disastrous for user companies. If their representatives were to work successfully in standardisation, or if they even attempted to push a proposal of their own they would not only have to attend all meetings, but to establish a reputation as a knowledgeable person (which will cause extra problems given the widespread view 'user = technically unsophisticated'). Gaining this reputation takes time, a fact which collides with most users' quests for quick solutions. Worse, few, if any, user companies will have a sufficiently large interest in standards issues to send people to committee meetings over any longer period of time. The resulting financial burden would be considerable, and especially in times of recession extremely few users will endeavour such undertakings.

Things look completely different for the IETF. Here, the technical merit of a proposal were said to be the single factor of overwhelming importance. In fact, according to the respondents this is almost the only consideration carrying weight during decision making. An exemplary response from a work group member:

> *"Technical merits, clarity of presentation, willingness to do the specification writing, willingness to implement spec, immediate utility of spec, interest by vendors and users. Yes, personality, etc. have some effect, but not dominant."* (WG member, 1995).

Yet, the above comment also reflects another characteristic of the IETF process. That is, it very much depends on individuals being prepared to do the actual specification and implementation work. Much of this work will require support of the respective employers. It may therefore be suspected that these active individuals are far more likely to be employed by either vendors or service providers, or academia than users. The former may hope to push their own proposals within the work groups, to be aware of the latest developments and to capitalise on the gained knowledge and experience. The latter have traditionally been closely associated with the Internet, and will normally find it comparably easy to justify standardisation activities. Users, on the other hand, will need to have a very strong business interest before actually being prepared to pay for working time spent on specifying standards.

In this context the IETF's requirement for two independent interoperating implementations required for a proposal to progress on the standards track is of major importance as well. Again, to some degree this does not exactly push user participation as they are far more unlikely to devote time and resources to a pilot implementation of a protocol than are, say, universities or vendors.

Opinions of work group members were almost equally split about whether or not it is necessary to attend the four-monthly IETF meetings in order to push a proposal. This appears to be less important than it is in the technical committees of the other bodies, but still far from being unnecessary or superfluous. It may suffice if someone, who needs not necessarily be the original champion, is there to support an idea.

General Perception of the Processes

Asked to characterise the respective standardisation processes they have been involved in and know of, opinions of committee members form the 'official' bodies (ISO, ITU, ANSI) differed widely; there was virtual unanimity among IETF working group members.

Most respondents from ISO, ITU and ANSI expressed a rather balanced view of the respective processes; acknowledging that consensus is important, that the lengthy processes, though laborious and sometimes frustrating, are required to reduce the risk of faulty specifications, to actually achieve consensus and guarantee fairness and openness of the process and thus ensure the widest possible acceptance of the standard, taking into account all views.

"In general, I would characterize the formal standards process as open to all interested/affected parties that

> *produces generally stable standards which are moderately*
> *successful in the marketplace (i.e., get built into real*
> *products that people buy)."* (committee member, 1995).

Yet, they also noted that at times the process is far too lengthy and
too formal, and that these attributes may - and sometimes do - thwart
a standard's take-off in the market.

> *"Formal, bureaucratic, thorough, pain-staking, arduous,*
> *satisfying, useful and necessary, slow-moving, evolving,*
> *subject to national interests, dependent on few dedicated*
> *individuals in each area of standardization, consensus*
> *process is both frustrating and satisfying, rewarding, and*
> *economically troubled."* (committee member, 1995).

'High-quality' and 'stability' were the most important positive
characteristics attributed to the standards produced by voluntary,
consensus-based processes.

> *"Formal processes that produce high quality standards*
> *documents which represent a high degree of consensus among*
> *the National Body participants."* (committee member,
> 1995).

Very few interviewees expressed enthusiastic or unambiguous views,
neither positive nor negative. Most respondents were rather neutral in
characterising their respective body's process. Despite this generally
observable attempt to be fair and unbiased, however, the overall
impression resulting from the responses is a negative one. Respondents
clearly noticed the weaknesses of the processes they are involved in,
and that there is very little they can do about it.

As far as perceptions of the process adopted by the IETF were
concerned, respondents particularly stressed the fact that in their
views this process is far superior to the 'traditional' ones adopted by
ISO, ITU, or ANSI.

> *"The IETF has the smallest and most sensibly designed*
> *process of any of the standards bodies active at present, and*
> *because of this it is lightyears ahead of any of the other*
> *standards groups. (I have also participated in ANSI and*

ISO standards work as well as in the EMA (Electronic Mail Association), so I have a reasonable basis for comparison)." (work group member, 1996).

Comments on the strengths and weaknesses of ANSI's, ISO's and ITU's processes largely came down to one prevailing observation. That is, ironically - they are the same. The processes' paramount strength - i.e. being taken serious by its participants; leading to reasonably mature and stable recommendations, accepted by a broad constituency; being open and observing due process - at the same time represents the major weakness, in that it leads to specifications that may have missed the window of opportunity, have been overtaken by the technical development and/or the market (i.e. de facto industry 'standards'). Yet, there is little one can do about this dilemma between 'stable specification' and 'timeliness'.

"Its major strength -- its inherent fairness -- is also its major weakness. To insure fairness, ISO/ITU imposes formality and process. But formality and process impose overhead. The amount of process makes things slow." (committee member, 1995).

Being open to everyone was seen as another major strength of the voluntary consensus process. This held at least for the Work Group level considered here, albeit with one reservation: you have to be able to afford it. Apart from that, virtually everyone can participate at the technical level (with the ITU being somewhat more selective than ISO), and all ideas will receive consideration.

Respondents from IETF WGs were in agreement particularly on the perceived strengths of their process. Many responses exhibited a considerable degree of what can only be viewed as either enthusiasm or, indeed, naivety. Most consider the requirement for independent and interoperable specifications as the strongest point of the process, thus once more highlighting the technology-centric view already noted earlier as being characteristic for the IETF. The comparably small formal overhead and the resulting speedy process were also seen as major strengths, as was its openness - *"everyone can speak"* -. Yet, not unlike the comments from members of the other bodies, this was also associated with a weakness by quite a few. "Naysayers" and "loudmouths" stand a good chance of delaying and possibly even obstructing the work; the process does not foresee any mechanisms to adequately deal with such individuals. Likewise, it tends to split complex problems into small, easily comprehensible pieces, thus running the risk of losing the big picture.

> "IETF is very weak in operational deployment of services. A number of proposals just don't scale in todays Internet. IETF is weak in solving big complex problems. These are split in smaller manageable pieces and solved, but the context of the bigger picture is often lost." (work group member, 1996).

Finally, the dependence on a sufficiently high number of people prepared to do the work, and capable of actually doing it, was seen as another potential problem.

> "Strengths: focus on implementation, openness to anyone, attempts to stress technology over politics, minimal BS, strong academic representation.
> Weaknesses: not able to move fast enough, openness to anyone, politics are intruding, no good strategy to deal with industry as opposed to ietf leading thingsm, hard to find good people to lead things (chairs, iesg, iab)." (work group member, 1996).

Potential Improvements

Inadequate mechanisms for distribution of, and access to the final specifications were considered by many to be a major barrier to the success of international standards issued by ITU and ISO. With the exception of a brief period in the early nineties, during which most ITU recommendations were freely available via the Internet, these documents could (and still can) only be purchased at a considerable price. ISO standards have always been rather expensive, too expensive in fact to make them readily available to many who might wish to implement them. Draft specifications are virtually inaccessible for the interested public. This is particularly crucial when contrasted with the IETF approach of making all specifications freely available, including preliminary ones.

> *"Reduce the cost of stnadards, at the limit in distributing them 'freely' on the Internet (WWW or FTP). This is a great debate these days. ISO sees a revenu problem associated with copyright violation."* (committee member, 1995).

Along the same line, respondents were also in agreement that use of readily available technology, especially electronic communication tools, would serve to speed things up. Internal use of e-mail seemed to be the exception rather than the norm, and even where committee distribution lists existed they were not necessarily used for technical discussions between meetings. It did not really come as a surprise that committee members would love to have electronic means at hand for discussion and distribution of documents. Some respondents also suggested that electronic discussions would help to broaden participation.

> *"Better use of Internet, web pages, ftp sites, electronic mail, on-line discussion groups, and perhaps even video-teleconferencing. Less use of paper."* (committee member, 1995).

Slowness of the process was identified as another major obstacle. Suggestions like *"start with complete proposals"* (like e.g. the 'Public Available Specifications' upon which ISO JTC1 may base its output) and *"more work done by the editors prior to the meeting"* aim at accelerating the process while at the same time attempting to retain high-quality output.

Whilst better use of technology would certainly contribute to faster publication of standards, and yield a higher degree of acceptance, more important reasons for the process's slowness were seen elsewhere. They considered other, more strategic issues to be of major importance in the long term. For instance, it appears that cooperation between different committees, even within the same organisation, was considered far from being satisfactory, potentially resulting in duplicated efforts and maybe even contradicting specifications. Accordingly, improving the internal organisation and coordination would also contribute to more efficient and faster work. The same holds for inter-organisational coordination, e.g. for cooperation with the regional bodies like ETSI and with industry fora.

> "... Simplifying the structure of the overall organization. Making the structure of the groups more logical so that redundancy is avoided and charters are more clear. Enhancing communication between groups by allowing more rapid and less formal mechanisms to communicate. And, speeding up the standardization process by means such as allowing rapid standardization for groups willing to do the extra work to make things happen quickly. I think this can be done without compromising carefulness by enforcing the checks and balances, but allowing them to happen more quickly." (committee member, 1996).

Finally, a number or respondents suggested that the whole process of writing technical standards in the field of information technology should be changed. In addition to the above they proposed to adopt a more project-like approach, where dedicated experts are being paid to develop standards under rigid project management and to a realistic but tight schedule (pretty much the approach ETSI has adopted). In such projects all stakeholders would need to be represented, including especially the user community. In particular, sufficient user requirements were seen as a mandatory prerequisite for any standards setting activity. Subsequent validation of the standards was also considered important. Finally, the strategic importance of standards would have to be made very clear to all parties. All in all, a process implementing these suggestions would come very close to the model of an ideal standards setting process introduced earlier.

There were very few improvements suggested from IETF work group members, most of which related to scaling. This included the need for more volunteers, rules how to decide when 'rough consensus' is reached, as well as mechanisms how to address more complex problems. Yet, no solutions, nor even realistic suggestions were proposed.

> "I think its gotten to be very difficult to find qualified WG chairs and Area Directors. These are all volunteer activities, and the demands (esp. for ADs) can be enormous.

And especially when the growing Internet constituency can lead to more conflicting opinions than used to be present.
So this is a serious problem, but I'm not sure what to do about it. The self-selected volunteer nature of IETF participation is a key strength, but it is a two-edged sword, since a few loud-mouth jerks can really make life miserable for everyone else in the group. But what's the alternative? I can't think of any that don't have even more serious problems." (committee member, 1996).

However, one astonishing recommendation was made, as it represented a clear contradiction to the valued openness of the IETF process. This respondent stated that it would be necessary to introduce

"Core groups and specific listings. There is too much dead wood on the mailing list and so on." (committee members, 1996).

If this became reality, the IETF would be more elitist than any of the other bodies.

5.3   On User Participation in IT-Standardisation

This section outlines and discusses the views related to user participation in the standards setting process, as expressed by some of its stakeholders. For the purpose of this discussion these include user companies, the individual committee members and, to a lesser degree, the standardisation bodies themselves. Their respective views and opinions on (increased) user participation in the standards setting process and related problems have primarily been compiled through interviews and questionnaires, but were also drawn from official publication (particularly for the different standards organisations). The focus, however, will be very much on users and committee members.

As could be expected stakeholders' opinions differed widely. An initial guess would be that the 'official' point of view calls for stronger participation of user representatives. In an increasingly competitive standardisation environment the idea would be that user participation can help raise a specification's chance of survival in the market place. It is - or at least one would want to think it is - in every standards setting organisation's interest to produce specifications that meet the demands and requirements of their prospective users, and thus stand a chance to be actually employed as a basis of products or services.

On the other hand, one could imagine that work group members will hardly be pleased by the idea of an increasing number of participants. To make matters worse, these new members may be expected to be not as technically sophisticated as standardisation 'professionals' might deem necessary. Accordingly, here one could anticipate major reservations against a larger number of user representative on the committees. Yet, assuming that individual committee members also like to see the specifications they are producing being turned into products, one might also expect that user participation is considered useful if restricted to e.g. requirements collection and reviewing, as opposed to fiddling about with the more technical aspects.

Looking at the issue from yet another angle, one could expect users themselves to be quite ambivalent in their views. Leading edge users, strategically employing state-of-the-art technology to support advanced applications and organisational structures are more likely to have clear requirements they need to be met. They may therefore decide to carry these requirements into the standards setting process. To have at least a realistic chance of success, however, their efforts should be backed by sufficient resources. That is to say, if leading edge users at the same time happen to be sufficiently large potential customers (i.e. Boeing, General Motors, British Airways, Reuters and the like) they may well be in a position to be successful in pushing their requirements through.

In contrast to that, one would expect that less sophisticated, and less prosperous organisations without far-reaching requirements will tend to consider involvement in standardisation being just not worth the effort. They will either try to get by on what they have got, to talk to their service providers and/or vendors in order to get quick 'customised' solutions (with all the risks and problems associated with this approach), or to solve the problems internally by integrating 'home-made' enhancements (with largely the same problems as customised solutions). Moreover, active involvement in the standards setting process will probably be regarded as being far too expensive and time consuming. What's more, the eventual outcome of such involvement lies too far in the future, and is far too uncertain, as to be of any perceived real benefit.

5.3.1   The Committee Members' Views

The idea of increased user influence had advocates among the respondents, yet was far from being uncontroversial. A considerable number of cons and reservations were voiced by committee members, which was basically what could have been expected. However, there were also outspoken supporters of more user input to the committee work. In fact, and maybe somewhat surprisingly, these supporters formed the majority. Still, a significant degree of reluctance to let user representatives have a greater say in the process was apparent as well. Finally, a third group was in support of increased user participation under certain conditions, or within only limited areas where these respondents felt users could contribute. These three different lines of thought will be presented and discussed in more detail further below. Prior to that, however, we need to have closer look at how user requirements are actually fed into the process, from where they typically originate, and what committee members felt could be done to improve the situation, if anything at all.

5.3.1.1   Integrating User Requirements!?

The formal procedures of the 'official' standards setting bodies give the impression that well-defined user requirements are essential. Indeed, it seems that without adequate requirements from the user side no activities are initiated at all. Still, the question remains whether the procedures are adhered to during an activity, and particularly how the reality in the work groups and committees looks like with respect to 'integrating user requirements'.

Both formal and informal cooperation was acknowledged by the respondents from ITU, ISO and ANSI. Typically, formal cooperation is on a liaison basis, that is, the user group participates in meetings and receives the written output, but has no right to vote. There is also informal cooperation through personal contacts, or through organisational delegates wearing the additional hat of a user group representative.

> "*Relevant user groups are granted liaison status with committees; in some cases the liaison is 'formal', meaning that paper is transferred, in other cases a representative of the user group attends meetings regularly.*" (committee member, 1994).

Yet, it seems that cooperation is at the discretion of the respective committee, and that it is very much by chance if cooperation in whatever form occurs at all.

Given the informality of the IETF process, it is hard to identify any cooperation that goes beyond 'whoever shows', i.e. there are no dedicated user representatives, but delegates from user companies or organisations participate in the WGs just like everyone else.

> "*People who are members of the IETF are members of the IETF, not members of some user group.*" (committee member, 1996).

This may be an overly naive view; quite a few WG members did see themselves as representing certain constituencies. Still, the fact remains that no distinction has been made by members of IETF WGs between the different affiliation backgrounds participants come from. Users, like vendors, service providers, and other groups are supposed to work for the benefit of the Internet.

Yet, one respondent (representing a vendor) noted that real user requirements do make it into the IETF process, via representatives from service providers or vendors.

> "*This is usually done by proxy through vendor representatives. In our case, we participate in the IETF process with the requirements of our user base very close. We have to build products that appeal to our users, so we very actively solicit input from the user community. We then represent that position during the standardization process.*" (committee members, 1996).

Another approach, adopted and eventually cancelled by ISO JTC1/SC18 and, more recently, by ITU-T as well, is to employ a 'user requirements' WG (the term 'service definition group' was used by ITU).

> "SC18 made a big show of developing user requirements; it even had a whole working group devoted to the process. I think the effort largely failed because (1) nobody could agree on what a user was, (2) the other WGs tended to look at WG1 (the user requirements group) as an impediment, and (3) when budgets got tight, nobody could afford to send real users to meetings just to oversee a process." (committee member, 1994).

However, it looks very much as if this approach was a failure in the eyes of many committee members - if they happened to know about such groups at all. Whilst overall the comments ranged from "... invaluable to the standardisation process ..." to "... at best as not necessary and at worse a hindrance ...", most interviewees from both organisations conceded that they really had no idea what the respective group did, or that they did not have sufficient experience (if any) with their work to comment on it.

A popular perception on dedicated user requirements groups held by a number of respondents can be summarised as follows:

> "Unlikely to be valid representatives and often negatively regarded by those who believe they do the 'real work'." (committee member, 1995).

This seems to be a major issue here. If a 'user requirements' group were established, they would have a major credibility problem with two different facets: first, the group would need to prove that it actually is a representative of the whole user community, and not just representing, for instance, some very large specialist users or users of specific products only. Second, it would be an uphill struggle to convince members of the technical groups that they did valuable work and contribute significantly to the overall process. Especially the latter, rather more psychological problem is almost impossible to overcome in the short term (if at all). Given the fact that these groups were disbanded by both ITU-T and ISO, it would seem that these are indeed serious problems.

For the following considerations it may be worthwhile to make a distinction between the ITU SGs and ISO/IEC JTC1, and ANSI JTC1 TAG, and the IETF. Both the ITU and ISO committees are technical work groups, which are effectively at the bottom of the whole formal standardisation process, in charge of doing the actual technical specification work. The TAG is ANSI's 'Technical Advisory Group' to JTC1, i.e. rather more a management group than a technical one. Being somewhat removed from the technical process their perception of how user requirements are integrated into the technical work may be expected to differ from views expressed by members of these technical groups, who have to face those problems as part of the normal standardisation work, and to reflect much more the 'how it should be' than how it actually is. Finally, with the smaller degree of formalism characteristic for the IETF, little distinctions may be expected between users and representatives from other constituencies (see above).

In spite of the well defined formal user requirements procedures in place, reality looks slightly different:

> "There is a formal mechanism, prior to the development of a standardization project. Sometimes, however, the list of requirements is prepared after the work on a project has started." (committee member, 1994).

Indeed, from the responses by ISO and ITU members it can be concluded that users only played a minor role in the compilation and formulation of what is taken as their requirements. A very pointed statement as to who identifies the initial user requirements comes from a particularly long-standing committee member, who remarked that this would be:

> "Whoever has the money to push it in ITU or ISO. It is never the users." (committee member, 1995).

To be more precise, it are largely the technical people who specify user requirements. This holds despite the official procedures in place.

"For proactive standards development, the user requirements are most often generated by the technical people currently participating on the standards committee, based on their knowledge of their own organization's requirements. ......" (committee member, 1994).

Whilst this assessment was shared by more than 70% of the respondents from ITU and ISO, it reveals a fairly common, yet potentially disastrous situation. It is well known - e.g. from the usability literature - that what designers think users want is not necessarily what users actually need.

Another aspect worth mentioning is that the term 'user requirement', or rather 'user', is not always taken too seriously.

"Usually, user requirements need to be identified before standardisation work can begin. However, the term *user* is often not taken very serious, e.g., any person is a user in the end, i.e., anybody can take the role of a user when user requirements need to be established." (committee member, 1994).

As one consequence,

"There is, unfortunately, a problem in determining REAL user requirements. Doing this scientifically would take billions; generally, the representative experts are trusted. If, however, an expert wants to influence a standard, they can try to insert a 'bogus' requirement that would help lead toward a particular design." (committee member, 1995).

This strategy is well suited to jeopardise any attempt to compile, and follow, real user requirements. Even worse, participation of 'real' users (i.e. representatives of user companies or user associations acting on behalf of their members) will be of little use if it is that easy to push requirements of whatever origin. To make user involvement in the process meaningful some mechanism would be required to determine who actually represents the users' side.

Despite the different scope of the ANSI JTC1 TAG there were no differences to ISO and ITU with respect to the initial integration of user requirements into the process. ANSI members too conceded that initial requirements are primarily established by technical people, without any prior formal requirements definition process.

> *"Initial requirements can either be from a company sponsor (often based upon a technology they are developing) or from the committee itself who recognize a technical area they feel is in need of standardization."* (committee member, 1995).

Differences surfaced with regard to mechanisms for how to integrate requirements during the standardisation process. Whilst potentially damaging effects of the current practice were stressed especially by ISO committee members, most ANSI members emphasised that there is ample opportunity to have user requirements considered during the process:

> *"User requirements can be integrated at any point in the process from the creation to the final vote. Public Press Releases are placed in the public record describing the start of a project, or the vote in the search for consensus. Every public comment or concern must be responded to in writing by the appropriate committee before the project can reach it's final state as an approved national, or international standard."* (committee member, 1995).

Whilst this is true in theory, from comments made by other members one could suspect that these procedures resemble a paper tiger.

> *"No* [mechanisms to integrate user requirements either prior to or during the standardization process] *on the part of the standards organizations themselves. In fact there was a recent proposal to attempt to get user organizations more involved in the standards development process which was defeated. Basicly the attitude was that if users wanted to be involved, they should join the relevant committees and participate in the process. (This of course conveniently ignores the fact that most users could not afford anything of the sort.)"* (committee member, 1995).

At the same time, they stressed that vendors and service providers have a strong incentive to listen to their customers' needs, and thus to introduce these requirements into the process.

Another difference to the technical committees was revealed in another comment made by a TAG member.

> *"What I think I see is a proposal either at the JTC1 level or the TAG level to initiate an activity in a particular area, which is then voted on and if accepted a working group is set up. I strongly suspect there's a fair amount of behind the scenes politicing before such a proposal is made or a vote taken (in fact I know there is)."* (committee member, 1995).

This "amount of politicing" can be attributed to the fact that the TAG is in charge of more strategic decisions - as e.g. proposing a new standards initiative - the form and outcome of which may well effect company strategies far more than the 'simple' technical decisions taken elsewhere.

As could be expected, responses from members of IETF WGs told a story slightly different from those of the other bodies. In general, the responses indicated that WG members didn't really care where the requirements underlying a standards setting activity came from, and whether or not they were real. Whereas a number of respondents noted that user requirements were made up by technical people, the overall view seemed to be 'who cares'.

> *"By the time IETF WG's (usually) get to see a proposal, where the requirements came form isn't always clear. It is comparatively rare (thogh not unheard of) for a requirements spec to actually originate in the IETF itself. Given that they originate outside, whether they come from users (or marketeers perceptions of users' needs), or technical people, or ... is hard to determine (and rarely relevant)."* (WG member, 1996).

This is not really surprising given the underlying IETF approach that people in the work groups act as individuals rather than representatives of a company or some other constituency. As stated in the 'Tao of the IETF' [RFC, 1994],

"The IETF is the volunteers who meet three times a year to fulfill the IETF mission. ... There is no membership in the IETF."

A WG member put it a little stronger:

"Organizations are not represented at all. The IETF is a group of individuals, not representatives. People who think otherwise are in need of (and end up getting) a course correction. The closest the individuals in the IETF come to organizational representation is when they talk about a particular product or body of code they work on and how some action being considered in the IETF will affect it." (WG member, 1996).

Again, this may be overly naive, since several respondents saw themselves as representing their respective employer or some other constituency. In any case, however, the current situation is about to change, caused by the recent commercial success of the Internet, which changed the largely academic Internet into something potentially profitable for vendors and service providers.

"Was research institutions (and some government) Now taken over by "routing companies" Cisco and so on. Currently the sw vendors are pushing and dominting my area, most notably netscape and Microsoft." (committee member, 1996).

If this is actually going to happen the IETF may eventually (have to?) transform itself into an organisation very much akin to ITU.

5.3.1.2 (More) Users on the Committees?

Given the 'official' standards setting bodies publicly expressed opinions on increased user participation in the standardisation process one might wonder if these views are shared by those who would have to live with more users in the committees - i.e. the current WG members. To come to the purely numerical result first: yes, a majority of members would welcome stronger user participation in and, even more so, stronger user orientation of the standardisation work. However, this does not give the whole picture by any means. For one, this view was far from being unanimous. A broad range of reservations were articulated, as well as a number or pre-requisites that would have to be met if more users were to be welcomed. Moreover, there were significant variations in the responses from members of the different committees.

In simple numerical terms, 46% of the overall respondents were in favour of increased user participation, 33% were against it, both without any reservations. The remaining 21% supported stronger user participation in principle, but would like to see certain limitations regarding the circumstances under which they would welcome more users. These figures underpin the strong ambivalence about (increased) user participation. Three quotes may serve to summarise the different lines of thought. Those in favour typically pointed out that standards, and products based on these standards, would stand a better chance of being accepted in the market place if standards development were based on real-world requirements rather than on what some people think might be a requirement. To achieve this goal, their prescription was to get more users involved.

> *"Yes, because sometimes we get the impression that experts are alone in their corner and then we start to doubt if they are connected to reality or not. Having users involved as much as industry and governements would mean gretaer consensus, greater balance of requirements and greater applicability."* (committee member, 1994).

In contrast to that, opponents commented that more users would mean more process, reduce the signal to noise ratio in the committees and, typically, that users do not really know want they want.

> *"I am sorry to say the contrary of what is generally expected but I do not believe in the interest of users' opinion, at least in Telecommunications. Users need to transmit the maximum of data to the best price. After that, they do not care if it is IP, X.25 or Frame Relay. Or if they care, it is because it is writen in their newspaper that this technique is the best one!*
> *Telecommunication domain is very complex. And most of users have not the time (and it is not their job) to analyse technical things in that matter. I believe that users' needs are best defined by operators people, in the condition that there was a good link, internally to the operator's company,*

with the client (genreally through sales people)." (committee member, 1995).

Popular pre-conditions that would have to be met to make user participation meaningful in the eyes of the third group of respondents included 'for requirements review only' or 'depends on what is being worked on':

> *"Greater user participation in generating and reviewing the user requirements would be of significant benefit. User participation in defining the details of a system to system interface would be of less benefit. If the standard is for user to system interface, then user participation in the definition would be more useful. A system to system interface requires technical decisions, based on what is technically feasible, and should be driven by those companies which will have to provide the products."* (committee member, 1994).

The motivation behind this view was very similar to the one expressed by the first group; user participation was sought not to work on the technical nuts and bolts of the standard but to increase its final credibility and acceptance. An increase in the number of users in the committees was believed to achieve this goal.

The overall impression from many of the responses was that to a considerable degree users were seen as inadequately technically knowledgeable. This perception led to the major concern about an increase in user participation, also expressed by respondents otherwise sympathetic towards the idea of stronger user involvement: the fear that the process would be slowed down even further, thanks to user representatives who would use up major portions of the limited and precious time available at meetings.

> *"Lack of user experience in developing technical solutions would interfere with the development of standards."* (committee member, 1996).

This central theme could be observed across all standards setting bodies. Almost per definition users were considered less knowledgeable in terms of technical bits and pieces than people working in the committees.

"In general, it would not be useful to have users attend standards committees, because users are not knowledgeable about 'engineering' solutions." (committee member, 1996).

Whilst this may be true in some cases, it seems questionable that user representatives per-se indeed lack technical knowledge and experience. This holds particularly for representatives from large user companies, who more often than not have to struggle with inadequate standards and implementations and frequently have to design their own solutions to get round these problems.

Another popular perception was that users are sometimes out of touch with reality as far as their wishes and perceived requirements are concerned. They were said to want networks and services to be faster, cheaper, and prettier, but not to be able, or unwilling, to specify what exactly these wishes mean in technical terms, and to recognise if and when their requirements are unrealistic.

"End users typically generate comprehensive wish lists without an understanding of the trade-offs that a manufacturer has to make." (committee member, 1995).

Users were also seen as not necessarily willing to buy what they required in the first place. These two concerns are interrelated. Users may rightly ask for additional functionality to be integrated in developing standards, or maybe even for new additional standards. Yet, if chances are that they will not buy the products based on these standards there will be little, if any, inclination to listen to them.

"It is frequently the case that a participant from a user organization may not know the direction that his organization wishes to take; in fact the organization itself may not have a well-formed plan. The classic example is OSI, where the U.S. federal government led the way with GOSIP and induced many companies to spend large amounts of money on both standardization and product development, and then failed to buy the resulting products." (committee member, 1995).

Despite all reservations, the one major benefit almost unanimously associated with increased user participation in the standards process was 'closer to reality'. That is, with more active users in (parts of) the process, the final specifications were supposed to be closer to their needs and enjoy broader acceptance in the market place. Thus, there would be a

> "Better chance of the specification being usable and " what the customer wanted". Better chance of implementation and take up." (committee member, 1996).

Moreover, standards would be implemented more readily as it could be proved that they meet actual needs and would be bought if and when available. This, in turn, again implies that user input was primarily considered important for acceptance of a standard in the open market rather than technical brilliance.

> "Apparantly recognized user requirements would encourage rapid and large-scale implementation of the standard. And user participation is a direct way to obtain accurate user requirements." (committee member, 1995).

How to make users participate in the process was another controversial issue. For example, the idea of user participation through dedicated user groups, representing a broader constituency with a stronger financial basis, enjoyed some support. However, this approach might cut both ways, as it would also rise new questions regarding the legitimation of the representatives. Moreover, funding would remain an issue.

> "What qualifies a user? EVERYONE has some agenda. How do you keep other organizations (vendors, manufacturers) from influencing user groups (or even creating their own)." (committee representative, 1994).

In any case, respondents were clear that user representatives would need a clear mandate and would be required to work continuously with the respective groups.

> "Only if the participation is consistent and by the same representative each time. A major problem in standards development is new people coming in to each meeting and re-hashing topics that had been previously discussed. As

previously stated, a standard is an agreed upon solution, not necessarily the best solution, and new people coming in to each meeting can usually find a better solution that is not agreeable to all participants." (committee members, 1994).

An alternative approach proposed by some basically provides for occasional participation of user representatives plus input via e-mail or correspondence. They suggested that funding required for user participation be provided by third parties with an interest in an increase in user participation, prominently including governments which were supposed to be interested in standards accepted in the open market.

Many interviewees from ANSI, ISO and ITU identified a major obstacle to user participation which had nothing to do with technical sophistication, slower processes or market issues. Rather, it was largely rooted in the current standards setting process as such, and in lack of funding which had become a major problem, predominantly for users, but increasingly for service providers as well.

"These costs are increasingly becoming an issue; it is now very difficult to obtain adequate funding and to justify attendance of meetings. The major question asked here is: 'is this part of our core business?'." (service provider representative, 1995).

Against this background of tight budgets and insufficient understanding on the users' part of the benefits of standardised solutions there were considerable concerns about how to actually increase user participation in the technical committees. A broad variety of suggestions were made, including the employment of cognitive psychologists to research user requirements and the establishment of special demonstration sessions for user representatives. Yet, a strong majority of respondents (except for the IETF) pointed out that it would be necessary for users to attend meetings and have their voices heard, whilst at the same time stressing their belief that this is an unrealistic solution because of massive funding problems.

> *"I really don't know; face-to-face participation in the formal standards process is expensive, and even large user groups may not have a budget that can support full-time representation. And while e-mail eases communication bottlenecks, it is still not as effective as an actual meeting for trashing out differences of opinion and building consensus."* (committee member, 1994).

In fact, it appears that almost all major problems associated with a stronger user representation in standards committees (except those directly related to the process as such, as e.g. a slower process) inevitably came down to funding: who is going to pay to enable user representatives to attend meetings, and to actively participate in the work of standards setting bodies? All other concerns committee members might have in relation to more user representatives in the meetings were dwarfed by this problem.

One popular suggestion to circumvent the whole problem of user participation, requirements compilation, and meeting real market needs was to shift the whole issue to the market, and let the users demonstrate their influence there.

> *"Why shouldn't users use the market place to vote their preferences? (If they are good products- buy them -if bad products- don't buy?)"* (committee member, 1996).

Similar propositions, stressing the users' hold over the industry through their purchasing power, can be found in the literature. Yet, the weakness in this idea should be fairly obvious: if you have bad standards, even those products fully implementing them would be far from being good. They would be as good as you can get them, but within the limitations established by the standard in the first place. If users want to exercise their influence in a meaningful way, there will be little alternative to contributing to profile development, maybe even to product design and, first and foremost, to standardisation.

As far as the IETF was concerned the virtually unanimous opinion on how users should participate in the process was along the line of "join the lists".

"Go to meetings, join the lists, read the documents, comment them, ask questions on the lists, volunteer to write requirements docs, help testing pilot applications, volunteer to write minutes, ... I'm against user committees. The only way for participations is as mentioned above. No formalities." (committee member, 1996).

This approach has the obvious advantage of eliminating the overhead (in terms of organisational efforts and possibly additional time) that may potentially come with user groups. Moreover, if it were true that the bulk of the standardisation work is done, and the decisions are made, on the respective lists of the WGs (as opposed to 'during the meetings'), this would be a very convenient platform for users to contribute, saving at least travel-related costs and time. On the other hand, given the extremely 'techno-centric' nature of the IETF work, this bears the risk that non-technical points raised by users would simply be ignored by the majority of 'techies' in the working groups.

5.3.2   The Users' Views

Whereas most of the committee members interviewed had articulate and clear views regarding the pros, cons, and consequences of user participation in the standards setting process, this did unfortunately not hold the other way round, i.e. for the companies studied. In fact, virtually all organisations in the case study that were in one way or another represented in standardisation bodies were either vendors or service providers themselves, or happened to have some interest in a specific, application-oriented area. In particular, none of the user companies (with just one exception) showed any interest in the type of infrastructure-related services to which e-mail and directory systems belong.

Three different types of user companies may be identified with respect to participation in standardisation activities:

- **Non participants**
  They form the largest group by far. The reasons for not participating in standardisation typically ran along the lines of *"No real benefits"* and *"We are toooooo busy for the most part"*. These arguments, of course, were little else but two wordings for

the same perception: that being active in standardisation is not worth the - or indeed any - effort.

- **Selective participants**
  Two (comparably small) companies reported activities in sectors they considered as being vital to their core business. In both cases this was the area of EDI (Electronic Data Interchange), and in both cases they acted on behalf of their respective constituencies. That is, they represented larger market segments, similar to e.g. a trade association (although the ties were less formal). In both cases, IT standardisation was recognised as being critical for the respective business domains, especially as companies in both sectors typically had to communicate with an extremely broad range of business partners and clients, and as EDI standards related to commercial practice. To enable that sort of communication, systems based on internationally agreed standards had to be in place. Also in both sectors, there was no single influential entity that could lead a standardisation process. Thus, it seems that a sufficiently urgent need for established standards may well push even smaller companies into the standardisation process.

- **Genuinely interested participants**
  Only one respondent was active in different standardisation bodies because of identified corporate needs and requirements. In contrast to the companies discussed above these activities were primarily in more general infrastructure related areas (as opposed to specific, business-critical applications such as EDI). It should be noted, though, that this company is a very large and proactive user indeed, with a track record in IT standards development. Size and global operations, however, do not seem to be sufficiently strong motivators in their own rights. Other equally large and geographically even more dispersed users did not show any tendency to become active in this area.

On the whole, the responses suggested even less interest on the users' side to participate in standards setting than could be anticipated from earlier analyses.

Even if elaborate requirements were available there would be little inclination to address perceived service inadequacies by seeking to influence standards setting. As many firms in the case study (including really large ones) simply bought their hard- and software off-the-shelf, they would naturally look to service providers and vendors to come up with solutions if problems arise. A typical approach may be summarised as:

> *"organization is not interested in standards issues, since we purchase software from Microsoft or Microsoft compatible. Thus we are happy to let Microsoft set the standard."* (user representative, 1996).

This response hints at a distinct 'not-our-business' attitude, which could be observed for a number of companies. They did not care how their system was installed, and whether or not any standards-based components were employed at all, as long as the provided functionality and connectivity were deemed sufficient. In particular, depending on just one supplier did not seem to be an issue, despite the well-known potential problems inherent to such a 'lock-in'.

Most of those users who went to standardisation meetings did so for almost identical reasons, particularly including knowledge gathering:

> *"... especially to gain experience, insight into other solutions, knowledge."* (user representative, 1995).

It is likely that this motivation will yield committee members that can be best characterised as 'observers'[21]. Whereas employees' experience, insight and knowledge are invaluable assets for a company in those areas that are in its business interest, they may be considered as less valuable in other areas. It is comprehensible that under these circumstances inclination was low to put time and money into efforts that do not directly contribute to a company's core business. Only two interviewees reported a 'real' motivation on the side of

---

[21] According to [Spring, 1995] this group of committee members characterises their main contribution to standardisation as the *"ability to listen attentively and monitor activities to ensure process is going in the right direction."*

their companies to participate. One of the EDI using companies attended

> *"To make sure that our business are met."* (user representative, 1995).

This seems to be the one motivation for users to participate. Unless they feel their core business interests are at stake, they will not be prepared to spend the money necessary to actively contribute to standardisation.

For one company standards committees to a considerable degree appeared to serve as a platform for pre-development cooperation with vendors - in addition to the motivations given above. That is to say, this company had shifted the contacts with potential vendors, at least in part, from bilateral talks into the standards setting process. This is indeed a pretty clever approach: if products had to be redesigned to meet their needs anyway, why not shift part of the work to the earliest possible stage of product development - standardisation. Moreover, they killed two birds with one stone by making sure that their requirements were considered from the very beginning, whilst at the same time having the vendors' staff on the committees work towards the company's goals (at least part time).

> *"All of the above* [push superior technical solutions, promote company solutions, represent company requirements, gain experience and knowledge] *as well as information transfer, education, and influence the standards to be able to scale and function in vast environments. We have found that essentially all vendors think too small and tend to come up with silly solutions which break after a few tens of thousands of nodes deploy them. Without our help they have not shown an ability to develop robust applications which can scale. Also, virtually no vendors come up with products which are actually deployable "as is". It usually takes us two years working with vendors before their "finished" products become robust enough to function in our environment. It takes longer if we haven't been working with them "up front" through their products' alphas and betas releases. Standards are a way to do some of that "up front" work and achieve a greater "level-set" between*

vendors. Sometimes it also achieves interoperability between vendors products which is one of the primary purposes of the standards exercise." (user representative, 1995).

Yet, only very large and influential users, preferably those with sufficient purchasing power, and a known reputation as being technically sophisticated and not just dreaming things up, will be in a position to pursue this approach. Another potential problem will occur if several such companies, yet with different needs and requirements, follow this approach. In this case, it would only work if the requirements of these firms were sufficiently similar to allow cooperation at this early stage, with the likely result suiting all needs. In any case, the interviewee thought this approach feasible.

"I wish that there was a way for the Fortune 100 to work together to get vendors to build products which we actually need and which are robust enough for our usages." (same user representative, 1995).

Under the above premises this would undoubtedly lead to products and, assuming continuing cooperation in the committees, standards which were very useful for the big players. Yet, at the same time problems for other, smaller and maybe technically less sophisticated companies would arise, as their specific environments and needs are not necessarily identical with, or even similar to, those of the larger companies. Such company size-specific issues, including e.g. scaling and, especially, implementation related problems, may be of the utmost importance to large companies running and maintaining their own communication infrastructures, but will be of extremely little interest to SMEs.

"If we take the IETF alone, we are frustrated by their lack of interest in practical implementation issues which directly impact the usefulness and viability of such critical standards such as DNS. Most of their standards have serious implementation deficiencies and many of them are simply unusable (e.g., BGP). If we take ISO standards then the situation is much, much, much worse." (same user representative, 1995).

The interviewee continued by blaming the standardisation bodies for ignoring all implementation related elements of a standard. It is conceivable that large companies would like to solve their specific implementation problems alongside the more fundamental problems addressed by a base standard, and doing so might even be a way of bringing in more users. On the other hand, there are several international organisations in charge of specifying functional standards and profiles. For implementation related problems their committees might be more appropriate places to discuss these issues - base standards should not be designed with a particular future application or infrastructure environment in mind.

Be that as may, a standard needs to be put to use, by integrating it into a service or a product (if you are a vendor or a service provider), or by building applications on top of, or around, it (if you are a user).

> "[We exploit the knowledge/expertise gained through participation in standardization] *through application design and development.*" (user representative, 1996).

Likewise, knowledge and experiences gained through participation in the standards setting process may not necessarily be exploited through new tangible artifacts alone. Rather, committee members are likely to be among the first aware of new directions and developments; indeed a committee may be the very place were a new development originates. This suggests that some users well see a potential competitive advantage resulting from participation, in that they may be able to immediately use the newly gained information to build leading edge applications, in addition to generally increased knowledge and awareness, which may be invaluable, but is hard to quantify.

> "*Hopefully we put it to work to design and deploy for competitive advantage from our IT investment.*" (user representative, 1996).

Responses were split about the perceived most effective and convenient way for organisations to participate in standardisation work. The overall impression from the responses was one of considerable uncertainty. Those organisations that had been active in standards setting stressed the need to go to meetings (which is very much in line with the comments made by committee members on the most efficient form of participation), several others felt that increased utilisation of electronic communication media, like e-mail, video conferencing or dedicated newsgroups, would be most useful (again in line with committee members).

In particular, however, nobody suggested a change of the process as such to better accommodate user needs, let alone made suggestions how this could be done. Apparently, this matter had not received too much attention thus far.

5.4   Summary and Analysis

An analysis of the relations between the different stakeholders in the process reveals the virtual absence of any users directly participating in standards setting. The main way of 'participation' is almost exclusively through a 'filter' of vendors and service providers. This filter, or barrier, between the standardisation process and the users (the ultimate customers) may be supposed to absorb many identified requirements. Moreover, it also contributes to the apparently popular, yet short-sighted approach to overcome functional shortcomings of systems and services through ad-hoc solutions provided by the respective service providers or vendors. This may(!) well be acceptable if the identified weaknesses are due to inadequate implementations of the standards, and if any enhancements solve the problems in a standard-compliant and backward-compatible way. Otherwise, the newly gained functionality may well cause incompatibilities with other implementations of the same standard, thus creating a situation standards were supposed to avoid in the first place. In addition, this strategy will easily lead the user into a dependence upon a particular vendor or provider. If this process takes place at different sites and within different companies, affecting several different implementations, the resulting incompatibilities may easily increase significantly, thus effectively undermining the very idea of standardisation.

Moving to a different topic, it is interesting to see that some of the commonly held beliefs about who actually makes the standards are justified. There is indeed the caste of long-standing 'professional standard setters' who serve as committee chairpersons, liaisons or editors, a vast majority of whom are indeed representing vendors and service providers, as are in fact the majority of all WG members. Only a very small group come from user companies, and a similar number actually see themselves as user representatives. A most interesting fact about these groups is that they are not identical. Thus, even if the popular call for more user participation were answered it appears questionable whether this could actually improve the situation, as many committee members from user companies see themselves as representing their employers rather than the user community. It is worthwhile to keep this in mind, as it follows that calls for an unconditional increase in user participation will not necessarily help strengthen the users' cause. From this it may in turn be concluded that actual 'user representation' cannot be achieved through the mere presence, and work, of representatives from user companies. Rather, either these representatives must also see themselves as advocates of the user community at large, or the requirements of the different user companies need to be sufficiently similar. The latter may safely be dismissed as unrealistic. Unfortunately, the former appears to be quite unlikely as well as it would require a very altruistic attitude on the side of the sending user company. This suggests that the only realistic way to achieve meaningful user representation is through a coordination of efforts, for instance through a dedicated user association representing its members' interests. Otherwise, there is a real danger that increasing the number of 'user representatives' would primarily mean turf wars not only between different vendors and service providers, but also between users.

With the exception of the strong user representation within the ANSI TAG (which is not a technical but a strategic group, and thus not quite at the centre of this study), there are little surprises regarding the composition of the different work groups. Yet, there is a striking difference between the single organisations regarding the respective role the individual work group members assume. There is no dominating faction within ISO, whereas strong majorities of representatives within both ITU and ANSI consider themselves as representing their respective companies. In contrast to that, IETF is led by 'techies'. This difference is nicely reflected in the members' comments on those factors they see as being influential in decision making in their respective committees. In the absence of a dominating group it is the individual that in many cases leads a group within ISO; for ITU and ANSI the need for being present at meetings to defend a proposal is seen as being most important, and IETF members put a proposal's technical merits on top of the priority list. In particular, aspects such as 'meeting user requirements' or 'likely to be accepted on the market' were of marginal importance. Today, the actual make-up of a committee is of little importance when it comes to taking up the user's stance.

One would be tempted to argue that at first glance users should get more out of anticipatory standardisation; whether or not a widely used industry standard receives the blessings of official standardisation will not make too much of a difference in most cases. In contrast, meaningful anticipatory standards could help keep IT systems simple and manageable. Unfortunately, this is very much a theoretical perspective. User requirements to a considerable degree depend on individual local environments. Identification of generally valid requirements is therefore extremely difficult, if at all feasible. Moreover, as environments change over time (e.g. with the advent of new applications or business processes), predicting future requirements is next to impossible. Even worse, with vendors and service providers dominating the committees, it may be assumed that these groups also establish (user) needs as they see fit. Whilst these needs might indeed be based on requirements defined by some of their customers, no mechanisms are available to make sure that these are actually general requirements and, accordingly, that standards based on these requirements will serve a wider community.

Even proactive standards based on real requirements, and addressing a real market need, are not necessarily a full success. Again, the case of X.400 provides us with a classic example. The widely identified urgent need to interconnect the various proprietary e-mail systems triggered the initial work done within the International Federation for Information Processing (IFIP) in the mid to late seventies. Eventually, the task was transferred to the then CCITT (later ITU-T), which published the first X.400 series of recommendations in their Red Book in 1984. During the late 1980s to mid-1990s the procurement policies of almost all major Western governments prescribed OSI-based systems. One should have expected X.400 to thrive in this extremely favourable environment. It did not. Yet, a closer look reveals a number of issues that stood in the way of X.400's ultimate success in the market place, some of which are directly related to the outcome of the standardisation process. For one, crucial parts of the first version of the specifications were extremely sketchy (as e.g. the encoding of body parts and the security features) or altogether non-existent (as e.g. the message store and interworking with the directory service). It would appear that whatever was available had to be published as a CCITT series of recommendations at the end of the 1980-84 study period in order to avoid another four year delay. Likewise, X.400 was first published before the OSI presentation layer standard was ready, and was written to sit directly on top of the session layer (this was corrected in the 1988 version, but not without a lot of difficulty). It may well be assumed that implementations based on these inadequate initial specifications contributed heavily to the less than satisfactory utilisation of X.400 based services.

The non-inclusion of a message store in the initial specifications already points to another problem: the disregard of technical developments that occurred in parallel with the standardisation process. Accordingly, a technical environment was assumed for X.400 that represented state-of-the-art in the late seventies to early eighties; for example, it was supposed that both MTA and UAs would by and large be implemented on e.g. mini computers (i.e. continuously running systems), with 'dumb' terminals as input/output devices. Yet, the diffusion of PCs meant that more 'intelligent' end-systems became available which would, however, normally be switched off at the end of a working day.

Moreover, X.400 was supposed to be the ubiquitous e-mail system, providing functionality to the desktop. In fact, this is likely to be an important contributor to X.400's problems in the market, as here again technical development overtook standards development - although at a later stage - as LAN-based e-mail systems became the systems of choice for internal communication in virtually all organisations. It must be stressed, though, that this intended ubiquity represented a major departure from the original rationale for X.400's development, which was to serve as an interconnection medium for proprietary systems.

These two developments - the diffusion of PCs and LANs in the mid to late eighties - rendered the idea of 'X.400 to the desktop' virtually obsolete. In more general terms, the time span between the start of the standards setting activity (preliminary work started in the mid/late seventies) and the completion of the final documents led to a missed window of opportunity. Other systems (i.e. PCs and LANs) had occupied the major market segment of corporate internal communication systems. Somewhat ironically, this left X.400 with the backbone market for which it had been intended in the first place.

Although the initial specifications failed to provide for several important features X.400 systems have always been considered as extremely complex and hard to manage. Indeed, X.400 aimed at providing a solution to all e-mail related problems. As all voting members within CCITT committees came from PTTs or equivalent organisations - who at that time still enjoyed a monopoly situation - they were not really inclined to follow a more user-friendly, gradual approach, with a first specification evolving along with upcoming new requirements. Rather, they were in a position to follow a 'take it or leave it' approach, and design a system that clearly reflects PTTs' ways of thought, and met their specific needs, as opposed to those of the users (as reflected e.g. in the concept of Administration Management Domains, ADMDs).

One explanation offered for the failure of OSI is based on the proposition that it failed to provide for a smooth transition from previously used networks; it had been designed without taking into account the characteristics of older networks. That is, any transition required some form of 'jumping'. In particular, X.400 was allegedly 'installed-base hostile' (see e.g. [Hanseth, 1996]). This claim is justified to some extent. X.400 was indeed 'installed-base hostile' in a way, largely due to the fact that it was considered an integral part of the OSI initiative, and accordingly initially required the use of underlying OSI protocols, implementations of which were not readily available in 1984 (and which have never been really popular anyway). In particular, use of the OSI Transport Protocol Class 0

(TP0) on top of X.25 was mandatory for interconnection to the public X.400 network[22]. These strict requirements regarding the underlying communication protocols implied that a prospective user company had to install a complete new OSI-based infrastructure if it wanted to employ X.400, a very costly exercise in terms of time and money, not to mention training and other end-user related issues.

On the other hand, the originally envisioned X.400 system, as an enabler of interoperation between proprietary e-mail systems, was certainly not 'installed-base hostile'. Quite the reverse, it was supposed to enable the separate heterogeneous elements of this installed base to communicate. A closer look at the then installed base shows that it comprised almost exclusively of heterogeneous proprietary systems; in particular, the Internet was little else than a network for (American) research institutions[23]. Moreover, X.400 was designed to take advantage of the widely installed base of X.25 networks, which at that time represented the most widespread packet-switched network infrastructure (at least in Europe).

Eventually though, the increasing popularity of the Internet delivered another major blow. It provided services well beyond the functionality of e-mail (as e.g. file transfer, newsgroups and, later, the World Wide Web), many implementations were freely available or came as an integral part of an operating system (as e.g. in the case of Unix), and systems based on these implementations were comparably easy to install and maintain. The exponential growth of the Internet since the mid-nineties was another major incentive to join this bandwagon.

In summary, it may be stated that a very complex, yet still inadequate first specification which additionally imposed stringent technical constraints, in combination with a lengthy standardisation process that allowed other technologies to firmly establish

---

22 This contributed considerably to the overall costs of running an X.400 installation, as X.25 was a costly service.

23 In 1986, the then ARPA-Internet had some 2000 hosts interconnected by 56 kbps links.

themselves in the market, led to the comparably poor utilisation of X.400. Indeed, the combination of these factors was far more important in this respect than the Internet, the popularity of which started growing exponentially only more than ten years after the first X.400 specifications.

Despite the undeniable general need for open, vendor and platform independent communication, standardisation apparently failed to realise that a protocol stack as complex as OSI would be useful only for a handful of large, technically sophisticated organisations (like e.g. Boeing or General Motors). And finally, the process eventually came up with such a broad variety of different service definitions and protocol specifications that rendered the single specifications virtually useless, and created the need for standard profiles in the first place. Accordingly, OSI must be considered a failure in the market place even although it correctly anticipated general initial requirements.

The X.500 directory service is a similar case, yet it differs from major other elements of the OSI suite in that it has so far managed to remain on the agenda. Again, general requirements were correctly anticipated when first standardisation efforts started in the mid eighties; a global, uniform directory service is high on the priority list of virtually all users. However, the service design is overly complex. Although products implementing X.500 have been on the market since as early as 1985, although more than thirty different implementations were available about ten years later, and although even the Internet has been experiencing a steadily increasing interest in, and growth of, X.500-related activities, the service is still far from being widely utilised on a global basis.

Of course, in addition to the above reasons, the Internet has become increasingly popular since the early nineties, and has in fact marginalised OSI. This is not least due to the fact that the Internet protocol suite is readily available on virtually all major platforms, comes for free in most cases, is comparably easy to handle and does not cause major installation and maintenance problems. The base protocols are simple (newer protocols are becoming increasingly complex, though) and easy to use. These characteristics are particularly important for the huge number of smaller companies, which have little resources and/or inadequate technical knowledge, and which do not run their own network.

The tremendous success of the Internet, especially when compared to OSI, has been considered by many as an indication of the superiority of the underlying standards setting process. *"The Internet standards development process is by far the best in the business."* At first glance, this view appears to be legitimate. After all, the Internet (together with its predecessor, the ARPA-Net) has been with us for almost thirty years, and has managed to transform itself from the initial four-node network of 1969 to the multi-million-node ubiquitous infrastructure it is today. What's more, its core protocols (i.e. IP and TCP) have remained largely unchanged throughout this transformation process, thus again demonstrating the flexibility and adaptability of the output of the Internet's standards setting process (i.e. the protocol specifications).

The IETF process[24] indeed differs considerably from those adopted by the more traditional 'official' bodies like ITU and ISO, primarily due to its lesser degree of formality and, probably more important, a different underlying design paradigm. In fact, many aspects make the Internet standards setting process stand out. These include the extensive use of e-mail distribution lists for discussions, which everyone with an interest in the topic can join, specifications which are openly available throughout all stages of the process, and the requirement for demonstrated interoperability of different implementations. These features would deserve to be considered more closely by ITU and ISO for integration into their respective processes as well, and have also been called for by number of interviewees from these organisations. Individual participation, as opposed to e.g. ITU's organisational participation, represents another major difference.

The most important distinction, however, is the Internet's evolutionary and modular design approach. Unlike ISO and ITU, the

---

[24] Please note that I am solely referring to the work group level. In particular, I am not discussing strategic foresight (or lack of it) of the IESG or the IAB.

IETF does not normally attempt to produce all-embracing specifications, but prefers to design relatively small modules that are able to interoperate. This approach enables a flexible adaptation to changing environments even of dated communication protocols, and allows to react quickly to emerging new requirements. Moreover, this way an 'installed-base hostility', which may easily be the kiss of death for an otherwise promising new technology, and for which OSI has been blamed by many, is avoided. The fact that so far the Internet has been able to scale may largely be attributed to this approach.

Still, and despite these very favourable characteristics, one should be careful with an overly enthusiastic evaluation of the Internet's standardisation process, and a few rather more critical remarks should be in order.

Prior to the World Wide Web (WWW), the Internet had by and large been a research network, with its governing bodies dominated by people primarily from academia and research. One should think it was a comparably simple and straightforward task to identify the needs of this rather homogeneous research community, and to specify protocols that actually address these needs. Standards setting work strived primarily to achieve technical excellence, and was largely uninfluenced by politics and corporate strategies.

The Web, on the other hand, enabled wide-spread commercial utilisation of the Internet, and brought it to the homes, thus opening up completely new markets. Indeed, the advent of the World Wide Web represented a major - if not the - turning point in the Internet's history, the effects of which have already been noticeable in standards setting as well.

As commercial interest in the Internet has been growing, so has the number of members of the IETF work groups, including especially representatives form service providers and vendors. Against this background it may be anticipated that corporate strategies are playing an increasingly important role, and that 'individual participation' will turn into 'organisational representation'.

Similarly, the process' dependence on the availability of the 'right people' to do the work - and the chronic lack of them - bears the risk that strong, knowledgeable individuals, backed by interested companies and supplied with sufficient funding, may move into dominating positions within the groups (e.g. by volunteering to do specification and editing work, or by demonstrating working implementations). Ultimately, this could turn an IETF WG into something akin to a corporate R&D group (or maybe a marketing group). These trends have been confirmed, and indeed stressed, by IETF interviewees, who also noted that the current process is ill equipped to address the problems that come with such increased participation and commercial interests[25].

With much of the work of the IETF work groups being done via distribution lists, and with meetings accordingly considered by many as being less important, it should be easier for user representatives to contribute. In reality, however, things look different. Users are as under-represented on the distribution lists and at the meetings as they are on ITU-T and ISO committees. The claim that "everyone can speak", made by several IETF WG members is as true for the IETF as it is at least for ISO. However, this does not imply that everyone actually does speak (or is indeed listened to, for that matter). By and large, vendors, service providers and, to a lesser extent, academia dominate the lists and the meetings, and little, if anything, is being done to change this situation. On the contrary, IETF WGs are experiencing problems as the Internet is becoming commercially more interesting. The IETF's process provides no mechanisms how to deal with 'naysayers' and 'loudmouths', and it does not scale well. These facts may be explained by the history of the Internet, where in the early days some enthusiasts would sit down and do the specification of a standard and the hack some time late at night, and that was

---

25 The increasing commercialisation may well have consequences well beyond standards setting, and effect the very nature of the Internet as such. The preliminary results of a recent Delphi survey, for example, suggest that most experts belief that the Internet will split up into different topical segments, including those for commerce and education, respectively, within the next ten years. The current debate on the proposed Internet II for academic purposes moves along the same line. It remains to be seen how standardisation will be organised within these segments.

about it. These days, the process suffers from its legacy; it simply has not been designed to address large, complex problems that come with today's complex IT infrastructure, to deal adequately with the commercialisation of the Internet.

Without formal mechanisms in place to prevent the process from delaying tactics, being taken over by actively participating disruptive people, and/or domination of commercial interests, there is a real risk that what has been considered the strengths of the process in a strictly technically oriented environment (e.g. rough consensus, no voting, openness to anyone) will prove to be major obstacles in an environment influenced by politics.

A recent development in the IETF may serve to underpin this view. It relates to the Simple Network Management Protocol (SNMP). Work on SNMPv2, to become the successor to the original and increasingly inadequate SNMP, started in 1992. The core specification was granted Proposed Standard status in 1993. However, it was not accepted by the industry, and very few vendors actually implemented it. Complaints were voiced primarily about the complexity of the design of the security and administrative framework[26]. The WG was rechartered in late 1994, and two competing proposals emerged, which were complemented by two additional positions, including the 'silent majority', representing those who apparently were put-off by the hostile environment that had become the norm in this group, which was monopolised by a few individuals. Eventually, the group was abandoned and the SNMPv3 group was chartered in 1997. In early 1998, SNMPv3 specifications were submitted to the IESG for consideration as Proposed Standards. This brief example shows that the IETF is beginning to experience major problems in cases when 'rough consensus' cannot be reached. This may turn out to be a major problem, especially if stakes are high, as they are in the field of network management.

---

[26] This is particularly noteworthy since simplicity and brevity have always been high on the agenda of IETF work groups. On the other hand, the fact that such comments caused the IETF to rethink the proposal and take up specification work again is highly laudable.

Many user representatives reported very limited interest by their company in standards in general, and even less in active participation in standards setting. Those who did participate were pretty much discontent with the process, and its outcome. It should be noted here, though, that by and large they judged the results of the standards setting by the quality and usefulness of the implementations they had in place (or rather by the lack of it).

Committee members' comments suggested that an increase in the number of users on the committees would be met with a considerable degree of scepticism (see below). Most interviewees agreed, though, that user requirements to work from would be most helpful; they also shared the official view that such requirements would increase a standard's chance of survival in the market. However, views were split again with respect to how this could be achieved. The list of potential alternatives how to integrate user requirements into, and indeed make users participate in the standardisation process can be summarised as follows:

- **Individual participation by users**
  This is not seen as a realistic alternative for the time being. The reasons for the users' absence include the financial burden, perceived as being out of all proportions to the likely benefits.
  If a user went that extra mile to try and push requirements in a WG, technical sophistication would have to be proved to overcome prejudices on the side of the 'techies' in the group against users who dream up wishlists and subsequently fail to buy what they had previously asked for.

- **Liaisons**
  A committee's liaison organisation receives the output produced by this committee and may participate in the process, but has no right to vote. This could be a very useful mechanism, if it were mandatory to liaise with appropriate user representatives. Unfortunately, it is very much at the discretion of the committee chairpersons whether or not to liaise, and with which organisation or committee. Moreover, appropriate groups are hard to come by.

- **Dedicated requirements groups**

  Both ISO and ITU followed this approach, and both subsequently disbanded the committees in charge of defining user requirements (or service definitions, as ITU called it). To make things worse, a rather more psychological problem has played a major role here: members of the technical committees, who consider themselves as those doing the real work, expressed reservations concerning the quality of the output, and indeed the legitimacy of these groups (if they knew them at all; apparently cooperation was not necessarily quite as close as it had originally been intended to be).

- **'Proxy' vendors**

  A very sensible approach, at least in theory, would be to use vendors as 'proxies', i.e. to let them do the work in the committees based on the requirements identified by their user base. Unfortunately, this strategy has potentially disastrous drawbacks. The user just cannot be sure that the vendor will really forward his requirements to the committees. They may, for example, conflict with a larger customers' needs, or with the vendor's strategy, or they may simply be considered as just not worth the effort. Users can exercise little control over vendors in such cases, and they can never be sure if they are really listened to. Moreover, the issue needs to be addressed whether vendors actually can be credible representatives of users who are not their customers.

- **Trade associations**

  User representation through trade associations would overcome some of the problems to be associated with the participation of individual users (e.g. high costs, lack of purchasing power). However, arguments against requirements group would hold as well, and trade associations would have an additional credibility problem in that they represent only their respective particular constituency rather than the user community at large.

- **User coalitions**

  The major difference to trade associations lies in the fact that they do not represent a particular market sector, but the totality of their respective members, which may be far more representative of the overall user community.

In a period when even service providers and very large users are struggling to finance participation in standards setting, costs for involvement are all the more significant for smaller companies. As they are likely to have requirements different from those of the large users, they will benefit little, if at all, from standards that have been influenced by large users only. In this context, the development of MAP is a case in point; one of its major drawbacks was the absence of small and medium companies during the specification phase. This dominance of sophisticated users contributed in the overly complex MAP specifications, and their ultimate failure.

Another major drawback to be associated with the current approach of a 'techie'-led development can be revealed by a second look at what the usability literature teaches us. Lindgaard, for example, observes that:

"Perhaps most importantly of all, developers often fail to realize that they themselves are not 'typical' end users; they believe that, because they are also computer users, they are so similar to end users that they do not need to verify this similarity through experiments, observations of users, or other types of interaction. They therefore fail to realize that their often implicit understanding of users' needs reflect their own perspective which is not necessarily shared by the end users." [Lindgaard, 1994]

This is exactly what can be observed happening on the technical committees. Technical experts go to these meetings. They identify requirements - indeed are forced to do so in many cases due to the lack of user representatives. Yet, not only is it questionable whether they really do know sufficiently well what is needed by the human end-user, but their insight into the needs and requirements of even of their own company, let alone others, may also be doubted (the latter being more important in this context).

Both the intra- and inter-organisational contexts in which systems are to be implemented must be taken into account prior to and during design. This, in turn, implies that even if technical experts in the committees were aware of the needs of their own organisations - and knew what has to be done to meet these needs - this would not necessarily imply that the result can simply be applied to other organisations as well. It may also well happen that a service or a particular service element is most useful within the context of one organisation, but unsuitable in another. In this case the company-centric approach will not yield any useful results. Unfortunately, as has been discussed earlier, such company-centric views still prevail among committee members, including user representatives. This is another strong argument in favour of coordinated user representation in standardisation.

Yet, if user coalitions were to channel the needs of their constituencies into standardisation it would be necessary to first align these requirements. Organisational issues would have to be resolved at this stage, and this would require strategists rather than engineers, though not necessarily at the committee level, but at the level of the 'channelling' entity.

If the above scenario were established properly, the resulting construct would very much resemble a dedicated requirements group, albeit one with great responsibilities and, in fact, power. This group would have to provide the initial requirements from which the technical groups could work, monitor the progress and make sure that the technical realisation still meets all requirements. If need be, they would also have to interfere with the technical work, and provide appropriate guidance if they found requirements were not incorporated adequately. This would require considerable technical expertise on this group's side. Thus, the frequently made assertion regarding the desirability of the suppliers' sole responsibility for the technical realisation of a standard does not hold.

Apart from the financial, technical, organisational and strategic problems to be solved, a psychological one would still remain. There is a lesson to be learnt from the fact that both truly global players in standardisation decided to disband their requirements groups. Financing participation had been an issue, but problems played a major role as well. In particular, this holds for the perceived credibility of these groups. A general agreement on their role would have to be established, and it would need to be very clear that they are really representing the user community at large (rather than just parts of it), and that they do have the competence, the strategic and also technical knowledge, if needed, to provide valuable input to the technical work. Interference at technical level should be informed, and be avoided at all if possible.

A few words should be said regarding the popular suggestion to employ electronic communication media to better support user participation. Whilst this should definitely be done, it probably will not help very much, apart from accelerating the process (which could be a good thing). Considering the overwhelming importance attributed to personal presence at meetings, e-mail and video conferences would contribute little in terms of meaningful user participation. On the contrary, it could potentially be used by interested parties to claim increased efforts to enable user input, knowing that this input is likely to be ignored altogether by those who actually attend a meeting.

References

[Hanseth, 1996]   Hanseth, O. et al.:
                     Developing Information Infrastructure: The Tension
                     Between Standardization and Flexibility
                     Science, Technology & Human Values, vol. 21, no.
                     4, 1996.

[Lindgard, 1994]   Lindgaard, G.:
                     Usability Testing and System Evaluation
                     Chapman & Hall, 1994

[RFC, 1994]   IETF Secretariat, Malkin, G.:
                     The Tao of IETF - A Guide for New Attendees of the
                     Internet Engineering Task Force
                     Internet RFC 1718, 1994

[Spring, 1995]   Spring, M.B. et al.
                     Improving the Standardization Process: Working with
                     Bulldogs an Turtles
                     In: Kahin, B.; Abbate, J. (eds): "Standards Policy for
                     Information Infrastructure". MIT Press, 1995

Further Readings

Aden, M.; Harris, M.: "A Practitioner's Guide to Standards and the
Government.". ACM StandardView, vol. 1, no. 2, 1993.

Alexander, D.:"Infrastructure evolution and the global electronic
marketplace: a European IT user's perspective". In: Hawkins, R.W. et
al. (eds): "Standards, Innovation and Competitiveness". Edward
Elgar Publishers, 1995

Bach, C.:"The Standards Process: Evolution or Revolution". ACM
StandardView, vol. 3, no. 1, 1995.

Branscomb, L.M.; Kahin, K.:"Standards Processes and Objectives
for the National Information Infrastructure". In: Kahin, B.; Abbate, J.
(eds): "Standards Policy for Information Infrastructure". MIT Press,
1995.

Cargill, C.F.:"Information Technology Standardization - Theory, Process and Organizations. Digital Press, 1989

Dankbaar, B.; v. Tulder, R.:"The Influence of Users in Standardization: The Case of MAP". In: Dierkes, M.; Hoffmann, U. (eds): "New Technologies at the Outset - Social Forces in the Shaping of Technological Innovations". Campus/Westview, 1992

Davis, F.D. :"Perceived Usefulness, Perceived Ease of Use, and User Acceptance of Information Technology". MIS Quarterly 13 (3), September 1989.

Farrell, J.:"The Economic of Standardization: A Guide for Non-Economists". In: Berg, J.L.; Schumny, H. (eds): "An Analysis of the Information Technology Standardization Process". North-Holland, 1990.

Ferné, G.:"Information Technology Standardization and Users: International Challenges Move the Process Forward". In: Kahin, B.; Abbate, J. (eds): "Standards Policy for Information Infrastructure". MIT Press, 1995.

Fischer, P.:"The Role of the User in the Standardization Process - Workshop Report". In: Berg, J.L.; Schumny, H. (eds): "An Analysis of the Information Technology Standardization Process". North-Holland, 1990.

Foray, D.:"Coalitions and Committees: How Users Get Involved in Information Technology Standardisation". In: Hawkins, R.W. et al. (eds): "Standards, Innovation and Competitiveness". Edward Elgar Publishers, 1995

Genschel, P.:"Standards in der Informationstechnik (Standards in Information Technology)". Campus Publishers, 1995.

Hawkins, R.W.:"Standards-making as technological diplomacy: assessing objectives and methodologies in standards institutions". In: Hawkins, R.W. et al. (eds): "Standards, Innovation and Competitiveness". Edward Elgar Publishers, 1995

International Telecommunication Union:"Strategic plan 1995 - 1999". ITU 1994

Jakobs, K.; Procter, R.; Williams, R.; Fichtner, M. ::"Corporate E-Mail in Europe - Requirements, Usage and Ways Ahead:"Proc. 4th Int. Conf. on Telecommunication Systems, Modelling and Analysis, 1996

Johnson, J.L. at al.:"The Role of the Government in Standardization: Improved Service to Citizenry". ACM StandardView, vol. 1, no. 2, 1993.

Larmouth, J.:"Understanding OSI". http://www.salford.ac.uk/iti/books/osi/osi.html

Libicki, M.C.:"Information Technology Standards - Quest for the Common Byte". Digital Press, 1995

Lindgaard, G.:"Some Important Factors for Successful Technology Transfer:"Diffusion, Transfer and Implementation of Information Technology", North-Holland, 1994.

Markus, M.L.:"Finding a Happy Medium: Explaining the Negative Effects of Electronic Communication on Social Life at Work". ACM Trans. on Information Systems, vol. 12, no. 2, April 1994.

Naemura, K.:"User involvement in the lifecycle of information technology and telecommunication standards". In: Hawkins, R.W. et al. (eds): "Standards, Innovation and Competitiveness". Edward Elgar Publishers, 1995

Nielsen, J.:"Usability Engineering". AP Professional, 1994.

Organization for Economic Co-operation and Development:"Information Technology Standards: The Economic Dimension". Information Computer Communications Policy, no. 25, 1991

Organization for Economic Co-operation and Development:"Information Technology (IT) Diffusion Policies for Small and Medium-Sized Enterprises (SMEs)". OECD, Paris 1995.

Office of Technology Assesnt:"Global Standards - Buidling Blocks for the Future". OTA-TCT-512, 1992

Repussard, J.:"Problems and Issues for Public Sector Involvement in Voluntary Standardisation. In: Hawkins, R.W. et al. (eds): "Standards, Innovation and Competitiveness". Edward Elgar Publishers, 1995

Rutkowski, A.M.:"The Present and the Future of the Internet: Five faces". Keynote Address at Networld+Interop '94, 1994.

Rutkowski, A.M.:"Today's Cooperative Competitive Standards Environment For Open Information and Telecommunication Networks and the Internet Standards-Making Model". In: Kahin, B.; Abbate, J. (eds): "Standards Policy for Information Infrastructure". MIT Press, 1995.

SNMP Research:"Backgrounder on the SNMPv2 Standardization Process". http://www.snmp.com/pressrel/v2-background.html, 1996.

Solomon, R.J.; Rutkowski, A.M.:"Standards-making for IT: Old vs. New Models". Conf. on the Economic Dimension of Standards, 1992

Spring, M.B.; Weiss, M.B.H.:"Financing the Standards Development Process". In: Kahin, B.; Abbate, J. (eds): "Standards Policy for Information Infrastructure". MIT Press, 1995.

Sproull, L. and Kiesler, S. :"Reducing social context cues: electronic mail in organizational communications". Management Science 32, (11), 1986.

Wagner, C.S. et al.:"Open Systems Standards in Manufacturing: Implications for the National Information Infrastructure". In: Kahin, B.; Abbate, J. (eds): "Standards Policy for Information Infrastructure". MIT Press, 1995.

Weiss, M.B.H.:"The Standards Development Process: A View from Political Theory". ACM StandardView, vol. 1, no. 2, 1993.

Yaverbaum, G.J. :"Critical Factors in the User Environment: An Experimental Study of Users, Organizations and Tasks". MIS Quarterly 12 (1), 1988, pp 75 - 88.

Chapter 6

Overall Analysis and Conclusions

The previous chapters addressed various aspects surrounding the links and associations between users, standards, standardisation processes, and implementations. This chapter will try and demonstrate how these different pieces fit together to form a coherent picture. There are some lessons to be learned from this picture, which will also be discussed.

I will first briefly recap and review the principal findings of the case studies - and the issues they raised - which are a major starting point for the subsequent analyses. Some conclusions can be drawn from relating the case studies with findings from the literature on technological innovations, including the necessity to introduce a distinction between 'infrastructural' and 'business relevant' technologies when discussing innovations.

Subsequently, the issue of adequate user representation in standards setting is raised. A 'user coalition', i.e. an entity in charge of compiling, aligning, priorising and representing its stakeholders' requirements appears to be the only meaningful solution. In particular, simply increasing the number of user representatives on standards committees would be counterproductive. This is primarily due to the context-specific nature of requirements, and to the fact that real, non-trivial requirements emerge only after years of experience with, and usage of, a particular system or service. The conclusions reached so far suggest the need for a reorganisation of the standards setting process. The major elements and properties of the new process include a viability analysis to precede the actual technical specification work, which in turn comprises several iterations to allow for emerging requirements to be integrated. Moreover, the implementation of the specification, and its exploitation in a working environment are also integral elements of the suggested process. Contrary to common belief it turns out that a speed-up of the overall process is not necessarily a desirable goal per se.

It has to be stressed here that the conclusions presented in the following refer to electronic mail systems in large, international organisations. Likewise, only four major standards setting bodies were studied (ISO, ITU-T, IETF, and ANSI). Thus, conclusions drawn are valid only with these qualifications and should not be generalised. Additional future work will be necessary to establish if (some of) these conclusions are valid for other technologies, different environments, and other standardisation bodies, respectively, as well.

6.1   Issues Arising from the Case Studies

The findings from the survey establish the empirical basis for the subsequent analyses. The major findings, plus the issues they raise, will be addressed in this section.

Within most companies the introduction of corporate e-mail followed a hybrid strategy, typically comprising four distinct, though normally overlapping phases. In these companies early initiatives introduced e-mail at departmental or site level, without any overarching corporate strategy. This happened in parallel at different sites, and eventually resulted in compatibility problems due to the different types of systems purchased. The resulting problems - it was not unusual for a company to have more then ten different e-mail systems in operation at the same time, interconnected through point-to-point gateways - led to severe internal and external communication problems and eventually caused central IT departments to interfere. Following that, a centrally managed backbone (typically X.400-based) was introduced, and attempts were made to reduce the number of local systems supported. Finally, some of the more technically more sophisticated companies recognised e-mail as a mission critical service and started integrating it into their business processes.

A different introduction strategy could be observed at a few companies that are either smaller or were founded comparably recently. They pursued a top-down strategy, thus avoiding some of the problems mentioned above. However, this held only for the first system generation, subsequent upgrades (e.g. from mainframe-based systems to LAN-based ones) caused problems similar to those outlined above. Moreover, the degree of acceptance appeared to be poorer compared to the bottom-up alternative.

These typical 'corporate histories' of e-mail may help explain another result of the study. The vast majority of user companies did not have any major functional requirements on e-mail systems which have not already been covered by the functionality specified in the standards (X.400 in particular). Almost all requirements that were not met could either be attributed to incomplete implementations of the specifications, or must be considered as being outside the scope of a standards document, and relating e.g to local implementations. It appears that more sophisticated requirements will only emerge if the system is integrated into business processes.

The study also sought to address the engagement of users and their approach towards user requirements in standards setting. Many popular preconceptions on how standards committees work were confirmed by the committee members themselves. For instance, decisions within the committees are taken for a variety of reasons, technical merits being but one of them, with e.g. outspoken supporters being more important for a proposal to be accepted. Both the statistical information obtained through the survey and comments made by respondents confirm that committees are to a considerable degree dominated by seasoned veterans who know all the nuts and bolts of the process (with the exception of the IETF, where the young age of the organisation is reflected in both the average age of the single work group members and their short average time of association with the IETF). Likewise, the views expressed by many interviewees back the notion of a process being far too slow and painstaking to meet the fast changing demands of today's market and the speed of technological progress. To improve this situation in the short term, suggestions made by respondents ranged from better use of electronic communication media to free availability of the documents, not least to elicit public comments. In fact, whilst most suggested improvements were of a rather 'tactical' nature, the broad consent regarding shortcomings of the processes indicated the urgent necessity for improvements.

Exploring the attitudes of both users and standards committee members regarding the pros and cons of (increased) user participation in standard setting revealed that most committee members would generally welcome such an increased participation in the groups, the major motivation being the hope to learn about real-world requirements. Many felt that committee work is too far removed from the users. However, this was not an unconditional welcome; popular reservations included the request for a clear mandate, continuing participation and adequate technical knowledge on the side of the user representatives. Most users, on the other hand, did not appear to be very much interested in 'wasting' scarce resources on participation in standardisation. Rather, they looked to their service providers or vendors when problems occurred, or possibly even try to solve these problems in-house. Only a handful of very advanced users, or those that have a vested business interest in the technology were actually sending representatives to committee meetings. This lack of user involvement may be expected to have considerable impact on the standards setting process; the exact nature of which needs to be analysed.

Changing Contexts

A users' specific needs and requirements regarding IT systems are not normally fully understood prior to system implementation. Two different mechanisms may be identified that influence the requirements on a corporate IT system. First, usage contexts changing over time will result in equally changing requirements. Secondly, requirements may change within each such context, as experience in system usage grows and new ways of system exploitation are found. Moreover, many of these changes may be induced from the outside (e.g. through new technologies or requirements from business partners) and are thus both inevitable and unpredictable from the outset. This, in turn, suggests that top-down strategies for the introduction of highly distributed, de-centralised and only loosely coupled systems such as e-mail may in fact be not too beneficial in the long term. The benefits typically associated with top-down strategies (including smooth introduction and homogeneous systems causing little technical problems) are not likely to last very long. In fact, they may not last long enough to compensate for the strategy's potential drawbacks, which include resistance to change at unit, departmental or individual level as well as a lost opportunity for individual and organisational learning. As one possible result of a top-down introduction strategy organisational learning is confined to single-loop learning (at the very best), whereas a decentralised structure promotes the more desirable double-loop learning[27].

---

[27] With single-loop learning errors are detected and corrected, but the correction has no impact on the company's policy. In contrast, double-loop learning involves questioning and potentially subsequent modifications of a company's policies and goals as result of the error.

These rather more theoretical considerations have been confirmed by findings from the case study, which show that it may well take a number of years following the initial system implementation until specific corporate-wide requirements were identified. For example, the e-mail system in a large organisation has typically been shaped by a sequence of different and changing environments within which it had to be implemented and run. These environments differed widely in terms of e.g. technological and organisational contexts. In many cases e-mail was originally implemented at departmental level. In some of these cases systems were chosen to meet department-specific, possibly unique requirements, reflecting the respective local contexts. Rather more commonly, however, they just happened to be available eventually, almost by accident. The integration of those departmental systems into a corporate-wide installation represented a major switch of contexts, and accordingly a change of requirements. As a result, the desirable characteristics of the system changed dramatically, and another phase of the overall implementation process had to be initiated to accommodate the new context. Subsequently, other context changes occurred, e.g. through the need to communicate with the outside world, and especially to open the internal system to customers and business partners.

Further findings from the case studies show that companies could pursue a top-down introduction strategy only for the first generation of e-mail systems. Subsequent implementations followed the same patterns as did their counterparts in those organisations which followed a bottom-up 'strategy' from the outset. That is, implementation of later systems generations were triggered by internal or external needs rather than deliberate strategic planning, which resumed only within some companies at a later stage when other usage contexts were considered, possibly also as a result of some organisational learning.

Infrastructural Technologies

A remarkably indifferent attitude regarding corporate e-mail was demonstrated by most companies. This came as some surprise especially since a massive body of literature exists on the diffusion and management of innovations, providing guidelines on how to introduce, utilise and manage corporate IT, as well as the organisational changes potentially induced by IT systems. The search for an explanation for this apparent lack of interest first leads to the observation that large organisations deploy technology in very different contexts for very different purposes. This holds for technology in general, and all the more for information technology. IT artifacts can be found on plant floors, in R&D labs, and on secretaries' desktops; the different purposes they serve include production automation, number-crunching, and accountancy.

Despite these different application areas, at a very general level IT artifacts may be categorised as being either 'specific' or 'generic', i.e. 'business relevant' or 'infrastructural'. A car manufacturer's robot may serve as a representative of the former, a secretary's fax machine as a typical example of the latter. In particular, a company's communication system (e.g. the internal telephone network, or the corporate e-mail system) was in many cases considered as being infrastructural technology. In terms of innovation theory, the major distinction between these categories is their different degree of exposure to context-specific requirements. That is, business relevant systems are very much shaped by the particular environment within which they are deployed. In contrast, requirements on infrastructural technology will not vary much between contexts, a common characteristic of which is the fact that within most companies they are not, or only to a very small extent, integrated into business processes. Figure 6.1.1 attempts to illustrate the distinction between 'infrastructural' and 'business relevant' (IT) technologies.

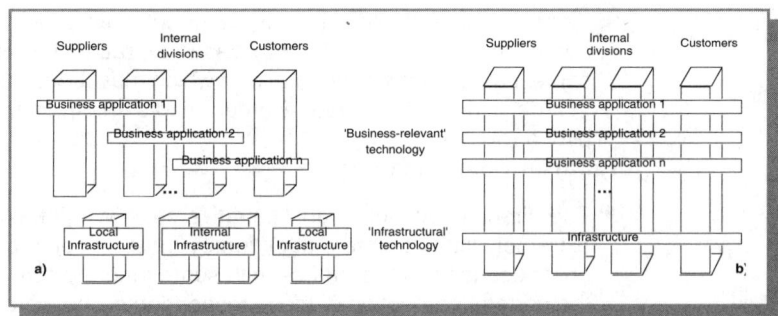

Figure 6.1.1:
'Business Relevant' vs 'Infrastructural' Technology
(based on [Benjamin, 1993])
a) Today -infrastructure and applications are separated
b) Ideal situation - integration of common infrastructure and applications

Figure 6.1.1a shows how an organisation's IT infrastructure and its business relevant applications are typically separated; in most cases they have been developed independently. Ideally, though, the infrastructure should be transparent for the application and the user by offering both the functionality and the performance necessary to make distributed or remote applications appear to be installed locally. It should also extend across organisational boundaries. This situation is shown in Figure 6.1.1b.

The need to quantify the corporate benefits to be gained from enhancing such infrastructural services in several cases hampered attempts to upgrade corporate e-mail systems, which were widely considered as part of the 'infrastructure'[28] by the case study companies. Investments in this area were hard to justify as they would yield largely indirect or intangible benefits[29]. Indeed, most companies represented in the case studies adopted a very reactive approach towards infrastructural systems. That is, although infrastructural technology may well have been enhanced to meet identified new requirements, in a vast majority of cases this only happened once the situation had become intolerable (e.g. through an unacceptable percentage of lost messages). Likewise, in terms of

---

[28] Firms invest where they perceive they will get benefit. However, their perceptions are not necessarily based on rational calculation. In the context of incomplete information - which must be assumed here - we see that decisions are shaped by other factors - 'fashion trends' and media hype play a role, too.

[29] The directory service is an illustrative case in point. It has thus far received extremely little corporate attention by most; in some cases, it was installed only because it came for free with some other system. This holds despite the general perception of those respondents who were in charge of managing corporate e-mail systems that an adequate directory service was becoming increasingly crucial for the smooth functioning of their company's communication infrastructure. Indeed, the existence of an adequate global directory service has been considered a necessary condition for the further emergence of the global information infrastructure.

Ward's cyclic model of an application[30] (depicted in Figure 6.1.2a), e-mail belongs into the 'support' cell, which again points to its (current) infrastructural nature. However, it should also be noted that deployment of corporate e-mail does not normally follow Ward's application life cycle. Rather, the typical development of corporate e-mail suggests that Ward's cycle should actually be a spiral (as depicted in Figure 6.1.2b).

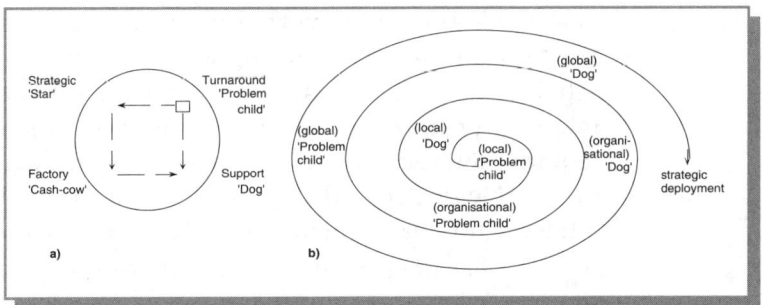

Figure 6.1.2:
Application Life Cycles
a) For applications (according to [Ward, 1987])
b) For e-mail (according to my case studies)

To summarise: we have identified a need to differentiate between categories of technology. Two such categories were distinguished for technological artifacts. They may be either 'infrastructural' or 'business relevant'. Less specific requirements may be expected for the former, due to an environment which is more consistent across departments, companies, and even business sectors. On the other hand, the environment of the latter typically exhibits strong, organisation-specific particularities, and thus a need for local innovations. Users appear to be more prepared to invest in 'business relevant' technologies, where potential return on investment is more obvious and tangible. Moreover, with requirements on the underlying

---

[30] Ward's model assumes that an application starts life as a resource consuming 'problem child'. Eventually, it becomes a strategic 'star', still costly, but now generating high benefits. Subsequently, it turns into a 'cash cow', generating high benefits, but using few resources. Finally, it becomes a 'support' application, no longer critical, but still valuable. Each application traverses this cycle exactly once.

infrastructure being less specific in most cases, comparably straightforward installations may be feasible here.

The above findings suggest that the observation that *"... it is unusual for a firm to go into developing and pursuing strategies for the development of technology when its main line of business lies elsewhere ...."* [Bierwert, 1992] is not quite correct. Rather, irrespective of a company's core business it appears that the perceived strategic importance of an IT system is the yardstick by which a company's willingness to start its own development activities has to be measured - i.e. whether it is classified as 'business relevant' or 'infrastructural'. Accordingly, a specific e-mail strategy requires the recognition of e-mail as a strategic service in the first place. Neglecting the crucial enabling role of an adequate infrastructure has in many cases led to an environment suffering from the fact that investment in infrastructure technology was given low priority.

Business Relevant Technologies

Which technological systems are actually considered as 'business relevant' by a company very much depends on the respective organisation's commercial interests. Accordingly, this will vary between companies; a car manufacturer, for example, may look to robots or systems for Computer Integrated Manufacturing (CIM), a publisher may be interested in Desktop Publishing equipment, and an innovative bottling line might attract a brewer. However, 'business relevant' has a broader scope than these purely production-oriented technical systems. In the service industry EDI may well fall into this category as well. In the banking and retail sectors, for example, EDI has already streamlined both intra- and inter-organisational processes to a considerable extent, a development which may be supposed to continue. The same sector was, for instance, among the earliest industries to use mainframes, which have long since been seen as being crucial thanks to their ability to process massive amounts of financial transactions and to handle large volumes of data. In particular, this shows that a system considered by one company as being 'business relevant' may well have 'infrastructural' status for another, a phenomenon that may, for example, be observed in the case of e-mail where perceptions regarding its business value differed between firms.

For each company technologies that relate to its core business - and its core competence - will naturally attract most interest, particularly if they hold the prospect of a quantifiable return on investment. Although demand for standard software has been growing faster than that for special customised software systems, tailor-made solutions are still preferred if the system is *"... affecting the primary business of firms, especially for areas closely linked to production and marketing ..."*. [Buschmann, 1989].

Very specific requirements and processes are most likely to have been developed primarily in the areas of a company's core business interests. These, in turn, stand in the way of a straightforward installation of a system. It is here where long-standing, time-honoured traditions characterise the environment, and where technical systems as well as production and business processes were designed to optimally meet the demands of their specific environment. A new system to be implemented here will have to be customised to a similar degree as have been the other artifacts in this environment. Accordingly, efforts will have to go into the design of a dedicated system, and its subsequent integration. Accordingly, it may be concluded that innovations are most likely to occur under these circumstances, i.e. when 'business relevant' technology is to be implemented[31].

The case studies have also shown that only those few companies which considered e-mail as a strategic tool, i.e. as 'business relevant', were prepared to implement a system that really met their needs. This situation is highlighted by the representative of one of these companies, who remarked that his organisation frequently had to build its own innovator level tools to achieve the desired functionality because of inadequate products. In contrast to that, the

---

[31] Indeed, it appears that recent research into innovations has almost exclusively focussed on what must be considered as 'business relevant' technologies, including robots for manufacturing plant, EFTPOS-systems in retailing, corporate cash management, home and office banking and ATMs in banking, and CIM in manufacturing.

case studies revealed that where an e-mail system was not considered as 'business relevant' it had typically been a matter of buying it off-the-shelf.

As most authors discussing the theory of innovation have so far failed to address infrastructural systems it appears that a closer cooperation and interaction between business studies and social sciences in general and SST in particular would be very fruitful.

6.2   Standardisation, Innovation and Implementation

It appears to be safe to say that standards-based components are going to play an increasingly important role in implementation processes. However, it is not yet clear how these different processes relate to each other.

In those cases where a suitable combination of standardised components meets the needs of a particular environment, standards establish the framework within which the implementation takes place. This is most likely to happen in the case of 'infrastructural' artifacts or systems. Alternatively, especially if 'business relevant' systems are concerned, standards may be considered as contributors to a system implementation, and to potential innovations. This contribution is likely to be through single component standards, as overall, system-wide standards are most unlikely to materialise for complex IT-systems. Yet, in this case these components will only play a minor role in the overall implementation.

The implementation arena as a major locus where innovations currently materialise - and where the social shaping of technology accordingly takes place - is to some extent complemented by activities within the standards committees in which the underlying groundwork upon which innovations will draw is done. In the case of electronic mail systems, for instance, much of the underlying communication-oriented systems exclusively comprise standardised services. Regarding the more application-oriented parts of the overall system, i.e. the e-mail service itself, we note that implementation-specific particularities become more important; it is primarily at this level where the integration into the existing IT environment takes place, and where accordingly innovations will (have to) occur. This holds all the more for applications utilising e-mail.

In any case, it follows that standardisation processes are important for innovations, and that they must not be ignored when discussing innovation processes. This argument may even be taken one step further, suggesting that major similarities exist between innovation and standardisation processes. Indeed, it may well be possible that lessons learned from the well-researched field of innovation may be applied to standardisation processes. This proposition may appear to be a little far-fetched; after all, there is a major, decisive distinction between the processes of standardisation and innovation - their respective scope. Whilst this is certainly true - and will be discussed below in more detail - there are indeed also major similarities between the two processes.

For one, users have a considerable influence on innovations. In fact, they could establish themselves in a position to dominate innovation and standards setting processes alike. As it currently stands, however, users' diverse and individual needs prevent them from playing the important role they could play - at least in standards setting.

Members of standards setting committees tend to see themselves as company representatives. This holds particularly for members from user companies. It may accordingly be concluded that they only contribute specific requirements that originated form their respective environments. It follows that here the local environment of the respective user representative's organisation has a major impact on the standards setting process in that it heavily influences the user requirements that are actually fed into the process. This impact in fact represents another correspondence between standards setting and innovation.

Moreover, both standardisation and implementation are major platforms for cooperation between vendors and users. Without this cooperation the outcome of the processes would most likely be far from satisfactory, due to the complementing roles users and vendors play, which are equivalent in both processes. It is the vendors' task to provide the technical knowledge and expertise. Users, in turn, contribute their specific knowledge about their requirements and environments, respectively.

These complementing roles imply that communication between the two parties is crucial in both processes. The 'technology-centric' view of the vendors needs to be aligned with the organisational and technical requirements of the users, a process that is essential during both implementation and standardisation, albeit with somewhat different foci. During implementation vendors need to gain a thorough understanding of the particularities of the context within which a system is to be implemented. Consequently, an active learning process has to take place on the side of the vendor. In standardisation, users need to contribute their specific requirements to the process; users assume the teacher's role here. Still, the underlying common need for communication remains.

Other factors that may shape technology will also be channelled into the international standards setting bodies' work groups. The respective corporate environments of the committee members' employers, for instance, will play a major role. The different visions of how a technology should be used, and the ideas of how this can be achieved are both formed by these local environments. It will exert a significant impact on the work of the committees, thus preceding, and possibly complementing the local implementation context as a major source of influence. This holds especially in the case of anticipatory standards, which specify new services from scratch, and thus offer the opportunity to incorporate to some degree the particular presumptions of the originating committee. In a more extreme case, work within the committees may even anticipate innovations that could otherwise potentially result from a local implementation. This may, for instance, happen if a strong user representative succeeds in promoting the particularities of his/her local environment as the basis of a standard.

Likewise, a reactive standard will transpose the environment from which it emerged; this will typically be the corporate environment of its inventor (i.e. typically a vendor or a service provider) who originally specified the system upon which the standard will be based. Thus, his/her visions will implicitly be embodied in the standard specification. Again, the correspondence between innovation and standardisation is obvious - both are shaped by a specific environment. Only in this case it is the vendor's environment that has a major impact on the standard.

Related to these observations, although on a personal rather than organisational level, we note that the processes leading to both technical design and technical standards are typically dominated by engineers, who in many cases lack an understanding of the non-technical components that need to be considered for both designs and standards alike. The accordingly rather 'technology-centric' outcome of both processes has frequently been criticised.

We can conclude that the work done within the standards committees has a major impact on innovations (in addition to design and the actual implementation itself). These activities are not unrelated; even local implementations of individual, customised systems are likely to include standards-based components. Standardisation will always influence innovations, either:

- directly, e.g. if a local implementation is done through integration and configuration of standards-based components, or

- as the basis of system design, in case of a customised solution comprising some standard elements being implemented, or

- as the locus of inventions.

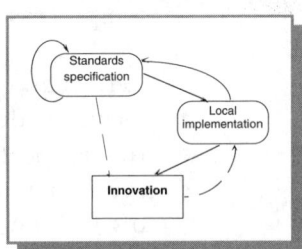

Figure 6.2.1:
Processes Contributing to an Innovation

Figure 6.2.1 depicts the close interrelation between the processes of standardisation and implementation, and the (potentially) resulting innovation. In fact, given the large number of standardised components available, the odds are that every innovation in the IT sector will at least in part be influenced by standardisation. It is time to turn to an analysis of the process of standardisation to gain some more insight into the particularities of the process, and its influence on innovations.

6.3   Users and Standardisation

So far the discussion suggests that the contribution of specific knowledge regarding the characteristics of the respective implementation environment represents the major role users have to play during an implementation process. That is, they have to feed their intimate knowledge of local particularities, which nobody else can possibly possess, into the process. Given the interrelation and similarities between implementation and standardisation processes, we may assume that users should be assigned an equivalent task for standards setting, again to optimally exploit their unique knowledge on their respective local environment. For standardisation purposes, this knowledge ideally takes the form of functional requirements, which then establish the basis from which standards can be developed. This conclusion is supported by practitioners and standardisation theorists alike; a majority of survey respondents, for example, stressed the fact that to them the contribution of real-world requirements constitutes the major role users are supposed to play in the process of standardisation.

Yet, 'requirements' is a very broad term, that not only refers to the technical domain, but is also closely linked to the particularities of the respective local environment. Accordingly, providing only functional and technical requirements does not suffice. Rather, organisational and other non-technical needs have to be considered, and user representatives need to be in a position to identify these needs. Thus, it would not make too much sense if only technical people were sent to the committees to represent users. Rather, corporate strategists and managers also need to get involved, to make sure that the non-technical issues are adequately covered as well.

If a user actually does participate, assuming the role of a user representative, as opposed to representing only a single company, survey findings show s/he will face credibility and communication problems. First, many respondents said they would need to be convinced of a proper mandate, to show that not just a particular company's special requirements are brought into the process, but more widely identified needs[32]. Typically, companies are sending their engineers to standards committees, and their views tend to be somewhat 'techno-centric'. Thus, it is not too surprising that committee members named technical sophistication on the side of the user representatives as a major prerequisite for meaningful participation. Thus, it would be necessary to convince committee members that representing a user in a standards committee does not necessarily require technical expertise, and that there are more aspects to standards than just purely technical functionality. Failing on the users' side to adequately address these issues will invariably weaken their position in the committee[33].

A major underlying obstacle here is rooted in a communication problem, and in the differences in views and perceptions of technology that can be identified between engineers and managers. Such problems in 'cross-profession' communication are not uncommon, to solve them requires learning by all sides; engineers need to gain some

---

[32] Apparently no such mandates are necessary for representatives of vendors and service providers. This may again be interpreted as an expression of the predominantly 'techno-centric' attitude of standards setting committees, whose vast majority of members are representing vendors or service providers. Their roles have never been questioned, although they obviously include the representation of the respective employers' commercial interests (which may or may not be in line with the overall best interest).

[33] It is worth noting here that despite the frequently voiced condition that users need to be technically sophisticated committee members also reported that a proposal's technical merits are significantly less important than the presence of its proponents at meetings (with the exception of the IETF, where technical merits is the one thing that counts). It might be suspected that 'technical sophistication' is put forward as an excuse to help keep users away from the committees. This would, however, need further data to work from.

understanding of the necessary organisational and managerial considerations, and managers need to get an understanding of at least the technological basics. This may sound trivial, but the reported major credibility and acceptance problems from which ITU-T's Study Group I, and its ISO sister group (i.e. those groups that were charged with identifying and compiling user requirements), suffered finally contributed to the abandoning of these groups.

The typical history of corporate deployment of e-mail, and of its perception as being primarily infrastructural, suggest that users will not only be unable to contribute initial requirements to a new standards setting initiative (others than very general ones), but they will also be unable to provide useful input for quite some time afterwards. This situation can only change if and when the status of e-mail (and of other IT systems with a similar corporate history) switches from 'infrastructural' to 'business relevant'. Even if this happens, it will subsequently take a considerable period of time to actually identify new, more advanced requirements. Although some are likely to emerge during implementation, others will only surface once the system has been adapted to, and especially integrated into, the local environment (e.g. into business processes) and experiences have been gained through its use, a process which may well take years.

If users are not (yet) in the position to contribute requirements, the standards setting process will not benefit very much from their participation. Therefore, we may conclude that in this case it will make little, if any, difference whether or not user representatives participate in the process, since they can only assume the role of technical experts - rather than that of a contributor of requirements - many of whom will be on the committee anyway (representing vendors). It follows from the above that this situation may easily occur in case of 'infrastructural' technologies, where users do not see any business incentive to contribute to standards setting. This additional lack of incentive comes on top of the reluctance caused by the general perception of the standardisation process as slow, inefficient, costly and yielding uncertain results.

Yet, the generally accepted principal role for user representatives in standards setting is to provide real-world requirements. However, we have seen that in most cases specific functional requirements cannot be available at the beginning of a standardisation project. Moreover, from the above discussion we have seen that unconditional user participation in standardisation is not a desirable goal per se, thanks to the largely context-specific - and thus very diverse - requirements that are to be expected. Instead, ways need to be found to achieve meaningful user representation.

Initially, an innovation may need only to be considered within a specific context (e.g. a single organisation), whereas standardisation addresses a far broader and more heterogeneous environment. An implementation takes place within the well-defined context of one single setting, taking into account, and being rooted in, its local characteristics and specifics. In particular, this holds for the identified functional requirements, which basically establish the technical aspect of the local context, and are identified by the one customer where the implementation takes place. In contrast, a standard needs to be useful to, and applicable by, a wide range of organisations across very diverse contexts. A broad range of potentially very different requirements from equally different environments will need to be addressed. Standardisation cannot try and accommodate some of these while ignoring others; rather, it has to be sufficiently generic to be easily adaptable to a variety of - ideally all - contexts.

An implementation process is inevitably bound to fail if there is no user participation; the involvement of numerous user representatives from different backgrounds significantly contributes to its success. Yet, the attempt to increase user influence in standardisation simply by raising the number of users on a committee will introduce a variety of additional, probably contradicting requirements. They may lead to highly complex standards, offering numerous alternatives and optional functionalities to suit all needs[34]; almost inevitably this would introduce incompatibilities between standard-compliant systems simply because of the different options that could be

---

[34] In fact, today's process tends to yield such results as well, the parallel standardisation of the three competing LAN technologies Ethernet, Token Ring and Token Bus to please DEC, intel, Xerox, as well as IBM and General Motors, being a case in point.

implemented, as it is the case e.g. with EDI standards. Against this background the frequently claimed need for more users on the standards setting committees requires some further analysis.

Given the huge variety of business sectors, organisational forms and business philosophies, the many different intra- and inter-organisational interdependencies, and all the differences that come with varying company sizes, not to mention regional or national differences in culture and legislation it is most unlikely that coherent requirements will ever materialise, apart from some very generic ones. Moreover, representatives of user companies do not necessarily see themselves as user envoys in general; rather, they are representing their respective employers. Therefore, there is a need for a mechanism to align the various requirements.

These considerations suggest that users should seek representation through a dedicated body (a 'user coalition'), responsible for voicing its stakeholders' needs and concerns in the appropriate standards committees. In any case, great care needs to be taken to ensure that such a body actually represents as broad a variety of users as possible, of all sizes and from all sectors, rather than acting as something similar to, say, a trade association representing only a single market sector. This broad market coverage is crucial for several reasons; for example, even basic requirements will differ between SMEs and large enterprises.

In fact, a user group - typically, though not necessarily a supplier-initiated organisation of users of e.g. a particular product or service - shares many characteristics with a user coalition - albeit in a different context - in that its scope is strictly limited to one product and one supplier, respectively. From a vendor's point of view these groups provide invaluable feedback, for instance on bugs, but also on requirements on future releases or new products. Here users play a role very similar to the one they should play in standards setting. Depending on the type of product, membership in these groups is very diverse, covering different industry segments and very distinct types of user companies. Thus, the diversity of users found to be crucial for user coalitions can be found here. Users, on the other hand, feel that membership in these groups is advantageous, and that vendors listen to what the groups say. It would therefore be extremely beneficial for the standards setting process if a similar situation could be created there as well.

There is also an economic dimension to this way of user representation, in that it offers the almost only realistic chance for those user companies which cannot afford direct participation to have their requirements filed with standards committees. Again, this holds particularly for SMEs, almost all of which currently stay clear of any standardisation-related activities. Finally, it will serve to reassure other committee members (i.e. representatives from vendor companies) that indeed a broad base of users is represented. Clearly, the alignment of requirements has to take place prior to actual standardisation to enable the user community to file an agreed set of requirements, and to speak with one voice.

The observations above trigger some further thoughts regarding the general desirability of direct user participation in standards setting, and indeed on the overall structure of this process.

6.4   A Proposal for a New Standardisation Process

The most frequently heard complaint about the process adopted by the 'official' standardisation bodies concerns their slowness and their lack of responsiveness to market needs and technological changes. Another point raised regularly is the danger of losing out to 'de facto standards', i.e. proprietary specifications or those developed by a consortium, which might, due to their speed of work and their commitment, eventually render the 'official' process obsolete. Indeed, this criticism seems to be justified given the lengthy and highly formal processes adopted by most standards setting organisations and ever shorter technology life cycles. However, in the light of the survey findings some reservations regarding these perceptions are appropriate.

We have seen that the implementation of a corporate IT system is far from being a simple and straightforward exercise. In many cases it starts as a highly distributed process, which only at some later stage may become largely centrally organised and managed. In the case of e-mail it typically took five to ten years before central IT took over. Since then, few of the organisations represented in the case studies have managed to harmonise their system to the planned degree, let alone to actually integrate e-mail into their business processes (if they intended to do so at all, that is). It is only now that few pioneering companies are in the position to identify functional deficiencies of the system, and can take appropriate action. One possible option at this stage - and actually pursued by some survey companies - is to contribute these requirements to the standards setting process through active participation. Two conclusions may be drawn from this observation:

- Users are hardly in a position to come up with meaningful specific requirements on a communication service if they have not already put the service in question (or a reasonably similar one) to more advanced use.

- It takes years of advanced service usage to reach this level of sophistication.

From this it may in turn be concluded that proactive standards cannot simply be designed on the basis of real user requirements because such requirements will not normally be available when standards are initially developed. This is underpinned and further stressed by the comparably general and sketchy level of the requirements compiled through the case studies even from long-standing users. Consequently, just speeding up the standards setting process will not yield any benefits in terms of usefulness and usability of the standards. Rather, mechanisms have to be provided that enable feedback of user experience into the standardisation process. Given the time it took e-mail users to develop specific technical requirements, it will take years before a standard reaches a reasonable level of maturity and usefulness.

We have already noted that a successful implementation relies on a close cooperation between users and vendors. Those joint efforts will not least result in a transfer of knowledge in both directions; users will learn about the technical nut and bolts, whereas vendors can collect information on requirements that will potentially be of extreme value for future implementations. Likewise, both groups need to work together during the specification of a standard, which is again going to result in knowledge transfer, albeit to a smaller degree.

We have also seen that direct user participation in standards setting is extremely limited today. Instead, indirect participation may occur through some kind of filter, established by vendors; that is, they are used as 'proxies' by their users in the hope that identified additional requirements are actually fed into the standardisation process. Assigning this role to vendors is a result of the necessary cooperation during implementation; after all, they should be sufficiently familiar with their customers' requirements to represent them on the committees. Yet, this is also a very dangerous approach, as no appropriate control mechanisms exist to verify that the requirements have actually been filed. Thus, whilst cooperation during the implementation process is sensible and necessary, it does not guarantee that user requirements will be fed into the standardisation process.

An alternative way of dealing with functional shortcomings revealed by the case studies is very much in line with observations of users in the context of configurational systems: innovations are being developed in-house, without worrying too much about standards-related issues. Like the approach outlined above, however, this one may be also disastrous in the long term, as it separates requirements from standards setting, with the inevitable result of less useful and usable standards. Moreover, it bears the risk of ending up with standard-based, but 'enhanced' systems, which may be perfectly integrated into their respective environments, but are unable to interoperate due to the incompatible, and non standard-compliant functional additions[35].

Table 6.4.1 shows the requirements likely to emerge during the individual phases of e-mail introduction and diffusion. Specific

---

[35] This observation alone suggests that the terms 'environment' and 'context' are in need of a redefinition. Until now, they are typically used to denote a *local* setting, in the sense of 'within an organisation'. As the need for inter-organisational communication increases, the actual environment within which implementations take place will likewise need to become inter-organisational. Ultimately, there will be only one, global 'environment'.

requirements will largely emerge during the integration phase, when usage of e-mail shifts from an infrastructural system to a business relevant one. Only during this late stage will companies have accumulated the knowledge and experience necessary to identify functional shortcomings.

E-mail development stages	Technical character-istics	Usage character-istics	Potential input to standards setting
Phase 0: None	none	none	possibly preliminary generic requirements
Phase 1: (Local) Introduction	local services (department level)	local use only	no additional requirements
Phase 2: Interconnection	interconnection via point-to-point gateways, (very) limited integration	primarily local use, increasingly company-wide	no additional requirements
Phase 3: Interoperability	interoperability through backbone, little integration	still primarily local use; 80 : 20 (internal : external) rule applies	some more advanced requirements possible
Phase 4: Integration	quite homogeneous system, integration into business processes	largely unknown	detailed requirements

Table 6.4.1:
Characteristics of the Phases-Based Introduction Process

Thus far, most enhancements to the standardisation process that seem to be necessary do not relate to the weaknesses commonly associated with this process, such as slowness, excessive formalism, and being infested with politics. Rather, it appears that continuous user input, particularly including experiences with early implementations, is the most important thing to facilitate production of useful standards. This suggests the need for a more iterative process, as it may be found in the field of systems design.

The picture of the typical standards development process today, as described in the respective bodies' rules and further detailed - and sometimes corrected - through the case studies is shown in Figure 6.4.1. A number of open issues emerge from this picture: for instance, it is not entirely clear who initiates a standardisation activity (apart from the formal rules), and on what grounds. The activity may be either reactive or proactive, it may or may not be based on user requirements, or it may only be supposed to serve a vendor's purposes. Moreover, until well after the completion of a standards project, it cannot be established whether or not a standard is economically viable. Given the huge amounts of money that have to go into the development of a single standard it is disastrous if a standard fails to deliver.

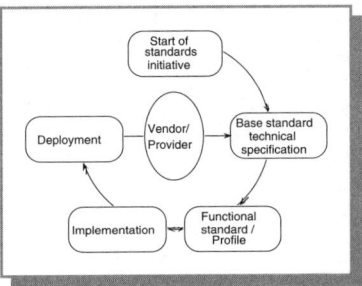

Figure 6.4.1:
Development and Subsequent Deployment of a Standard

The process exhibits some more potentially severe deficiencies. For one, no dedicated requirements elicitation phase precedes the process. As it currently stands, all requirements are largely made up by committee members, to a considerable degree reflecting vendors' and service providers' interests. Even worse, no formal mechanisms have been established to enable users to feed their working experience directly back into the process. Thus, to actually enable meaningful involvement, modifications to the process described above will be necessary.

Considering the above deliberations, the role users should ideally assume, the comments and insights gathered through the survey, as well as the conclusions outlined above, the model for a specification development process, as depicted in Figure 6.4.2, emerges.

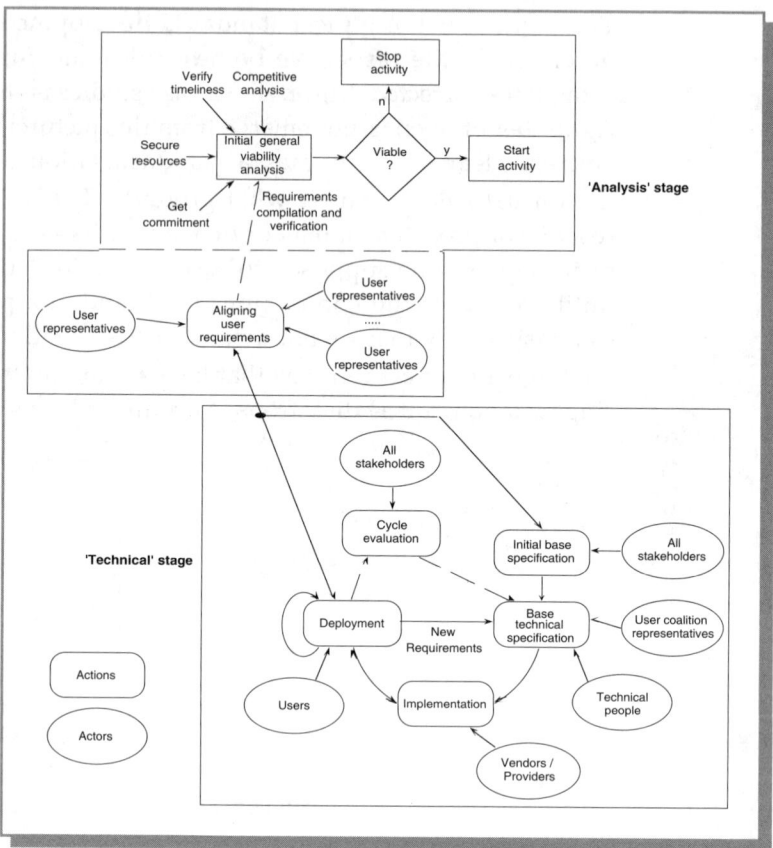

Figure 6.4.2:
The Improved Cycle of Specification Development
(the Cyclic Stage Model of Standardisation, CSMS)

This model aims primarily at the support of anticipatory standards setting. Yet, in doing so it draws upon an important reactive element, i.e. cycles of user feedback. These cycles allow users to - iteratively - contribute their experiences to the process. Up to now this property has only been available in reactive standardisation, where users had the opportunity to forward their earlier experiences[36].

This is a two-stage process, with an analysis stage preceding the technical work. During the former, a first compilation and verification of initial requirements from both the technical and the business perspective is performed, the required resources are secured and, if applicable, it is ensured that a window of opportunity will be met. The model draws upon ideas from the discipline of Participatory Design, which promotes equal participation of all stakeholders in process or system design. In fact, the process will not work properly without equal and balanced participation of all interested parties, and without a common understanding of the problems and issues at hand. This holds for both phases of the model.

Ideally, commitments from all stakeholders, including vendors, service providers and users to implement and to actually use the technology, respectively, would be obtained at the earliest possible stage. Such commitments would help ensure that requirements will indeed be addressed and that products based on this standard will eventually be purchased. Unfortunately, given the duration of the process, the pace of technological development and the resulting level of insecurity, such strong commitments are highly unlikely. However, a common understanding, together with a certain degree of commitment and trust on the sides of both users and vendors should be feasible.

Several fundamental decisions need to be taken before the actual (technical) standards setting work can commence. First of all, it is crucial to realise the impossibility of solving all potential future problems from the outset, and accordingly not to try and specify an all-embracing standard. Recent experiences show that attempting to specify such standards are bound to fail. For example, most of the largely proactive OSI standards, based on projected user needs, and designed to include all possible options, have not been accepted in the market. Accordingly, an evolutionary approach has to be adopted

---

[36] At least in theory, that is. Moreover, there was hardly a way to verify that the final system actually reflected these experiences.

(very much in line with the ideas underlying the Participatory Design approach). Work is based on a set of initial requirements, specified primarily by those who will actually use the system in the future. Subsequently, the specification can be refined based on experiences made during the deployment phase.

However, we have seen that at least the vast majority of corporate users of electronic messaging systems were not in a position to identify much more than very basic requirements on (standards for) these systems, even after having used comparable services for a lengthy period of time. From the above discussion it may furthermore be concluded that this lack of more specific requirements may generally be expected for infrastructural systems. This holds especially for the field of non-technical requirements (i.e. those emerging from e.g. work processes or organisational culture), which only surface after years of usage (if at all, that is). Regarding technical requirements, only rather general and generic ones may be expected to be available from the outset[37].

Obviously, the situation will be even worse at the beginning of a proactive standards setting activity, when very little or no prior experiences at all on the side of the users must be assumed. Thus, the set of initial requirements mentioned above will, in all likelihood, be little else but a comparably sketchy wishlist. Still, despite all its shortcomings, this - inevitably rather pragmatically compiled - list represents the state-of-the-art in user requirements, and will be a far more useful starting point for any standardisation work than - probably largely unfounded - assumptions regarding future 'user needs' which are primarily defined by vendors and service providers anyway, and upon which the standards setting process is typically based today.

---

[37] Quite surprisingly, and somewhat disconcerting, even the IETF had major problems when they had to specify requirements for the new IPng protocol. Those eventually identified were *"... presented without weighting ..."*, and were criticised for being *"... too general to support a defensible choice on the grounds of technical adequacy."* (quoted in [Monteiro, 1998]) - after more than twenty years of usage and literally thousands of person-months of experience.

Having assembled the initial requirements list, its single items have to be weighed with respect to their perceived importance, potential contradictions have to be sorted out, and finally a catalogue of mandatory requirements has to be agreed upon, to serve as the basis for the subsequent technical work. Furthermore, in the likely absence of well-founded, strong requirements during the early stages of the process, this catalogue will have to be 'living', i.e., requirements will be added and possibly removed as work progresses and practical experiences are gained.

Looking at the implementation of a new standard it needs to be considered if, and to what degree, it will cause changes to an already installed base. If it does, the nature an the extent of these changes must be evaluated carefully[38]. Again, a step-by-step approach to the introduction of changes is highly recommended, which particularly implies that only very few components of a network may be replaced at a time, and that an alignment phase has to follow each such change before another replacement may be done.

Moreover, a transition strategy needs to be advised. Whilst it would be desirable to have such a strategy in place prior to the technical work, it is most likely that in practice these will be developed in parallel. Indeed, as experience from the IPng standardisation process indicates, a working protocol fulfilling the initial requirements may well be standardised upon without an explicit transition strategy.

Ensuring backward compatibility is a closely related major issue here, as is avoiding installed-base hostility. Yet, as the final outcome of any major changes to a large installed base is not normally predictable, the only realistic way of approaching this problem is to use common sense, to apply a degree of pragmatism, to monitor the transition process closely, and to make sure that changes are indeed carried out gradually.

---

[38] Actor Network Theory (see e.g. [Callon, 1991]) tells us that a large, well-aligned actor-network - such as e.g. the Internet, or indeed any large, global network - is almost irreversible. It can only be changed into an equally well-aligned network.

These deliberations seem to suggest that the IETF process could be a solution, as it apparently addresses all issues raised. Indeed, some of the essential characteristics discussed above can be found in the IETF process as well, including particularly the evolutionary design approach, the importance assigned to backward compatibility, and the necessary degree of pragmatism. The step-by-step approach is indeed a cornerstone of the IETF process, which aims at standardising comparably small but interoperable components, which can be combined to provide the desired functionality. The installed base of the Internet alone makes backward compatibility an issue of overriding importance, and impossible to circumvent. This, too, has been realised by the IETF; even if a new version of a standard has been specified its predecessor may remain an Internet standard *"... to honor the requirements of an installed base."* Finally, given the highly dynamic environment within which the IETF's standardisation work takes place, a certain level of pragmatism is essential. Examples of how this may work include the tendency to prefer producing a quick solution over doing lengthy discussion on merits and disadvantages of different proposals, and the rather relaxed attitude towards the use of external specifications (both open and proprietary)[39].

Yet, there are also some important differences. First, the IETF does not have an explicit requirements elicitation phase, or indeed any mechanism to ensure that real user requirements actually establish the basis of a standards setting activity. Not unlike the situation to be found within ISO and ITU, it is normally up to the single work group members to define the requirements they subsequently work from. Second, the IETF process requires the availability of two independent, interworking implementations as a necessary condition for a proposal to proceed on the RFC standard track. Whilst this is an important step, and one that makes the IETF process stand out from its 'competitors', I feel it stops halfway through, as this requirement aims primarily at checking the correctness of the specifications, and

---

[39] Obviously, there is a risk that too great a degree of this pragmatism opens a loophole for interested parties to undermine the IETF process.

their interoperability, rather than exploring user requirements[40]. That is, the IETF does not care who is doing the implementations, since proof of interoperability is the only requirement. As a consequence, the implementations will be close to prototypes. In particular, they need not be employed in a real production environment. Yet, to gain experiences with, and to subsequently define real requirements derived from these experiences, it is important that the implemented system is employed in commercial working environments, and that experiences gained there will contribute to a more usable revised version of the underlying standard (as opposed to only demonstrate interoperability). Finally, IETF Work Groups are abandoned once they have achieved their goal; if a standard is in need of enhancements, a completely new group is set up.

The discussion of the issues that eventually led to the less than enthusiastic utilisation of X.400 has unveiled a number of problems that any new process needs to address as well. For one, inadequate first specifications led to an unfavourable perception of the service. In a standards setting process based on the CSMS the close cooperation between vendors and users during the technical work should guarantee that even initial specifications are solidly based on real world requirements (albeit potentially rather generic ones). This cooperation should also prevent excessively complex specifications. Moreover, since the process is very adaptive, potentially relevant new technical developments can easily be integrated if this is considered worthwhile. Likewise, the gradual development of specifications, and the continuing integration of emerging new requirements (and technologies) is one of the new process's most important characteristics.

Above, I have already argued that it is more useful to strive for a reasonably fast first specification based on generic initial requirements, and to enhance it subsequently when real requirements

---

40 *"A specification from which at least two independent and interoperable implementations from different code bases have been developed, and for which sufficient successful operational experience has been obtained, may be elevated to the "Draft Standard" level. [....] "interoperable" means to be functionally equivalent or interchangeable components of the system or process in which they are used."*

emerge from service use, than to aim at a full-fledged specification from the outset. In parallel, efforts should be undertaken to establish confidence that a viable technology will emerge.

Based on the requirements compiled, technical committees would then attempt to develop a draft specification, which is returned to the user representatives for review and, eventually, approval. Ideally, the engineers drafting the specifications would come from both sides, vendors and users, as this would help to keep the specifications in line with the requirements available. The group of user representatives should be composed of engineers as well as non-technical people to make sure that all facets of the requirements are met. There may be several iterations, with the proviso that a balance is maintained between evaluation and development. Subsequently, the first version of the final specification can be released for implementation.

During the following deployment phase, operational experiences will be gained within a variety of user environments. Eventually, the experience accumulated will be sufficient to identify shortcomings of the specification. The resulting additional requirements identified will serve as input to a second cycle, during which the specification will be enhanced accordingly. Prior to this stage, the specification will be 'frozen', i.e. no changes may be made. This does not include dealing with 'defect reports', i.e. reports on errors or ambiguities in the original specification, which have to be acted upon immediately.

We have now seen that standardisation as well can be based on a model exhibiting characteristics similar to those of the spiral model of software engineering. The most important commonalities include the prerequisite of an initial commitment from all parties involved, the early specification of underlying requirements, and regular checkpoints. The latter are used for risk analysis in the original spiral model, whereas their equivalent in the proposed model, the 'Cycle evaluation', has a broader scope in that potentially important external developments (e.g. relevant new emerging technologies) are also taken into consideration. Accordingly, this phase may well yield requirements in addition to those emerging from deployment experience.

The time of implementation of the final specification or system represents a major difference between the spiral model and the CSMS: whereas integration, acceptance test, and implementation conclude the activity according to the former, they are integral, and repetitive, elements of the latter. Likewise, the CSMS yields operational specifications (which need to be fully integrated into their respective environments) rather than prototypes. This is particularly important as many requirements will result from the particularities of implementations within the context of a specific environment. A prototype, on the other hand, is not normally integrated into its environment, and predominantly used to obtain feedback on the functional aspects of a specification, including especially the user interface.

Some particular characteristics of this process model are worth noting. For instance, it can be applied to industry consortia and official standards setting bodies alike; it does not make any assumptions regarding the process which eventually yields a specification (apart from the crucial role assigned to the user community). This is particularly important since both approaches to standards setting will be needed in the future, largely depending on the type of technology to be standardised. In some areas, such as basic telecommunications infrastructure services (as e.g. X.25, ISDN, and ATM), technical specifications need to be mature and have long-term stability to ensure that potentially large investments in such technology will not become obsolete too soon. Here, formal standards, based on a consensus of all interested parties, will be preferred. On the other hand, in less stable areas (as e.g. PC interfaces and peripherals) agreed specifications will have to be available quickly to establish a common basis for applications, and to avoid competing proprietary specifications. In such cases, where the expected lifespan of a specification may not be too important, less formal processes, as e.g. those typically adopted by industry consortia, will be better suited. The model also allows for a consortium to do the initial specification and subsequently have a formal body to transform it into a standard once it has sufficiently matured.

A process based on this model would have considerable advantages over the current one, but some (minor) potential drawbacks must also be conceded. Beginning with the latter, we first note that obviously the 'first round' of the process may take longer than it does today, due to the time required for the viability analysis. Second, the process stands or falls by input from the user community. Consequently, users' attitudes towards standardisation need to be changed. They will have to be convinced that active contribution to standardisation is in their interest, not just a waste of scarce resources.

Another issue relates to the need for cooperation between users, primarily during the first stage of the process. It could be argued that companies will be reluctant to publish and discuss their requirements, making them available to competitors, as they might see a danger of revealing too much of their strategic planning. However, successful work done within various consortia, for example, shows that users themselves apparently are not too worried by this issue.

These problems are more than compensated for by the benefits. For one, a viability analysis preceding the technical work will help reduce the number of unsuccessful standardisation activities. As a desirable side effect, this will also free resources, both financial and human, from projects that are not likely to produce any viable output anyway, thus compensating, at least in part, for the additional resources required to develop the viability analysis.

The second major advantage relates to the mechanism provided for user feedback. As pointed out above, the model is based on two assumptions. The first postulates that requirements will emerge over time, and that it may well take them more than a decade to develop (as it did in the case of e-mail). The second one postulates that a standardisation activity is not just a matter of setting up a committee, producing a standard, and disbanding it again (as e.g. the IETF does). Some European research programmes have adopted a similar, albeit less formal, approach. In these programmes, certain projects serve as testbeds at user sites; experiences gained from these sites may then be contributed to European standards bodies, typically ETSI. This approach has to some degree been borrowed from the usability domain, where 'learning-by-using' - typically through prototypes - is a popular way of identifying usability deficiencies in a software system. Reassessments can be done on a regular basis, thus making standards development more reliable, and easing the task of systems planning for the user community. They would ensure the start of new specification activities if and when sufficiently strong new requirements emerge. It follows that the user community must have the right to demand the specification of a new version of a standard.

Summarising the characteristics of the proposed model of a standards setting process, it can be noted that a viability analysis preceding the actual technical work should not only make standardisation more efficient, but should also reduce the number of standards, making life easier for both users and vendors. The feedback and monitor mechanisms for users will significantly contribute to standards that meet actual requirements. The price to pay is primarily constituted by the longer overall process. To compensate for this, the time allocated for the technical specification of a standard should be minimised, to enable timely first implementations.

6.5   Outlook

The conclusions reached, and the lessons potentially to be learned, have been based on a survey of representatives of large e-mail user corporations and members of those standards committees in charge of electronic messaging services. For this particular domain, I consider these conclusions as valid and well-founded. I also feel that some lessons may be applied to other services and environments with sufficiently similar characteristics; in particular, standardisation activities relating to the GII are potential beneficiaries. Considerable further work needs to be done to establish to which other environments the results of this thesis may be applied. For example, a categorisation of environments would be helpful to identify differences and similarities.

Regarding the social shaping of technology it would be interesting to examine the distinction between 'business relevant' and 'infrastructural' technology in more detail. While it can certainly be shown that the 'elevation' of e-mail from a mere interpersonal communication system to a mission-critical application boosted corporate interest in, and requirements on, the service, further empirical studies are needed to determine whether or not 'infrastructural' and 'business relevant' actually establishes a valid and useful categorisation. In the same way, it would be interesting to analyse in more detail users' perception of the importance of standardisation and implementation when it comes to those services or systems that are regarded as 'business relevant'. For example, it could be speculated that a greater deal of strategic thinking can be observed for 'business relevant' technologies, which might affect the fortune of a company.

If we accept the premise that corporate perceptions regarding value and importance of ('infrastructural') technology may indeed change over time, it would also be interesting to find out what exactly causes these views to change. Possible alternatives here include the internal accumulation of experience that eventually leads to such changes, and new technological developments, but also general hype about e.g. new applications or business processes. In particular, the potential existence of common trajectories should be investigated. In this context it would also be interesting to study the diffusion process of e-mail (and similar IT systems) in more detail. The processes that have been unveiled by the case studies suggest that the popular 'critical mass' theory is ill equipped to explain the introduction and diffusion of e-mail in large, globally operating and geographically distributed corporations.

One of the cornerstones of SST - unchallenged here - is the notion that technology is shaped by its context of use. This concept suggests that little similarities between organisations exist in this respect, and that it will accordingly be next to impossible to identify more than just a handful of common, specific requirements (i.e. requirements that from more advanced usage). From the standards setter's point of view, however, it would obviously be most helpful if unified requirements were available. Accordingly, additional research to establish if, and where, such common, cross-context requirements actually exist would be extremely helpful for requirements elicitation as a vital part of the standards setting process.

The proposed new model of the standards setting process is to a great extent based on the notion that specific user requirements will not normally be available at the beginning of a standards activity (this holds particularly for anticipatory standards). As this proposal is in stark contrast to the widely held position that strong permanent user participation in standards setting is a sine-qua-non, further research into the development of user requirements will be needed to back this suggestion which probably looks somewhat strange to some. Likewise, the proposal to start with a viability analysis plus a basic first implementation, rather than to specify a very elaborate system from the outset - as it is the case today - will raise a few eyebrows.

Putting it all together, standardisation is bound to play an increasingly crucial role, not only for the emerging information infrastructures, but also in implementation processes, and as an additional source of innovations. To be able to produce usable and useful standards the standardisation processes need to be improved. All stakeholders in the process stand to benefit if they can summon up the energy required to bring standardisation processes in line with reality.

References

[Benjamin 1993]　　　Benjamin, R.I.; Levinson, L.:
　　　　　　　　　　　A Framework for Managing IT-Enabled Change
　　　　　　　　　　　Sloan Management Review, Summer 1993.

[Bierwert 1992]　　　Biervert, B.; Monse, K.:
　　　　　　　　　　　Creating Applications of Information Technology
　　　　　　　　　　　in the Service Sector
　　　　　　　　　　　In: Dierkes, M.; Hoffmann, U. (eds): "New
　　　　　　　　　　　Technologies at the Outset - Social Forces in the
　　　　　　　　　　　Shaping of Technological Innovations".
　　　　　　　　　　　Campus/Westview, 1992

[Buschmann 1989]　 Buschmann, E. et al.:
　　　　　　　　　　　Der Softwaremarkt in der Bundesrepublik
　　　　　　　　　　　Deutschland
　　　　　　　　　　　GMD Studien no. 167, 1989.

[Callon 1991]　　　　Callon, M.:
　　　　　　　　　　　Techno-economic networks and irreversibility
　　　　　　　　　　　In: Law, J. (ed.): "A Sociology of Monsters: Essays
　　　　　　　　　　　on Power, Technology and Domination". Routledge,
　　　　　　　　　　　1991.

[Monteiro 1998]　　 Monteiro, E.:
　　　　　　　　　　　Scaling Information Infrastructure: The Case of the
　　　　　　　　　　　Next Generation IP in Internet
　　　　　　　　　　　The Information Society, vol. 14, no. 3, 1998.

[Ward 1987]　　　　　Ward, J.:
　　　　　　　　　　　Integrating Information Systems into Business
　　　　　　　　　　　Strategies
　　　　　　　　　　　Long Range Planning, vol 20, pp 19-29, 1987.

Further Readings

Blumberg, M.; Gerwin, D.: "Coping with Advanced Manufacturing Technology". In: Rhodes, E. and Wield, D. (eds): "Implementing New Technologies". Blackwell Ltd., 1994.

Boehm, B.: "A Spiral Model of Software Development and Enhancement". IEEE Computer, vol 21, no 5, May 1988.

Daniels, N.C.: "Information Technology.: The Management Challenge". Addison Wesely, 1994.

Fincham, R. et al.: "Expertise and Innovation - Information Technology Strategies in the Financial Services Sector". Oxford University Press, 1994.

Fleck, J.: "Innofusion or Diffusation: The Nature of Technological Development in Robotics". Edinburgh University PICT Working Paper, no. 4, 1988.

Fleck, J.: "Configurations and Standardization". In: Esser, J. and Fleischmann, G. (eds): "Soziale und ökonomische Konflikte in Standardisierungsprozessen". Campus, 1995.

Gattiker, U.E.: "Technology Management in Organisations". Sage Publications, 1990.

Hammer, M.; Champy, J.: "Reengineering the Corporation". Nicholas Brealey Publishing, 1993.

Howells, J. et al:: "New Technology and the Changing Bank - Retail industry Relationship". Edinburgh OICT Working Paper No. 31, 1991.

Martin, E.W. et al.: "Managing Information Technology: What Managers Need to Know". Macmillan Publishing Company, 1994.

Bradner, S.: "The Internet Standards Process -- Revision 3". Internet RFC 2026, 1996

Scarbrough, H.: "The Successful Exploitation of New Technology in Banking". In: Rhodes, E. and Wield, D. (eds): "Implementing New Technologies". Blackwell Ltd., 1994.

Williams, R.: Private Communication, December 1997.

List of Functional Requirements on E-mail and Directories

The requirements have been categorised according to their respective source, distinguishing between 'General' (G), 'Corporate' (C), and 'End User' (E). G-requirements typically refer to rather universal aspects, like e.g. reliability and transmission delay. The 'C' denotes those requirements related to more administrative aspects, take directory synchronisation as an example. E-requirements relate to the functionality available to the end user, including for instance receipt notifications or easy-to-understand error messages. It must be noted, however, that the distinction between C and E is somewhat artificial; end users will benefit a lot from a well-synchronised directory service, much the same as a feature-rich system will come in useful for a corporation. The distinction has been retained, however, since a major distinction in terms of scope remains between the different classes.

The following table lists the actual requirements, the associated class (G, C, or E), and some explanatory comments. Requirements on e-mail are given first, followed by those on a directory service.

Requirements	Cat.	Comments
The system must reliably send and receive messages.	G	Reliability may for instance be measured as the percentage of the mail sent that is received at the correct destination. Ultimately, the service should ensure that reliability approaches 100 percent. Information must be provided in case of a communication failure.
Users should be able to receive messages from any other users at any time.	G	There must not be any restrictions relating to time of day or sender (except when explicitly specified by the user).

Requirements	Cat.	Comments
It should be possible to interconnect different messaging services.	G	This refers to the interconnection of services like e.g. X.400 - SMTP or cc:mail - X.400, and includes especially the capability to exchange messages with binary data between different messaging services.
Interoperation between e-mail and other services is required.	G	In practice, this means gateways from an e-mail service to fax/ telex/ 'snail-mail'.
It is absolutely crucial that no information is altered in transit.	G	This holds even if several different services, providers and management domains are involved.
Messages and delivery notifications will have to be delivered to the recipients within a predefined time.	G	This is only a qualitative requirement; a quantitative figure mentioned was 30 min. No such goal has been specified for Internet messages.
The 'least cost route' should always be chosen.	C	This holds if a message is routed through transit ADMDs.
Mechanisms to detect and protect against viruses should be provided.	C	To prevent viruses to be distributed via executable programs included in messages or attachments.
It should be possible to specify mandatory routes.	C	If for security reasons messages must not transit through certain domains.
In case of a non-delivery notification supplementary information should be provided.	C/E	This could for example be used to trace the source of an error.

Requirements	Cat.	Comments
Multiple security levels are required.	C	To allow for serious (i.e.. primarily business) usage of e-mail security mechanisms to be provided include: • integrity: the message is transferred intact, without any changes or additions, • encryption: message content is only decipherable by the intended recipient, • authentication: originator and/or recipient are authenticated, • privacy: specifies access rights to messages. Observation of traffic patterns should also be impossible.
Consistent time stamps should be provided.	C/E	Based on e.g. ISO standard time zones or GMT.
Different national character sets should be supported.	C/E	At least within Europe with its considerable number of different national character sets this is understandable. These need to be mapped appropriately.
Multiple different binary attachments should be supported.	C/E	If several binary files are to be transmitted in one message, this is typically done using attachments. Unfortunately, these tend to cause problems for many gateways, which frequently simply discard them.
An External Body Part should be supported.	C/E	This could be used similar to attachments; to send binary files. A standardised encoding scheme would be required. As an intermediate step, service providers should offer conversion facilities for files. This conversion, however, must not alter the contents of the document.

Requirements	Cat.	Comments
User addresses must be unique.	C/E	This holds for both, the global part of the address (i.e.for instance the right hand part of an Internet address) and the local part (the left hand part of an Internet address).
Addresses should be as simple as possible.	C/E	In particular, there is no need for the service provider name to be part of the message (i.e. e.g. the 'ADMD' part of an X.400 address).
There should be no restriction on the maximum message size.	C/E	In practice, an upper limit of 10 MByte for a message plus attachments is considered acceptable. Larger messages should be compressed.
Messages must still be delivered as soon as possible after the target period has expired.	E	That is, it must always be attempted to deliver a message. However, user policies that require otherwise should be supported as well.
There must be facilities to divert messages.	E	For instance, if a user has temporarily moved.
It should be possible to switch off delivery or non-delivery notifications.	E	This may be useful in case of e.g. low-importance bulk mailings.
Users must have feedback about the message status.	E	This refers to the need to be informed if and when the message has been sent and received by the recipient(s) for whom it was intended. It also refers to information required after a system failure.

Requirements	Cat.	Comments
Users should be able to send the same message to more than one user simultaneously.	E	This can for example be achieved through the use of a distribution list (DL), providing for one dedicated group address. In this case, nested DLs need to be supported as well, including detection of possible loops.
The same contribution can be sent to more than one group with a single command.	E	This may serve to support group communication in a more convenient way.
Whiteboard services should be provided.	E	Functionality provided by whiteboards is similar to the on offered by Usenet-newsgroups.
A 'Call Barring' function should be available.	E	To have unsolicited mail barred, based e.g. on the originator or message size.
The user should be provided with mechanisms to conveniently manipulate messages.	E	This includes the capabilities to • store, merge or discard messages as required, • read messages in a structured order, • be made aware that a message has arrived, and about its priority, • immediately delete unwanted messages or to refuse their receipt, • define default configurations for certain tasks.
In case of a non-delivery notification it should be possible to have the message content returned as well.	E	This serves to help the originator identify the original message that could not be delivered.

Requirements	Cat.	Comments
There has to be an adequate global directory service.	G	Directories provide a support service crucial for electronic communication services, and especially important for e-mail. Their major fields of use include: • address and information look-ups, • provision of security mechanisms, • support of message service interoperability.
The directory should cover the full user population.	G	An information service which covers only a small fraction of users is of little benefit.
Information stored in the directory must be up-to-date and accurate.	G	This may be improved if users can directly modify information held in their own entries. However, experience indicates that this alone will not be sufficient. From the operator's point of view, an auto-registration of O/R addresses is most desirable, as is a global registration of management domain names through a dedicated authority.
Information stored in the directory has to be consistent.	G	A global directory service will be provided through a large number of interoperating servers. This raises the issue of information consistency. This point is of particular importance since the global service will be provided by public and proprietary services, which do not necessarily use the same protocols or support the same pieces of information.

Requirements	Cat.	Comments
The directory should be able to store a broad variety of information.	G	This holds particularly if the address of a yet unknown potential communication partner is to be retrieved. In addition to electronic addresses, postal addresses and phone/fax numbers should also be available.
The directory should be reasonably fast.	G	This requirement is not that crucial. Most look-ups will be done by applications, and a message delay in the range of tens of seconds due to a directory access may be tolerable. Things may look different if the service is accessed directly by a user. Replication mechanisms will be required to increase performance of the service.
Organisational contact details should be accessible through the directory.	C	Such details include an help-desk address as well as the switchboard phone number and the postal address.
There should be alternative access methods to a directory service.	C	Access via e-mail would be desirable as an interim solution.
The directory must be easy to use.	E	Again a straightforward requirement. However, it may be expected that the vast majority of directory accesses will be through applications (as e.g. e-mail).

Table A.1.1:
Requirements on E-mail and Directory ServicesCompiled from Literature
Categories: C = Corporate; G = General; E = End-user

In addition to the requirements listed below, other, more trivial ones have also been identified by several interviewees, including particularly reliability, notifications, security features, and interworking between different systems. However, only those requirements will be listed in the following that have not already been addressed above.

Requirements	Cat.	Comments
Mechanisms for directory synchronisation should be available.	C	Historically, different proprietary directory services have been employed by most organisations, leading to the urgent need of tools, mechanisms and/or services ensuring consistency of information throughout the organisation.
Interconnection of different management domains should be completely transparent.	C	Domain interconnection, that is, the seamless interconnection of different management domains (PRMD - PRMD, PRMD - ADMD, ADMD - ADMD) is required. This includes smooth interoperation between MTAs supporting different versions of X.400.
There is an urgent need for user-friendly addressing and naming.	E	By far the most popular single requirement. Current X.400 addresses have almost unanimously been identified as a 'pain in the neck'. They need to be short, guessable and straightforward, and should not carry routing information.
The contents of error messages should be in plain language.	E	Numeric codes and cryptic messages understandable only for experts have to be avoided to ensure that error messages can be understood by normal users.

Comfortable facilities for editing, retrieving and re-using of messages are needed.	E	The user should be provided with mechanisms that allow him to manipulate messages received or to be sent in a most convenient way. This includes the capabilities such as • hierarchical mailboxes, • filtering functions, • integration of a sophisticated editor, • refiling outgoing messages.
Auto-replies should be supported.	E	This refers to either the confirmation of read messages or to the generation of an explicit reply message at the recipient's side.

Table A1.22:
Requirements on E-mail and Directory Services Compiled from Interviews
Categories: C = Corporate; G = General; E = End-user

Questionnaires

User Representatives

Part 1: General

G1   Please provide some background information about your
     organization (number of staff, locations of
     branches/departments/subsidiaries.., etc).

G2   Please give some information on the structure and usage of
     messaging services in your organization (eg. which system(s)
     is/are being installed, how does the topology look like,
     number of users, number of messages/month, etc).

G3   Please provide some information about yourself, your tasks and
     responsibilities, and your department.

Part 2: E-Mail

E1   A little bit of history: when and how did e-mail emerge in your
     organization (top-down - ie following a management decision -
     vs bottom-up, ie. more or less isolated at different sites).

E2   Do you have an organization-wide e-mail strategy by now? If
     so, when, how and why has this strategy been specified, and
     who was in charge?

E3   What did your organization expect from taking e-mail on board
     (eg. more convenient internal communication, competitive
     advantage, less pressure from business partners)?

E4   Did you do a requirements analysis beforehand? If yes, are the
     results available (I would be particularly interested in specific
     functional requirements)?

E5   Did you (have to) do a cost/benefit analysis? If yes, are any
     information available?

E6   What were the initial criteria for the system of choice, and
     why did you select a particular system (eg. proprietary,
     SMTP/MIME, X.400)?

E7 Who was in charge of the introduction (eg. central IT department, local departments, third parties)?

E8 What were the major problems in introducing e-mail (eg. convince management, get funding, technical issues, ...)?

E9 What kind of user support do you provide (user training, dedicated support staff, help-desks, special manuals, ...), and who is in charge?

E10 What are the main application areas (interpersonal messaging, mail-enabled applications like eg. EDI, groupware, ...)?

E11 Which problems/drawbacks/shortcomings/flaws/.... have been identified - related to technical issues (eg. directories, security, gateways)? - related to organizational issues (eg. funding)? - related to end-user issues (eg. dissatisfaction, no-use)?

E12 Is there something like a list of essential/nice-to-have/unimportant functional requirements (eg. mandatory notification is essential, low transfer times are nice-to-have, video body parts are of no interest at all)? Again, I would be particularly interested in specific functional requirements.

E13 What will be the next steps (eg. integration of mobile users, enhance security, install uniform directory, interconnect to the Internet, ...)?

E14 Which major benefits have been identified?
E15 Are there any cost-related information available (ie. hard- and software, personnel, transmission)?

E16 Did e-mail have an impact on the organizational structure of your company?

E17 Do you have any evidence if use of e-mail has changed the way people communicate?

E18 Are there any established communication channels for your end- users to report on problems, additional requirements, make suggestions, etc?

E19   What is your overall assessment concerning the usefulness of the system?

E20   If the system has been successful, what has been the single most important contributor?

Part 3: Directory

D1   Does your organization operate a directory service? If yes, of which type (eg. proprietary, X.500)?

D2   Do you have some usage statistics available?

D3   What have been the major motivations for installing the service?

D4   Did you do a requirements analysis prior to installation?

D5   What were the major problems prior to/during installation?

D6   What are the major fields of application for the directory (eg. internal/external white/yellow pages, security, more general information system)?

D7   Which applications are the major beneficiaries of the directory (eg. e-mail, EDI, groupware)

D8   Do you plan to integrate any other data bases (eg. HR data bases)?

D9   What are the major problems identified during operation of the service (eg. integration, DIT population, interconnection, data management etc.)?

D10   What are the major functional flaws/shortcomings of the service (if any)?

D11   Again: is there something like a list of essential/nice-to-have/unimportant functional requirements?

D12   Who will be able to access your data (only internal users, business partners, public)? Why?

D13   Have you been participating in public pilots (as eg. Paradise)? Why (not)?

D14   What is your overall assessment concerning the usefulness of the directory service?

Part 4: Standardization

S1   Is your company active in user organizations (as eg. EEMA)?

S2   If yes, why, and what are the major activities?

S3   Has your organization been actively involved in standardization efforts? If yes, where (ITU, ISO, ETSI, IETF, ...)

S4   If not, why not (eg too expensive, too time consuming, don't see any real benefits...)?

S5   If yes, which department has been in charge of the standardization activities? Why?

S6   Why did/do your representatives attend standardization committee meetings (to push superior technical solutions, to promote company solutions, to represent customers' or company requirements, to gain experience and knowledge, ...)?

S7   How do you exploit the knowledge/expertise gained through participation in standardization (eg. design better products/ services, enhance usefulness of product/service for company/ customer, ...)?

S8   What are the estimated costs per representative per year?

S9   Are there any (technical) issues that you feel have not been addressed adequately by the standards committees (eg. name representation)?

S10   Are there any open (technical) questions your company would need a solution for (eg. MHS routing)?

S11   What would you consider the most appropriate way for your organization to promote standards-related issues?

S12   What would you consider as the best/most effective/most
      convenient way for your organization to participate in
      standardization work (representatives at group meetings, a
      dedicated user committee, ...)?

Committee Members

1   For how long have you been active in standardization? Where (eg. ITU, ISO)?

2   On which committees have you been active, and what have been your role(s) (eg. editor, rapporteur, member)?

3   Why did you attend the meetings in the first place (eg. boss told me to go, interested in topic, part of the job)?

4   How would you characterize your role in the process (eg. company representative, national representative, user´s advocate, promoter of technically superior solutions, ...)?

5   How would you characterize the ISO/ITU standardization process?

6   What are its major strengths and weaknesses?

7   According to your experience, what kind of organizations (ie. manufacturers, service providers, governments, users, PTTs, PNOs, research institutions) are represented in the committees?, and which are the most dominant ones (if any)?

8   How do standardization activities typically emerge (eg. based on products/services already available, based on an identified demand, others)? Can you give a typical example?

9   Who identifies the initial requirements (eg. technical people in the committee, other committees, user representatives, product specs)?

10 Are there any formal/informal mechanisms to integrate user requirements either prior to or during the standardization process, or for a new version of the documents?

11 Are there normally formal/informal cooperations with user groups? If yes, how?

12 How do you evaluate the usefulness of dedicated 'Service Definition' committees (like eg. SGI, or the old SC18, WG1)?

13   Again, according to your experience, what are the main factors influencing technical decisions taken (eg. supporters/opponents are present during discussion, reputation of supporters/opponents, purely the technical merits, solution has already been implemented somewhere, company/national/ group interests)? Please indicate their relative importance as well.

14   Are a standard's complexity, usefulness or usability of concern? If yes, what is being done about it?

15   How would you describe the respective outcome, ie. the final standard (eg. too complex, just great, should do)?

16   Do you think stronger user participation in the process might be of benefit?

17   If yes, how would you envisage getting users to participate (eg. go to meetings, set up additional 'user-committees', dedicated Service Definition groups)?

18   Which benefits would you expect from increased user participation (if any)?

19   Please identify prospective drawbacks/problems possibly resulting from increased user participation (if any).

20   Would you personally like to see a higher degree of user involvement in the process? Why (not)?

21   What improvements to the standardization process would you suggest (if any)?

The X.400 and X.500 Series of Recommendations - A Brief Introduction

X.400 - The Message Handling System (MHS)

This section provides a brief overview of the services offered by MHS. The introduction is followed by a description of those functionalities most crucial to the usability of the service, including interpersonal messaging, addressing, and security.

Introduction

MHS is a vendor-independent electronic messaging system, based on a store-and-forward architecture. It has been standardised by the International Telecommunication Union (ITU) in their X.400 series of recommendations [ITU 92a]. For a more detailed description please refer to these standards documents.

Figure A.1.1 shows the functional MHS model. The user, a human or an application program, accesses the Message Transfer System (MTS) through either a User Agent (UA) or a Message Store (MS). Once a message has entered the MTS, it is routed from Message Transfer Agent (MTA) to MTA until it reaches its destination MTA, which in turn informs the final recipient UA.

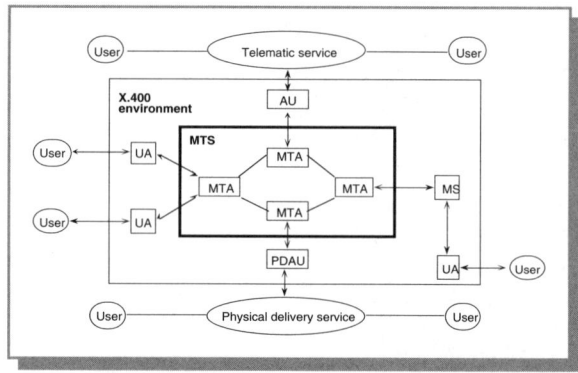

Figure A.1.1:
The Basic MHS Model
MTS = Message Transfer System; MTA = Message Transfer Agent;
UA = User Agent; MS = Message Store;
AU = Access Unit; PDAU = Physical Delivery Access Unit

Users without a UA but with access to other Telematic services (e.g. Facsimile) can also be reached via dedicated Access Units (AUs).

Moreover, a Physical Delivery Access Unit (PDAU) provides interconnection to the 'normal' mail delivery service.

A message consists of two basic components: the Envelope and the Content. The envelope carries information required by the system like, for instance, source address and destination address. The content is the piece of information to be delivered to the recipient (cf. Figure A.1.2).

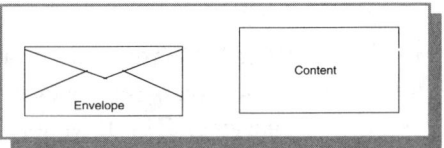

Figure A.1.2:
Structure of an MHS Message

The recipient of a message is identified by an Originator/Recipient Name (O/R Name), which may either be a directory name or one out of a number of different O/R address types, including the mnemonic O/R address, which is virtually the only form being used.

Groups of recipients can be reached through Distribution Lists (DLs). Each DL has an O/R name which identifies its expansion point, ie. the MTA where it is stored. DLs may be nested (cf. Figure A.1.3).

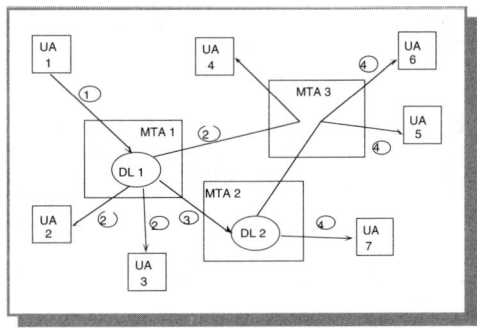

Figure A.1.3:
Use of Distribution Lists

A Message Store (MS) can be used to provide a more secure and continuously available storage mechanism, by providing some

rudimentary data base functionality. The MS interacts with the MTS
on behalf of its associated UA (Figure A.1.4).

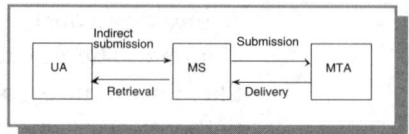

Figure   A.1.4:
The Message Store

The MHS recommendations provide for a set of functions extending the
basic transfer service, called Interpersonal Messaging Service (IPM
service). The IPM service is an extension of the basic transfer service,
offering a number of additional 'human-oriented' features closely
related to features already known from the office environment. This
includes for instance an indication of copy recipients or a subject
indication. In particular, interpersonal messages may carry different
types of information (multi-part body) including e.g. text, graphics,
facsimile and video (see Figure A.1.5). Body parts defined in the IPM-
specification include IA5-Text, Telex, Videotex, G3- and G4-
facsimile, encrypted, and voice, with the formats of the latter two
being left for further study.

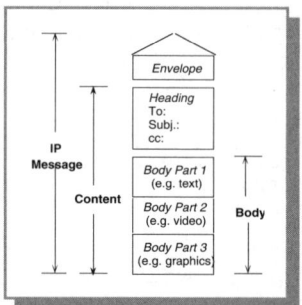

Figure   A.1.5:
IP-Message Structure

The MHS organisational model subdivides the global service into
different Management Domains (MDs), reflecting administrative
and/or organisational structures. A domain comprises at least one
MTA (see Figure A.1.6).

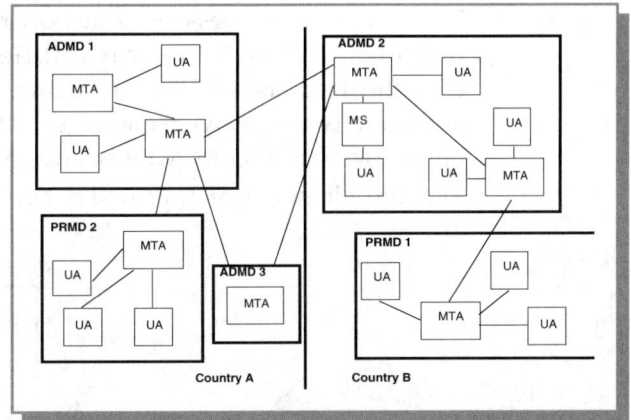

Figure A.1.6:
Relations Between Management Domains

There is a distinction between:

- **Administration Management Domains (ADMD)**
  An ADMD is operated by an administration (BT in the UK).
  There may, however, be more than one ADMD per country.

- **Private Management Domains (PrMD)**
  An organisation other than an administration may establish and
  manage its own PrMD. A PrMD may span country borders.

MHS can utilise the Directory Service (DS). Figure A.1.7 shows the
functional model of MHS - DS interworking.

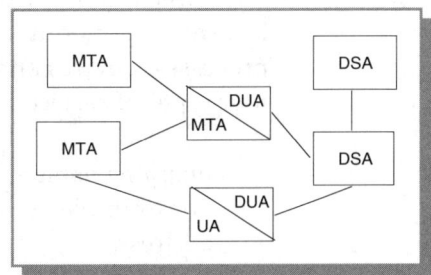

Figure A.1.7:
Interworking Between MHS and the Directory Service
DUA = Directory User Agent; DSA = Directory System Agent

In addition to its message transport related functionalities MHS also provides for security capabilities, including prevention of unauthorised users from misusing the system, and guaranteeing authenticity of received messages. The directory service is used for authentication. Figure A.1.8 below shows the X.400 security scenario, and the elements of the model between which the single services apply.

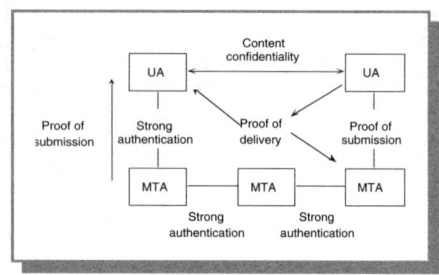

Figure   A.1.8:
X.400 Security Scenario

X.500 - The Directory Service (DS)

This section is intended to provide a very condensed overview of the subject. Those who have a deeper interest in the directory's functionality should read e.g. [Chadwick, 1994] or should refer to the original standard [ITU, 1993d].

Overall Functionality

The directory service provides a uniform naming scheme for, and information about a network's resources (including e.g. hosts, processes, devices and human users). In general, a DS has to provide four types of service:

- **mapping name → information**
  For example, an object's name may be mapped onto its network address.

- **mapping name → set of names**
  A set of objects is identified by one single name.

- **mapping information → set of names**
  This service establishes a 'Yellow Pages' function.

- **secure communication**
  Authentication and mechanisms for electronic signatures are provided.

Usually, the DS is described as a - highly distributed - Client-Server System (see Figure A.1.9). This may be characterised by a typically small number of hosts (the servers, the Directory System Agents (DSAs)) providing callable services to the other hosts of the system (the clients, the Directory User Agents (DUAs)).

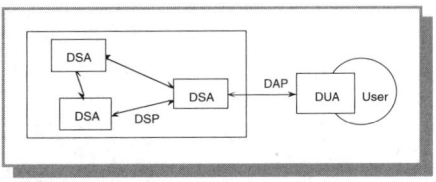

Figure A.1.9:
The General Directory Model
DSA = Directory System Agent; DAP = Directory Access Protocol
DSP = Directory System Protocol; DUA = Directory User Agent

In terms of the DS, resources are referred to as Objects. Every object is represented by an Entry (see Figure A.1.10), the totality of entries forms the Directory Information Base (DIB). An object's name and the information stored in an entry are composed of Attributes. An attribute is a tuple <AttributeType, AttributeValue>. Attributes may be structured hierarchically.

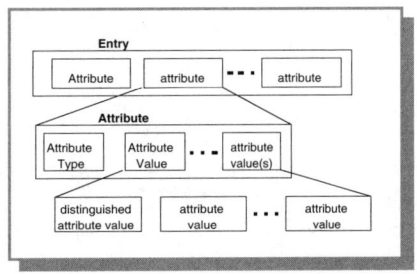

Figure A.1.10:
Model of an Entry (User Information Part)

A Relative Distinguished Name (RDN) is assigned to every entry, and thus to every object. Every RDN is non-ambiguous relative to its immediate superior. The sequence of RDNs of an object plus those of its superiors forms its Distinguished Name (DN, see Figure A.1.11). The DN is globally unambiguous. The directory also provides for alternative names, called Aliases. An alias entry holds a pointer at the object entry.

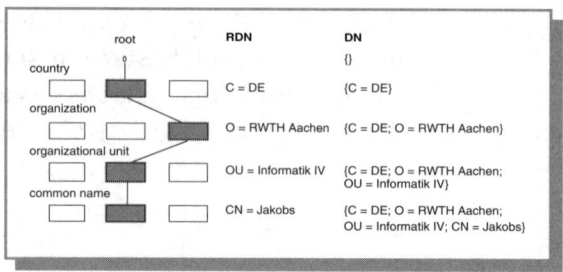

Figure A.1.11:
A Sample Distinguished Name (DN)

Several operations have been defined to search, access and modify the information, including Modify and AddEntry. With the exception of the latter these operations only effect leaf entries.

The directory's Schema (see Figure A.1.12) specifies the structure of the DIB; as this structure will in almost all cases be hierarchical, a Directory Information Tree (DIT) will thus be established.

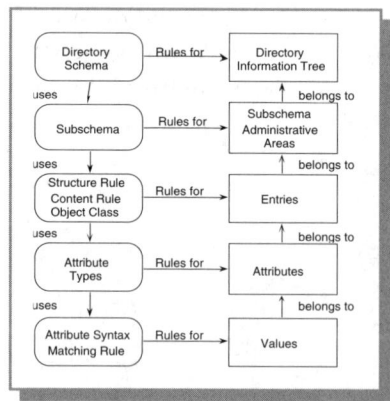

Figure A.1.12:
The Directory Schema

An Object Class definition specifies a set of mandatory and optional attributes for an entry of a given class (e.g. country, organisation), an Attribute Type indicates the type of information (e.g. country name or telephone number) stored in an associated Attribute Value with a defined syntax (e.g. printable string). The schema is composed from a number of Subschemas each valid within one particular management domain.

Every DSA has Knowledge about objects known to other DSAs (to provide for distributed operations). This knowledge is kept in References. To enable distributed operations different modes of DSA interaction have been specified:

- **Chaining**
  The DSA contacted forwards a request to exactly one other DSA, which in turn may forward the request if necessary.

- **Parallel Chaining**
  The DSA forwards a request to several DSAs in parallel.

- **Referral**
  The DSA returns hints at responsible DSA(s).

To increase both performance and availability of the service, data can be replicated. The directory provides for a Shadowing mechanism which enables the replication of part or all of a DSA's information to other DSAs, managed and controlled through Shadowing Agreements, negotiated between participating DSAs.

Different entities will need to have different views of the information stored in the directory. This fact is reflected in the definition of different Information Models, each of which offers specific pieces of data to its respective 'user'. The human user sees what is provided under the User Information Model, i.e. information typically related to other human users. Information related to the operation of the service will be provided for system administrators within the framework of the Operational and Administrative Information Model (e.g. information related to access control rights).

The Administrative Authority Model reflects the subdivision of the DS into (hierarchical) subdomains, each of which is administered and managed by an Administrative Authority. It is this authority's task to assign names and to specify the subdomain's subschemas. Information required internally for DSA operation is subsumed under the DSA Information Model. This includes for example knowledge information and information on shadowing agreements.

Access Control mechanisms allow administrators to implement security policies, i.e. to specify who has access to which information via which operation. The scheme is based on Access Control Lists.

The directory provides for two levels of authentication. Simple authentication is based on a user's distinguished name and a password and is primarily intended for local use, i.e. authentication for example between a DUA and its home DSA. Yet, this simple mechanism may not be sufficient for a number of applications, e.g. for those employed by strategic business-critical processes. Strong authentication provides for secure communication in an insecure environment. It makes use of properties of Public Key Cryptosystems (PKCS). Whereas every PKCS may be used to submit secret information, an additional property is required to make the system useful for authentication purposes as well - permutability. With a PKCS being permutable the secret key may be used to encipher a message. Thus, since the secret key is only known to one particular user, this user's identity may be verified by deciphering the message using the public key. Public keys are created and assigned by a Certification Authority (CA).

Finally, note that the X.500 directory serviceis based on the overall assumption that information stored will be long-lived. Although this assumption seems to be a little too optimistic, information may still be regarded as 'long-lived' when compared to data required for example for applications such as traffic control or mobility management. However, recent research suggests that X.500 is capable of handling even such highly transient data.

Index

Access control 235-236
Access Control Lists 236
Access Units 228
Adaptation 4, 79, 156
Addressing 39, 64, 112, 150, 217, 228
ADMD 152, 217, 231
Administration Management Domain 152, 231
Administrative Authority 236
Administrative Authority Model 236
Adoption 22, 26-27, 30, 32, 62, 75, 78, 80-81, 83, 92-93, 105
Advisory Group on Standardization 63
Agent 87-88, 92, 97, 228, 231, 233
Agreed User Requirements 69
Amendment 59
Analysis stage 195
ANSI 4, 15, 19-20, 35, 46, 103, 108-110, 112, 118, 120-122, 128,
                                                              131-133, 140, 149-150, 170
Anticipatory (standard) 114, 116, 150, 182, 194, 205
Approval Stage 57-58, 60
Area Director 67, 117, 125
ARPA-Net 155
Asynchronous Transfer Mode 28, 113
AT&T 62
ATM 11, 14-16, 28, 65, 113, 115, 201
ATM Forum 11, 15-16, 65
Attributes 233
AUs 228
Authentication 212, 232-233, 236
Backbone 86-90, 95, 152, 171, 192
Backward compatibility 197-198
Bangemann Report 2
Base (standard) 10-11, 14-16, 19-20, 40-41, 53, 70-71, 77, 147
Boeing 71, 127, 154
Bottom-up 80-81, 83-84, 92-96, 171, 174, 220
British Airways 127
BSI 11
Business process 33, 79, 90-91, 150, 171-172, 175, 179, 186, 190, 192, 204
Business Process Re-engineering 79

Business relevant (technology) 170, 175-180, 186, 192, 203-204

Case studies 5, 75, 77, 79-83, 89. 91. 93-97, 103, 142,
144, 170-171, 174, 176-177, 179-180, 190-191, 193, 204

Cc:Mail 87, 89, 91, 105, 211

CCIF 61

CCIR 61

CCIT 61

CCITT 18, 61, 108, 150-152

Central Secretariat 55, 57

Certification Authority 236

Chaining 235

Chairperson 55, 65, 108, 149, 159

Change agent 97

CIM 178

Client-Server System 233

Committee Draft 57-58, 69

Committee Stage 57

Company representative 33, 82-84, 86-89, 91-92, 111, 181, 225

Compatibility 12, 22, 26, 28, 30, 37-38, 52, 81, 93, 96-97, 113, 171, 197-198

Compatibility (standard) 26, 28, 38, 52

Competition 28-29

Competitive advantage 147

Computer Integrated Manufacturing 178

Consensus 11-12, 27, 35-36, 39, 57, 60, 67, 98,
111, 114, 120-122, 125, 133, 136, 141, 158, 201

Consortia 14-18, 24-25, 29, 32, 35-36, 52, 60, 65, 98, 115, 189, 201-202

Copy recipients 230

Corporate user 5, 37, 42-43, 77-78, 104, 196

Credibility 160

De facto (standard) 12-14, 16-17, 28-29, 106, 114, 122, 189

De jure (standard) 12-13, 16-17, 106

Decreasing return 26

Deregulation 117

DIB 233-234

Diffusion 4, 29, 51, 99, 151-152, 166, 174, 191, 204

DIN 11

Direct user 43, 189, 191

Directory 142,. 234-236

~ Information Base 233
~ Information Tree 234
~ service 76-78, 88, 90, 93, 113, 151, 154, 210, 215-218,
222-223, 231-232, 236
~ System Agent 231, 233
~ User Agent 231, 233
DIS 57-59
Distance learning 2
Distinguished Name 234, 236
Distribution list 67, 93, 124, 155, 157, 214, 229
DIT 222, 234
DL 214, 229
DN 234
Double-loop learning 173
DQDB 28
Draft International Standard 57-58
Draft Standard 63, 68, 112
DS 231-233, 236
DSA 231, 233, 235-236
DSA Information Model 236
DUA 231, 233, 236
Due process 11, 13, 32, 35-36, 50, 122
E-mail 4-5, 43, 67, 75-97, 99, 104-105, 113, 124, 140-142, 148, 150-153, 155, 163,
166, 171, 173-181, 186, 189-192, 202-204, 209-212,215-216, 218, 220-222
Early adopter 92, 95
ECMA 18
EDI 38, 91, 115, 143, 145, 178, 188, 221-222
EDIFACT 38, 115
Editors 149
EEMA 106, 223
Electric telegraph 8
Electronic commerce 78, 90, 115
Electronic Data Interchange 143
Electronic mail 26, 77-78, 93
Electronic messaging 78, 80, 82-83, 92, 98, 196, 203, 228
End-user 41-44, 80, 82-83, 95-99, 153, 161, 216, 218, 221
End-user computing 44, 95-99
Enquiry Stage 57-58

Entry 233-235
Ethernet 113
ETSI 11, 15, 18, 37, 49, 98, 125, 202, 223
European Computer Manufacturers Association 18
Exploitation plans 34
Fast track procedure 20, 59-60
FDIS 57-59
File transfer 153
Final Draft International Standard 57-58
Functional standard 10-11, 14, 18, 40-41, 71, 147
Funding 31, 82, 86-87, 139-141, 157, 221
Gateway 85-86, 88-89, 171, 192, 211-212, 221
General Assembly 55
General Motors 30, 71, 127, 154
GII 2-3, 21, 203
Global Information Infrastructure 2, 21
Globalisation 24, 30
Government 24, 31, 35, 43, 54, 62, 77, 102-104, 116-118, 135, 138, 140,
                                                    151, 164, 166, 225
HDTV 4
IAB 66-67
IBM 17, 29
ICT 21, 26, 29, 44
IEC 15, 54, 56, 59, 69, 73-74, 131
IESG 66-68, 117, 158
IETF 4, 15-16, 18, 33, 65-68, 70, 73-74,77, 103, 108-112, 116-117, 119-123,
                125-126, 129, 131, 134-135, 140-142, 146, 149-150, 155-158, 164,
                                                    170, 172, 198-199, 202, 223
IFIP 150
Implementation 4, 11, 14-15, 23, 30, 32, 36, 40, 42-45, 60, 62-63, 65,
                67-68, 70-71, 76-77, 79-81, 84, 92-96, 107, 112, 119-120, 123,
                138-139, 146-148, 151-155, 157, 159, 166, 169-174, 180-184,
                                    186-187, 189-191, 193, 197-201, 203-205
Implementor 103, 106
Incompatibilities 25, 38, 81, 85, 96-97, 107, 148, 187
Indirect user 43
Industrial revolution 8
Industry 12, 14, 16-17
Industry fora 8, 11, 125

Industry standard 14, 17, 51, 97, 150

Information Age 81

Information and Communication Technology 21

Information Model 235-236

Information society 1-2, 51, 206

Information system 80, 86, 166, 206, 222

Information technology 2-3, 11, 37, 46-47, 49-51, 73-74, 79,
                                     83, 95, 98-99, 113, 125, 165-166, 175, 206-207

Infrastructural (technology) 170, 174-178, 180, 186, 192, 196, 203-204

Infrastructure 2, 21, 46, 48-51, 91, 98, 142-143, 146-147, 153,
                                     155, 158, 164-165, 167, 175-176, 178, 201, 205-206

Innovation 22, 43, 46-50, 52, 96-97, 99, 164-166, 170,
                                     174-175, 177, 179-184, 187, 191, 205-207

Innovation theory 175

Installed base 197

Installed-base hostility 152-153, 156, 197

Intangible benefits 176

Intellectual property rights 9, 49, 52

Intelligence gathering 25

International Electrotechnical Commission 54

International Federation for Information Processing 150

International Organization for Standardization 8, 46, 50, 54, 73-74

International Radio Consultative Committee 61

International Radiotelegraph Conference 61

International Standard 8, 11, 27, 30, 37, 50, 53, 56-60, 71, 73,
                                     114, 123, 133, 182

International Standardized Profile 71

International Telecommunication Union 8, 50, 61, 73-74, 165, 228

International Telegraph and Telephone Consultative Committee 61, 108

International Telegraph Consultative Committee 61

International Telegraph Convention 61

International Telegraph Union 8, 61

Internet 2, 65-68, 70, 74, 76, 86, 89, 105, 109, 116, 120, 123-124,
                                     126, 129, 135, 153-158, 164, 167, 198, 206-207, 211, 213, 221

    ~ Architecture Board 66

    ~ Engineering Steering Group 66

    ~ Research Task Force 66

    ~ Society 66

    ~ Standard 65-66, 68, 74, 116, 155, 167, 198, 207

Interoperability 2, 11, 14, 30, 40, 48, 71, 80, 83, 97, 146, 155, 192, 199, 215

Interpersonal communication 78, 95, 203

Interpersonal messages 230

Interpersonal Messaging Service 230

Interworking Unit 87-88

Introduction 191

IP 79, 136, 155, 206

IPM service 230

IPng 197

IPR 9, 32

IRTF 66-67

IS 57-58, 86, 95

ISA 54

ISDN 2, 14, 201

ISO 4, 8, 11, 14-16, 18, 20, 33, 35, 40, 46, 50, 54-60, 65, 67, 69-71, 73-74,
76, 103, 106, 108, 110, 112, 118, 120-124, 128, 130-133, 140,
146, 149-150, 155,157, 160, 170, 186, 198, 212, 223, 225

ISO/IEC Directive 50, 56, 73

ISOC 66

IT 2, 4, 8-10, 13-14, 17-19, 23, 25, 31, 44-45, 48, 51, 59, 79-80, 82,
84-86, 95-96, 115, 143, 147, 150, 158, 164, 166-167, 171, 173, 175-176,
178, 180, 184, 186, 189-190, 204, 221

IT-infrastructure 91

ITU 4, 8, 11, 15-16, 33, 61-62, 64, 67, 69-70, 73-74, 76, 103, 106,
108-110, 112, 117-118, 120-123, 128, 130-132, 135, 140,
149-150, 155, 160, 165, 198, 223, 225, 228, 232

~ Constitution 61

~ Council 62

~ -D 61

~ Plenipotentiary Conference 61-62, 73

~ -R 61

~ SIO 62-70, 74, 76, 79

~ Telecommunication Development 61

~ Telecommunication Standardization 61, 63-64

~ World Conferences on International Telecommunication 61

ITU-T 14, 16, 37, 40, 55, 59, 61, 63, 65, 69, 108, 130-131, 150, 157, 170, 186

~ Advisory Group on Standardization 63

~ Recognised Operating Agencies 62

~ Recommendations 15, 63

~ ROA 62
~ Telecommunication Standardization Bureau 64
~ TSB 64
~ World Telecommunication Standardization Conference 63
~ WTSC 63-64
JTC1 .... 26, 50, 59, 69, 73-74, 109, 124, 130-132, 134
~ -TAG 109
Knowledge transfer 191
LAN 83, 88-90, 92, 105, 151-152, 171
Layer 14, 41
Learning process 39, 80, 182
Liaison 33, 55-56, 65, 70, 111, 128-129, 149, 159
Liaison Statement 70
Mail-enabled application 91-92, 94-95, 221
Mainframe 83-85, 87-88, 90, 171, 178
Management Domain 152, 211, 215, 217, 230-231, 235
Manufacturing Automation Protocol 71
MAP 71-72, 74, 161
Mass production 8
Message Handling System 228
Message store 151, 228-230
Message Transfer Agent 88, 228
Message Transfer System 228
MHS 105, 223, 228-232
Microsoft 17, 29, 105-106, 135, 144
Mini computer 151
Mission critical 91
MS-mail 89, 106-107
MTA 88, 151, 228-230
MTS 228, 230
Multi-part body 230
Naming 232
Netscape 29, 135
Network externalities 2, 38, 80
Network management 65, 158
Network Management Forum 65
Networking effects 26
New Work Item Proposal 56, 58, 69

Newsgroups 148, 153, 214
O-members 54, 59
O/R address 215, 229
O/R Name 229
Object Class 235
Object Management Group 65
Open system 38, 70, 107, 113-114, 167
Open Systems Interconnection 113
Operational and Administrative Information Model 235
Organisational learning 82, 93, 96, 173-174
OSI 14, 33, 40-41, 70, 79, 113-114, 116, 138, 151-156, 195
   ~ Reference Model 40-42, 70, 115
P-members 54, 56-57, 59
Packet-switched network 153
Parallel Chaining 235
Participatory Design 195-196
PAS originator 60
PAS submitter 60
Path dependencies 22
PC 83, 151-152
PDAU 229
Physical Delivery Access Unit 229
PKCS 236
Plenipotentiary Conference 61-62, 73
Post, Telegraph and Telephone administration 62
Preliminary Stage 56, 58
Preparatory Stage 57-58
Presentation layer 151
Private Management Domain 231
PrMD 231
Proactive (standard) 12, 14, 16, 112-115, 132, 143, 150, 190, 193, 195-196
Product user group 106
Profile (standards ~) 10-11, 14, 18, 40, 53, 70-71, 141, 147, 154
Project editors 108
Proposal Stage 56, 58, 69
Proprietary (standard) 12, 14, 17, 21, 26-30, 32, 35-36, 38, 60, 76, 79-80, 97, 107,
                        111-113, 117, 150, 152-153, 189, 198, 201, 215, 217, 220, 222

Protocol 2, 14, 65-66, 70-71, 86, 116, 120, 152-156, 158, 197, 215, 233
  ˜ specification 70, 154-155
PTT 37, 62, 64, 103, 108-109, 117, 152, 225
Public (standard) 12, 14, 16
Public Key Cryptosystems 236
Publication Stage 58
Publicly Available Specifications 60, 124
Purchasing power 146
Questions 64
Railroad 8
Rapporteurs 108
RDN 234
Reactive (standard) 12, 14, 16, 112-115, 176, 182, 193-195
Recognised Operating Agencies 62
Recommendations 15, 63
References 235
Referral 235
Regulatory (standard) 10, 12
Relative Distinguished Name 234
Replication 12, 216, 235
Request for Comments 65
Requirements elicitation phase 193, 198
Reuters 127
RFC 65, 68, 74, 76, 134, 164, 198, 207
ROA 62
Rough consensus 67, 114, 125, 158
Schema 234-236
Scientific or Industrial Organisation 62
SDO 4, 11, 13-14, 20
Security 93-94, 151, 158, 195, 211-212, 215, 217, 221-222, 228, 232, 236
Service definition 40, 69-70, 130, 154, 160, 225-226
Service provider 21, 30, 38, 42, 76-77, 94, 99, 102-104,106, 110,
                                                        117-119, 127, 129, 134-135, 140, 142, 144, 147-150,
                                                        156-157, 161, 173, 182, 193, 195-196, 212-213, 225
Session layer 151
Shadowing 235-236
  ˜ Agreements 235
Simple authentication 236

Simple Network Management Protocol 158
Single loop learning 173
SIO 62-70, 74, 76, 79
SMEs 188-189
SNMP 158, 167
Social interactions 24
Social shaping of technology 43, 180, 203
SST 180, 204
Stakeholder 5, 21, 24-25, 34, 101-102, 104, 107, 125-126, 148, 170, 188, 195, 205
Standardisation 3-5, 7-8, 12, 18-27, 29, 31-33, 35-38, 40, 48, 50-51, 54-55, 59,
                    62-63, 65-68, 74, 94, 101-104, 106-109, 111-116, 119-120, 126-127,
                    130-133, 135, 141-145, 147-148, 150-151, 153-154, 156, 159, 162,
                    165-166, 169-170, 173, 180-184, 186-187, 189-198, 200, 202-205
~ politics 24
~ process 5, 12, 25, 29, 32, 35-36, 40, 65-66, 68, 102,
                    106-108, 111-112, 116, 120, 130-131, 133, 135, 143,
                    148, 151, 153, 156, 159, 169, 181, 184, 186, 189-192, 197, 205
Standardization Bureau 63-64
Standards 1-5, 7-43, 46-71, 73-74, 76-80, 93-94, 96-99, 101-109, 111-116, 119-159,
                    161-162, 164-167, 169-173, 179-205, 207, 212, 223-226, 228, 232
~ anticipatory ~ 114-116, 150, 182, 194, 205
~ base ~ 10-11, 14-16, 19-20, 40-41, 53, 70-71, 77, 147
~ compatibility ~ 26, 28, 38, 52
~ de facto ~ 12-14, 16-17, 28-29, 106, 114, 122, 189
~ de jure ~ 12-13, 16-17, 106
~ Developing Organisations 11
~ Draft ~ 63, 68, 112
~ Draft International ~ 57-58
~ Final Draft International ~ 57-58
~ functional ~ 10-11, 14, 18, 40-41, 71, 147
~ industry ~ 14, 17, 51, 97, 150
~ International ~ 8, 11, 27, 30, 37, 50, 53, 56-60, 71, 73, 114, 123, 133, 182
~ Internet ~ 65-66, 68, 74, 116, 155, 167, 198, 207
~ proactive ~ 12, 14, 16, 112-115, 132, 143, 150, 190, 193, 195-196
~ professionals 108
~ profile 10-11, 14, 18, 40, 53, 70-71, 141, 147, 154
~ proprietary ~ 12, 14, 17, 21, 26-30, 32, 35-36, 38, 60, 76, 79-80, 97, 107,
                    111-113, 117, 150, 152-153, 189, 198, 201, 215, 217, 220, 222
~ public ~ 12, 14, 16

~ reactive ~ 12, 14, 16, 112-115, 176, 182, 193-195

~ regulatory ~ 10, 12

~ setting body 5, 8, 9, 11, 18, 33, 37, 53, 68-69, 71, 102,
                                      112, 128, 135, 137, 141, 170, 182, 201

~ setting process 21, 23-24, 31, 35, 104, 108, 125-128, 140, 142, 145,
                                 147, 155, 170, 173, 181, 186, 189-190, 196, 199, 203-204

~ statutory ~ 13, 17

~ track 67-68, 120

~ voluntary ~ 8, 11-13, 15-17, 34, 48, 114, 121-122, 166

~ war 3

Statutory (standard) 13, 17

Strong authentication 236

Survey 4, 25, 98, 108, 171-172, 184-185, 189-190, 194, 203

TAG 109, 131-132, 134, 149

TCP 79, 155

TCP/IP 79

Techie 86, 112, 142, 149, 159, 161

Technical Advisory Group 55, 131

Technical and Office Protocol 71

Technical Committee 4, 54-55, 59, 69, 119-120, 134, 140, 160-161, 200

Technical Corrigendum 59

Technical Management Board 55

Technological change 189

Technology-centric 112, 122, 182-183, 185

Telecommunication Development 61

Telecommunication Standardization 61, 63-64

Telecommunication Standardization Bureau 64

Telecommunications 38, 113

~ infrastructure 201

Telephone network 22

Teleworking 2

TOP 71, 74

Top-down 80-83, 85-87, 89, 92-93, 95-96, 171, 173-174, 220

Trade association 39, 143, 160, 188

Transport Protocol 152

Transposition Procedure 60

TSB 64

UA 151, 228, 230

Uncertainty 22-23, 147

United Nations 61

Unix 84, 88, 153

Usability 51, 76, 98, 103, 132, 161, 164, 166,190, 202, 226, 228

User 1, 3-4, 17, 26, 29-34, 37-44, 49-50, 74, 76-78,
80, 82-85, 87, 89-90, 92, 94, 98, 101-102, 104-106, 108, 110,
114, 119-120, 126-150, 152, 154, 157, 159-161, 165, 167, 169,
172-173, 177, 181-182, 184-191, 193-196, 199-200, 202-204, 210,
213-215, 217, 220-222, 225-226, 228, 232, 235

˜ agent 87, 228, 231, 233

˜ coalition 39, 160, 162, 170, 188

˜ community 31, 125, 129-130, 149, 160-161, 163, 189, 201-203

˜ companies 188

˜ corporate ˜ 5, 37, 42-43, 77-78, 104, 196

˜ direct ˜ 43, 189, 191

˜ group 69, 103, 106-107, 128-129, 139, 141-142, 188, 225

˜ indirect ˜ 43

˜ Information Model 235

˜ involvement 47, 101, 132, 137, 166, 173, 226

˜ participation 4-5, 37-38, 49, 51, 98, 103, 107, 120,
126-128, 135-142, 149, 163, 172, 187, 189, 191, 205, 226

˜ representation 141, 149, 160, 162, 170, 187, 189

˜ representative 4, 104-106, 111, 126-129, 137-141, 144-147, 149, 157, 159,
161-162, 170, 172, 181-182, 184-187, 200, 220, 225

˜ requirements 5, 39-40, 53, 68-70, 74, 78, 93-94, 106, 125,
128-134, 137, 139-140, 150, 159-160, 172, 181, 186,
190-191, 193, 196, 198-199, 204-205, 225

˜ requirements groups 130

Vendors 17, 21, 27-30, 32-34, 37-39, 42-44, 76, 94,
102-110, 112-117, 119-120, 127, 129, 134-135, 139,
40, 56, 60, 66, 101-102,142, 144-150, 154, 156-158, 160,
173, 181-183, 186, 188-191, 193, 195-196, 199-200, 203, 228

Viability analysis 170, 202-203, 205

Video conferencing 148

Voluntary (standard) 8, 11-13, 15-17, 34, 48, 114, 121-122, 166

Voluntary process 13

Window of opportunity 31, 33-35, 122, 152, 195

Workflow 78

Working Draft 57-58

World Conferences on International Telecommunication 61

World Telecommunication Standardization Conference 63
World Wide Web 153, 156
WTSC 63-64
WWW 124, 156
X.25 .... 12, 136, 153, 201
X.400 .... 76-77, 86, 88-90, 93, 105, 113,
                          150-154, 171, 199, 211, 213, 217, 220, 227-228, 232
X.500 .... 76-77, 90, 93, 113, 154, 222, 227, 232, 236